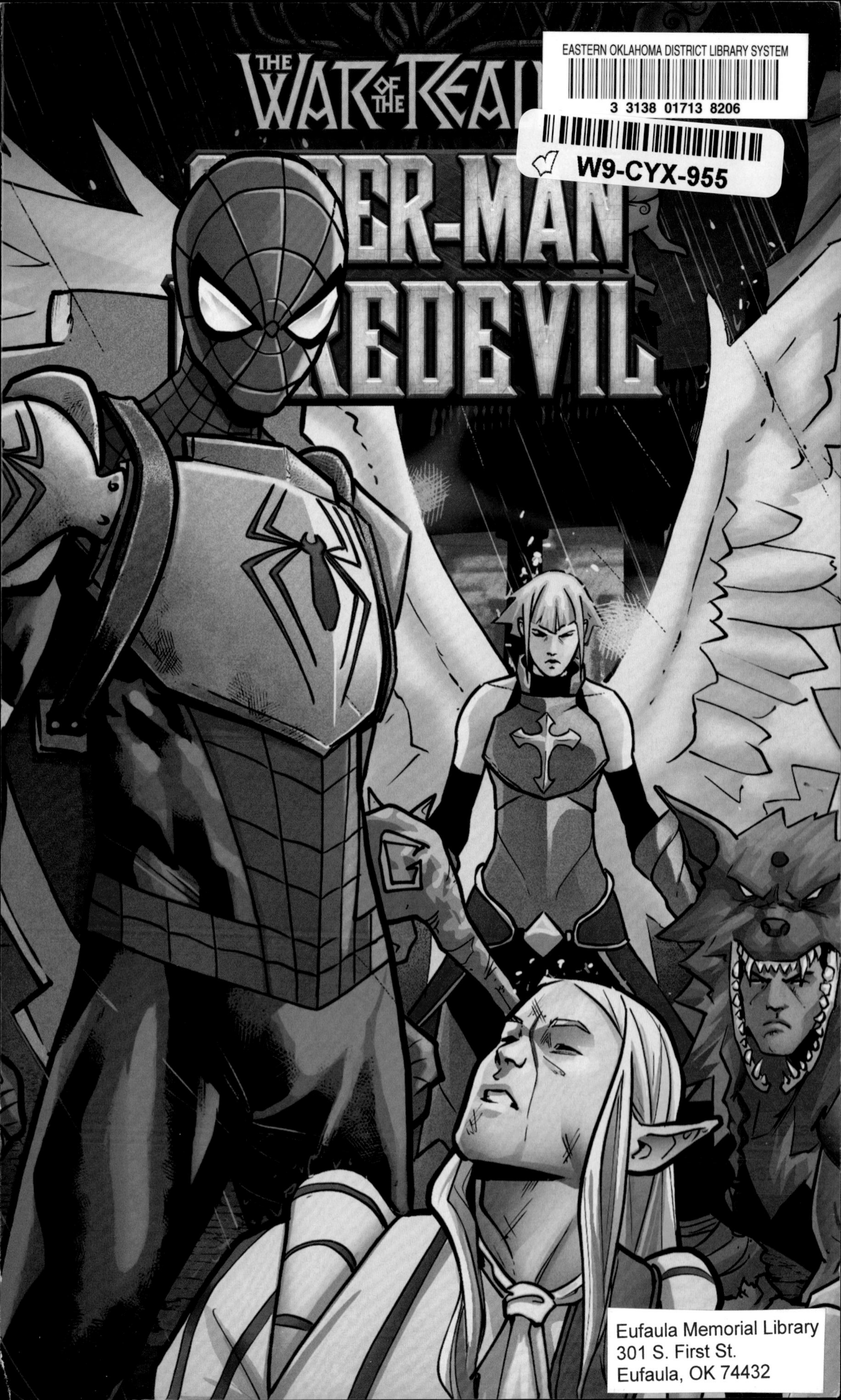
THE WAR OF THE

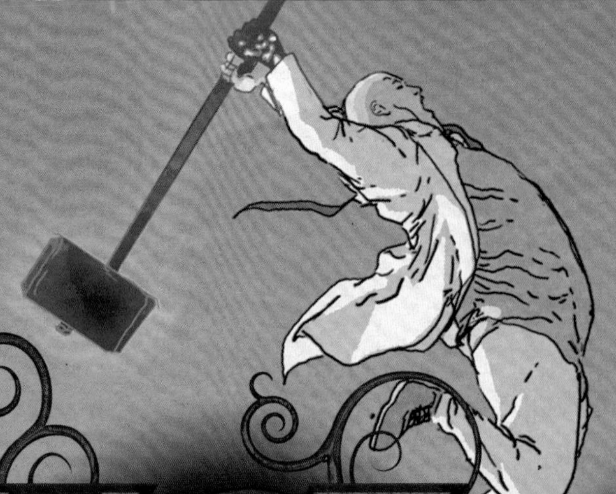

THE WAR OF THE REALMS

After laying waste to nine of the Ten Realms, the Dark Elf King Malekith and his powerful allies have finally brought the War of the Realms to Midgard — the last realm standing!

The Asgardians and heroes of Earth fought bravely but thus far have failed to halt the coordinated attack. Malekith and his powerful allies have divided the Earth among them, making a war that must be waged on many fronts. Malekith claimed Europe for the Dark Elves, gave Asia to Muspelheim, North America to the Frost Giants, Australia to the Trolls, South America to Nifflcheim, Antarctica to Roxxon and Africa to the Angels, who call it "New Heven." For its residents, it's anything but.

The invasion began in New York City. With Thor missing, it's up to humans, heroes and gods alike to save Midgard. But the war has only begun, and not every battle can be won…

COLLECTION EDITOR **JENNIFER GRÜNWALD** **CAITLIN O'CONNELL** ASSISTANT EDITOR
ASSOCIATE MANAGING EDITOR **KATERI WOODY** **MARK D. BEAZLEY** EDITOR, SPECIAL PROJECTS
VP PRODUCTION & SPECIAL PROJECTS **JEFF YOUNGQUIST** **ADAM DEL RE** WITH **JAY BOWEN** BOOK DESIGNERS

SVP PRINT, SALES & MARKETING **DAVID GABRIEL** **SVEN LARSEN** DIRECTOR, LICENSED PUBLISHING
EDITOR IN CHIEF **C.B. CEBULSKI** **JOE QUESADA** CHIEF CREATIVE OFFICER
PRESIDENT **DAN BUCKLEY** **ALAN FINE** EXECUTIVE PRODUCER

WAR OF THE REALMS: SPIDER-MAN/DAREDEVIL. Contains material originally published in magazine form as SPIDER-MAN & THE LEAGUE OF REALMS #1-3 and WAR OF THE REALMS: WAR SCROLLS #1-3. First printing 2019. ISBN 978-1-302-91928-3. Published by MARVEL WORLDWIDE, INC., a subsidiary of MARVEL ENTERTAINMENT, LLC. OFFICE OF PUBLICATION: 135 West 50th Street, New York, NY 10020. © 2019 MARVEL No similarity between any of the names, characters, persons, and/or institutions in this magazine with those of any living or dead person or institution is intended, and any such similarity which may exist is purely coincidental. **Printed in Canada.** DAN BUCKLEY, President, Marvel Entertainment; JOHN NEE, Publisher; JOE QUESADA, Chief Creative Officer; TOM BREVOORT, SVP of Publishing; DAVID BOGART, Associate Publisher & SVP of Talent Affairs; DAVID GABRIEL, SVP of Sales & Marketing, Publishing; JEFF YOUNGQUIST, VP of Production & Special Projects; DAN CARR, Executive Director of Publishing Technology; ALEX MORALES, Director of Publishing Operations; DAN EDINGTON, Managing Editor; SUSAN CRESPI, Production Manager; STAN LEE, Chairman Emeritus. For information regarding advertising in Marvel Comics or on Marvel.com, please contact Vit DeBellis, Custom Solutions & Integrated Advertising Manager, at vdebellis@marvel.com. For Marvel subscription inquiries, please call 888-511-5480. **Manufactured between 7/19/2019 and 8/20/2019 by SOLISCO PRINTERS, SCOTT, QC, CANADA.**

10 9 8 7 6 5 4 3 2 1

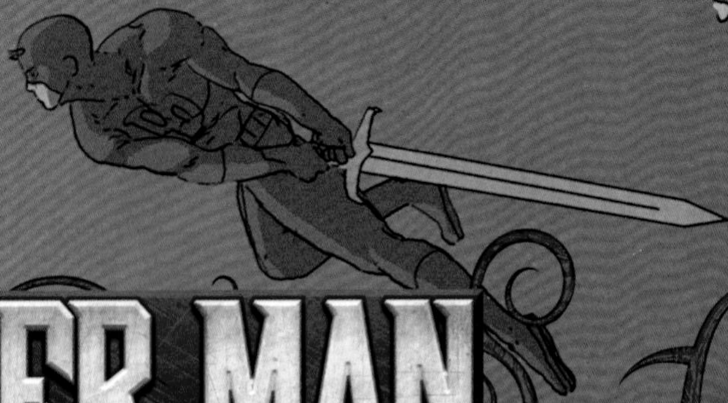

SPIDER-MAN DAREDEVIL

SPIDER-MAN & THE LEAGUE OF REALMS #1-3

Sean Ryan
WRITER

Nico Leon WITH Marco Failla (#3)
ARTISTS

Carlos Lopez WITH Andrew Crossley (#3)
COLOR ARTISTS

VC's Joe Caramagna
LETTERER

Ken Lashley & Brian Reber (#2) AND Cully Hamner & Brian Reber (#3)
COVER ART

Kathleen Wisneski
ASSOCIATE EDITOR

Nick Lowe
EDITOR

WAR OF THE REALMS: WAR SCROLLS #1-3

"THE GOD WITHOUT FEAR"

Jason Aaron
WRITER

Andrea Sorrentino
ARTIST

Matthew Wilson
COLOR ARTIST

VC's Joe Sabino
LETTERER

Alan Davis, Mark Farmer & Matt Hollingsworth
COVER ART

Sarah Brunstad
ASSOCIATE EDITOR

Wil Moss
EDITOR

Tom Brevoort
EXECUTIVE EDITOR

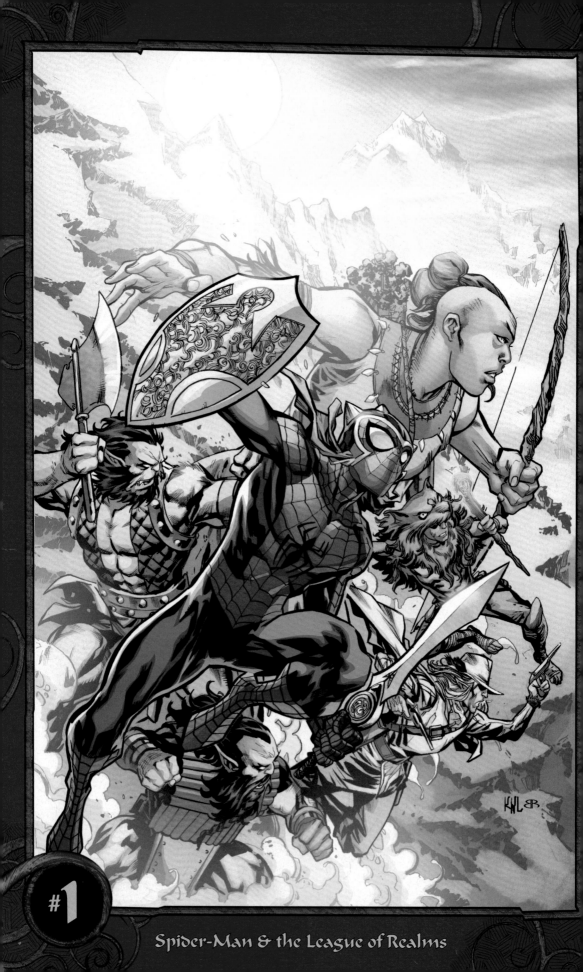

#1

Spider-Man & the League of Realms

When an enemy arose who threatened all nine of the extraterrestrial realms, the League of Realms was formed to join their strengths and bridge their ancient antagonisms. It wasn't easy: the League would have failed and splintered without the leadership of a true hero: THOR! ...Wait, did you think we meant--

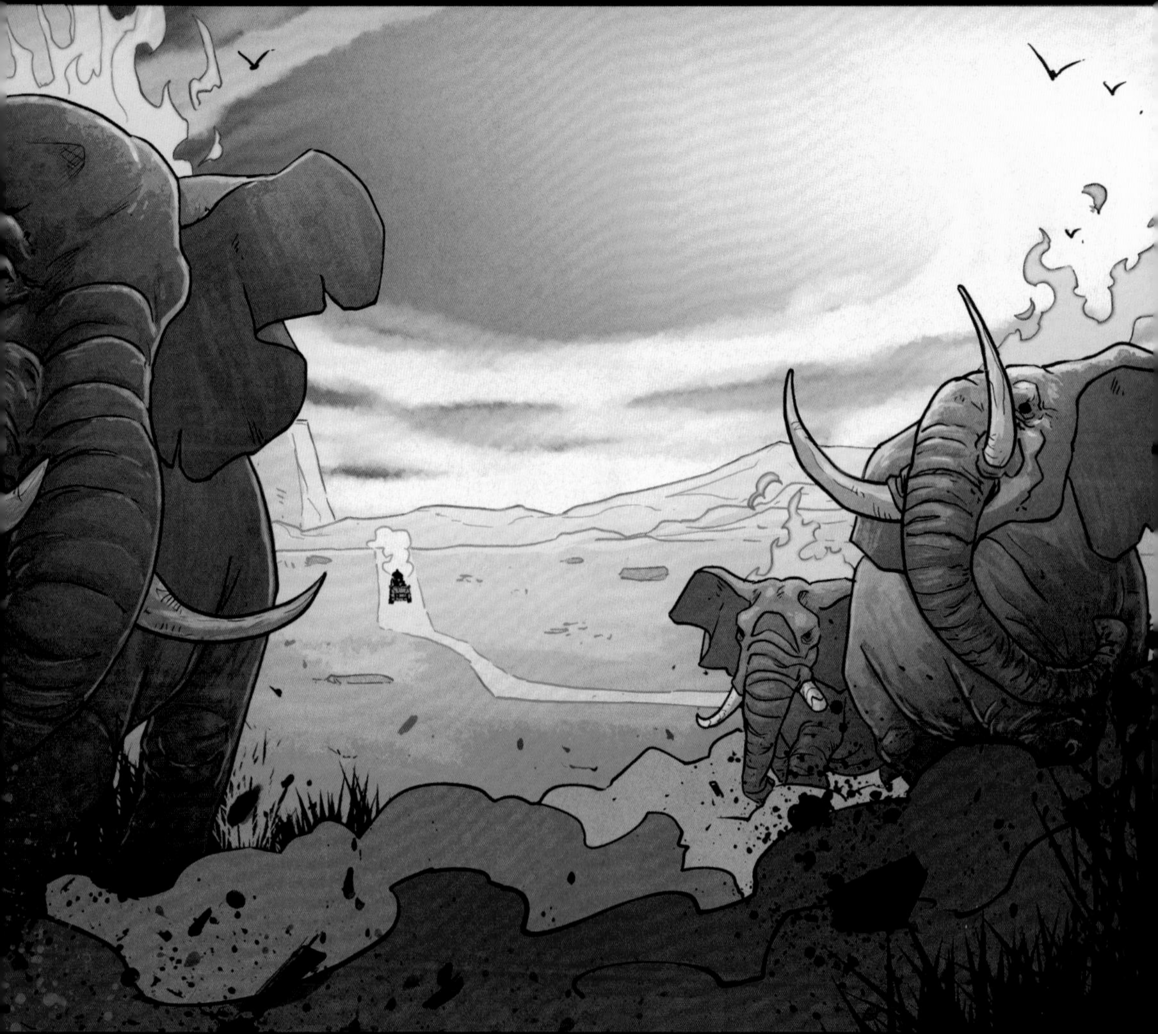

Spider-Man and the League of Realms:

"WHY WE FIGHT"

Part 1 of 3

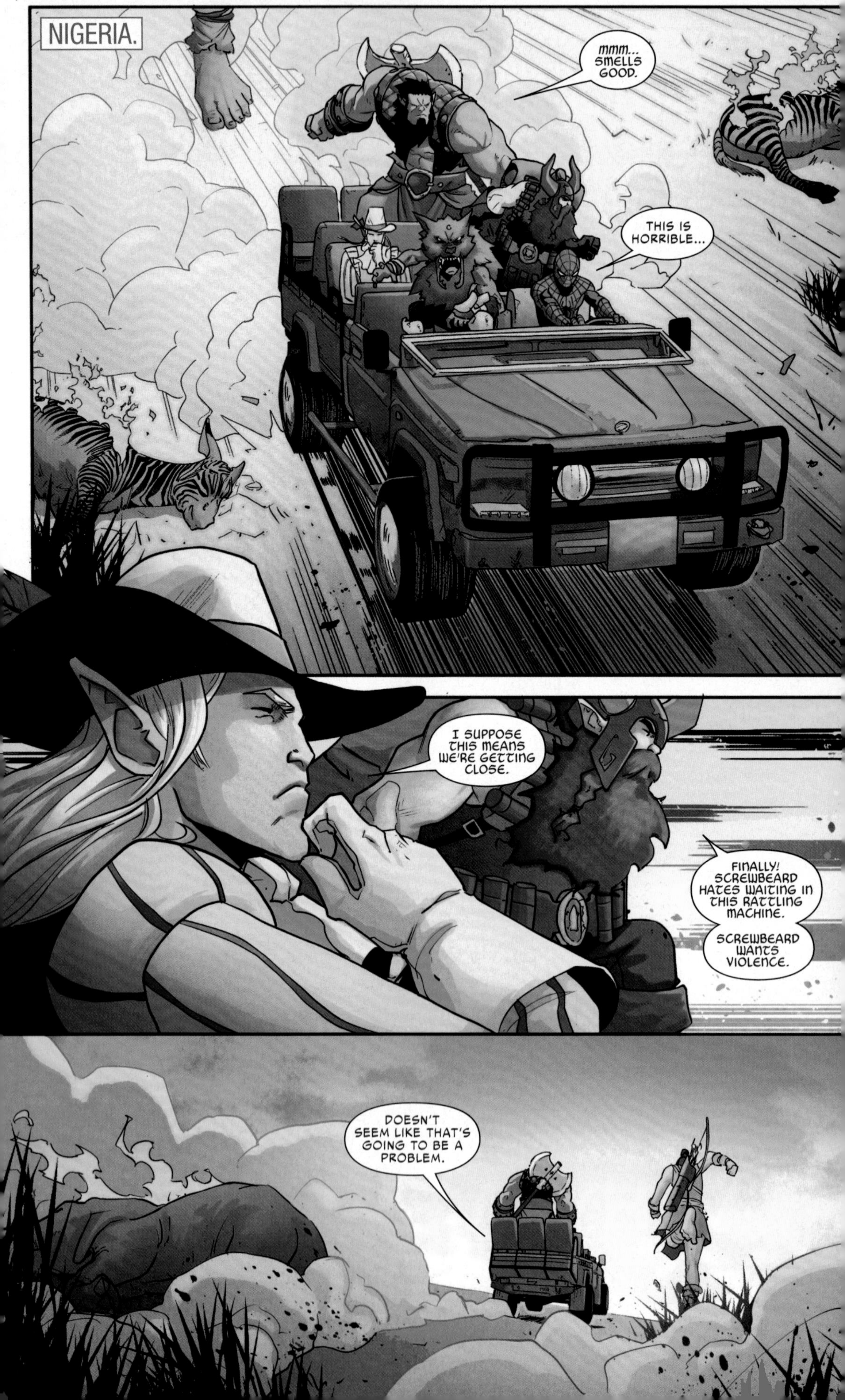
NIGERIA.
mmm... SMELLS GOOD.
THIS IS HORRIBLE...
I SUPPOSE THIS MEANS WE'RE GETTING CLOSE.
FINALLY! SCREWBEARD HATES WAITING IN THIS RATTLING MACHINE.
SCREWBEARD WANTS VIOLENCE.
DOESN'T SEEM LIKE THAT'S GOING TO BE A PROBLEM.

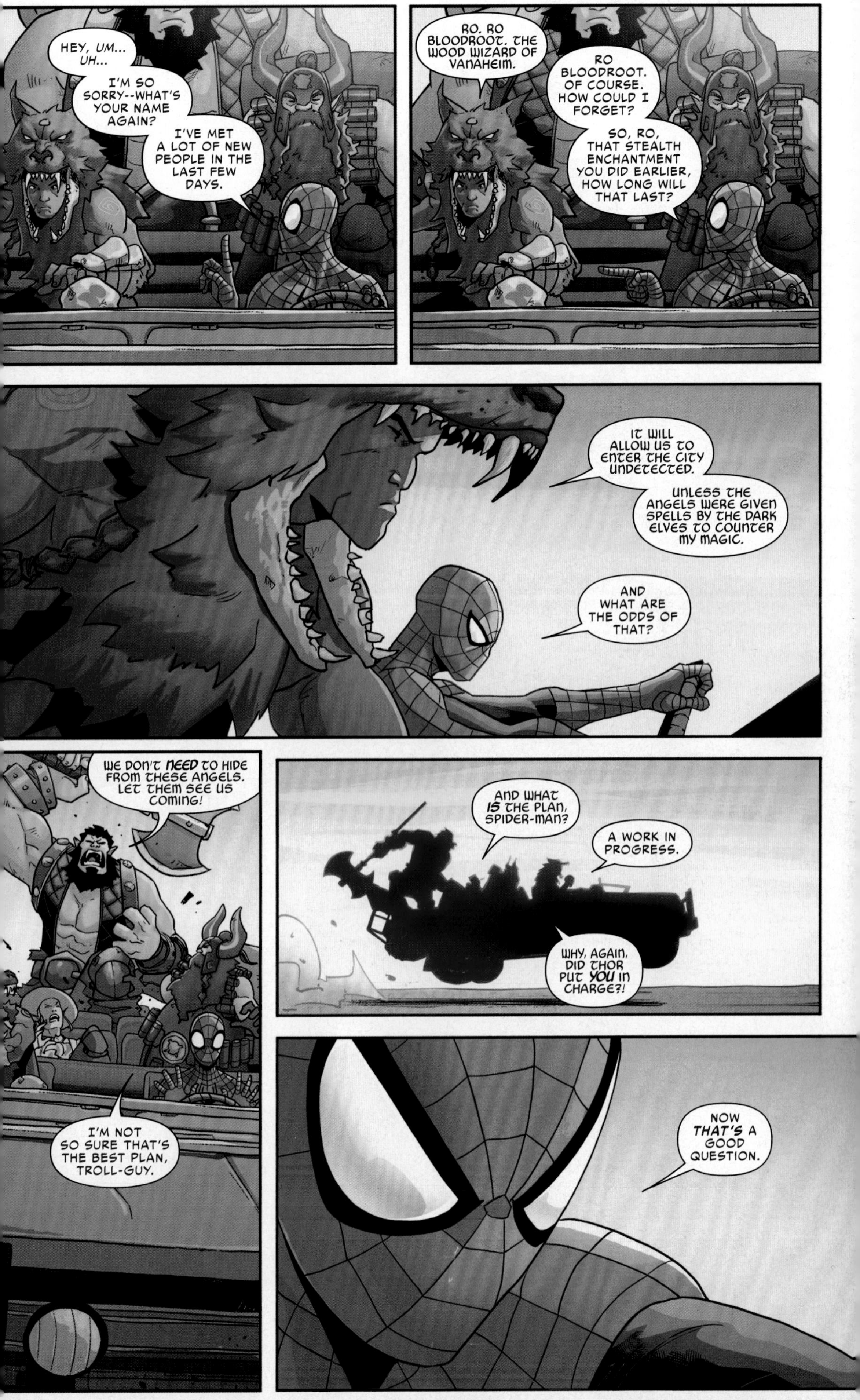
HEY, UM... UH...
I'M SO SORRY--WHAT'S YOUR NAME AGAIN?
I'VE MET A LOT OF NEW PEOPLE IN THE LAST FEW DAYS.
RO. RO BLOODROOT. THE WOOD WIZARD OF VANAHEIM.
RO BLOODROOT. OF COURSE. HOW COULD I FORGET?
SO, RO, THAT STEALTH ENCHANTMENT YOU DID EARLIER, HOW LONG WILL THAT LAST?
IT WILL ALLOW US TO ENTER THE CITY UNDETECTED.
UNLESS THE ANGELS WERE GIVEN SPELLS BY THE DARK ELVES TO COUNTER MY MAGIC.
AND WHAT ARE THE ODDS OF THAT?
WE DON'T NEED TO HIDE FROM THESE ANGELS. LET THEM SEE US COMING!
I'M NOT SO SURE THAT'S THE BEST PLAN, TROLL-GUY.
AND WHAT IS THE PLAN, SPIDER-MAN?
A WORK IN PROGRESS.
WHY, AGAIN, DID THOR PUT YOU IN CHARGE?!
NOW THAT'S A GOOD QUESTION.

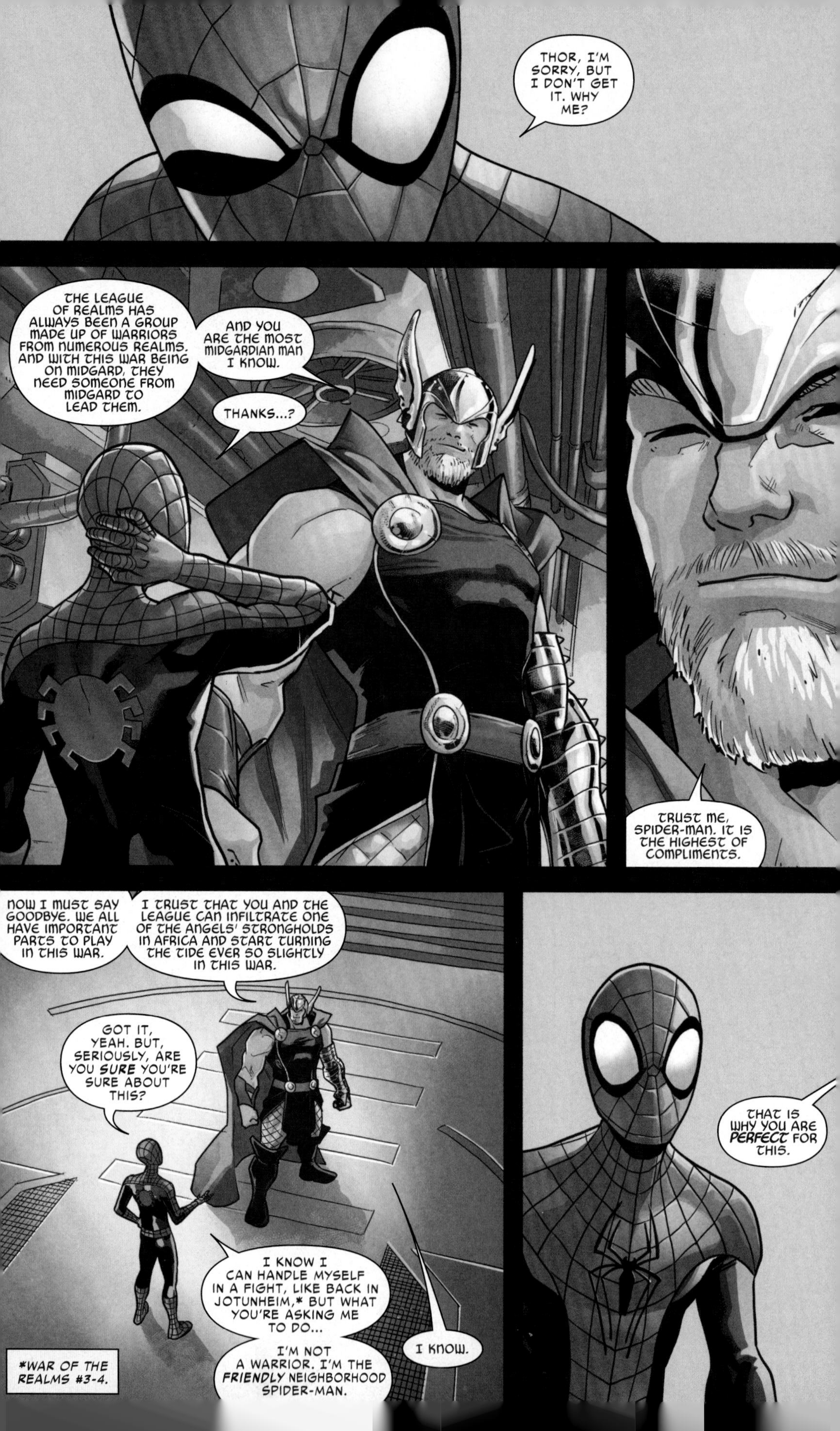
THOR, I'M SORRY, BUT I DON'T GET IT. WHY ME?
THE LEAGUE OF REALMS HAS ALWAYS BEEN A GROUP MADE UP OF WARRIORS FROM NUMEROUS REALMS. AND WITH THIS WAR BEING ON MIDGARD, THEY NEED SOMEONE FROM MIDGARD TO LEAD THEM.
AND YOU ARE THE MOST MIDGARDIAN MAN I KNOW.
THANKS...?
TRUST ME, SPIDER-MAN. IT IS THE HIGHEST OF COMPLIMENTS.
NOW I MUST SAY GOODBYE. WE ALL HAVE IMPORTANT PARTS TO PLAY IN THIS WAR.
I TRUST THAT YOU AND THE LEAGUE CAN INFILTRATE ONE OF THE ANGELS' STRONGHOLDS IN AFRICA AND START TURNING THE TIDE EVER SO SLIGHTLY IN THIS WAR.
GOT IT, YEAH. BUT, SERIOUSLY, ARE YOU SURE YOU'RE SURE ABOUT THIS?
I KNOW I CAN HANDLE MYSELF IN A FIGHT, LIKE BACK IN JOTUNHEIM,* BUT WHAT YOU'RE ASKING ME TO DO...
I'M NOT A WARRIOR. I'M THE FRIENDLY NEIGHBORHOOD SPIDER-MAN.
I KNOW.
*WAR OF THE REALMS #3-4.
THAT IS WHY YOU ARE PERFECT FOR THIS.

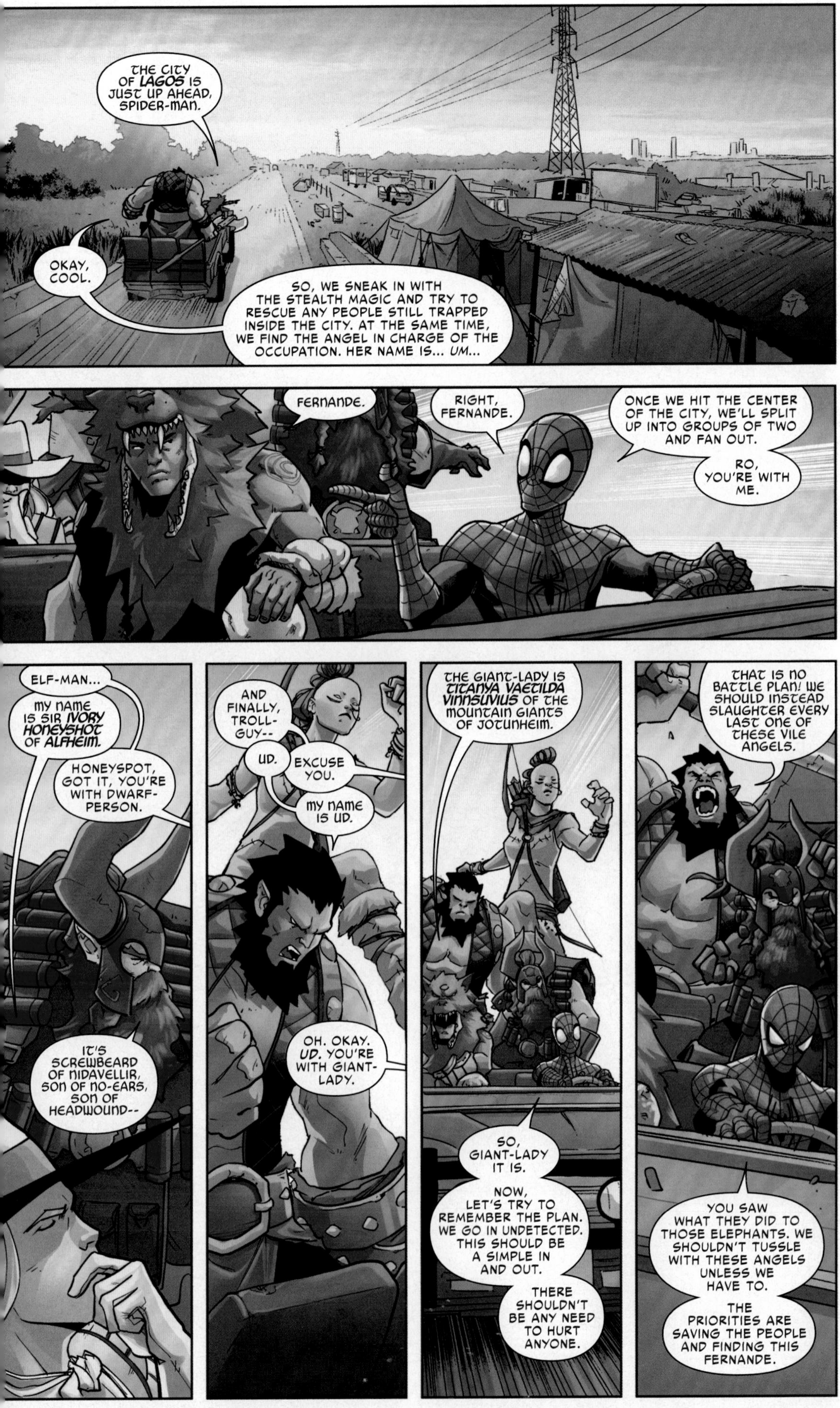
THE CITY OF LAGOS IS JUST UP AHEAD, SPIDER-MAN.
OKAY, COOL.
SO, WE SNEAK IN WITH THE STEALTH MAGIC AND TRY TO RESCUE ANY PEOPLE STILL TRAPPED INSIDE THE CITY. AT THE SAME TIME, WE FIND THE ANGEL IN CHARGE OF THE OCCUPATION. HER NAME IS... UM...
FERNANDE.
RIGHT, FERNANDE.
ONCE WE HIT THE CENTER OF THE CITY, WE'LL SPLIT UP INTO GROUPS OF TWO AND FAN OUT.
RO, YOU'RE WITH ME.
ELF-MAN...
MY NAME IS SIR IVORY HONEYSHOT OF ALFHEIM.
HONEYSPOT, GOT IT, YOU'RE WITH DWARF-PERSON.
IT'S SCREWBEARD OF NIDAVELLIR, SON OF NO-EARS, SON OF HEADWOUND--
AND FINALLY, TROLL-GUY--
UD.
EXCUSE YOU.
MY NAME IS UD.
OH. OKAY. UD. YOU'RE WITH GIANT-LADY.
THE GIANT-LADY IS TITANYA VAETILDA VINNSUVIUS OF THE MOUNTAIN GIANTS OF JOTUNHEIM.
SO, GIANT-LADY IT IS.
NOW, LET'S TRY TO REMEMBER THE PLAN. WE GO IN UNDETECTED. THIS SHOULD BE A SIMPLE IN AND OUT.
THERE SHOULDN'T BE ANY NEED TO HURT ANYONE.
THAT IS NO BATTLE PLAN! WE SHOULD INSTEAD SLAUGHTER EVERY LAST ONE OF THESE VILE ANGELS.
YOU SAW WHAT THEY DID TO THOSE ELEPHANTS. WE SHOULDN'T TUSSLE WITH THESE ANGELS UNLESS WE HAVE TO.
THE PRIORITIES ARE SAVING THE PEOPLE AND FINDING THIS FERNANDE.

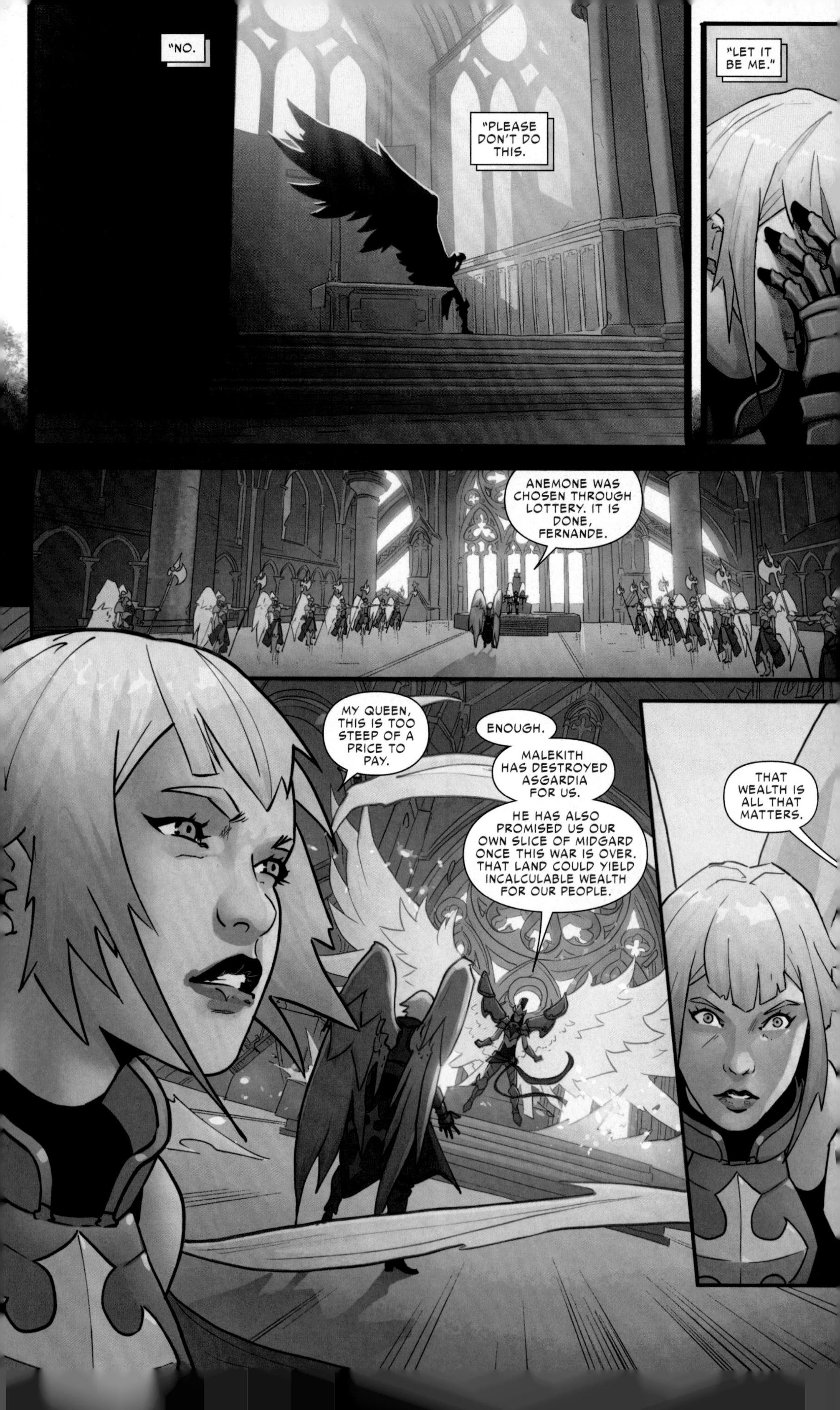
"NO.
"PLEASE DON'T DO THIS.
"LET IT BE ME."
ANEMONE WAS CHOSEN THROUGH LOTTERY. IT IS DONE, FERNANDE.
MY QUEEN, THIS IS TOO STEEP OF A PRICE TO PAY.
ENOUGH.
MALEKITH HAS DESTROYED ASGARDIA FOR US.
HE HAS ALSO PROMISED US OUR OWN SLICE OF MIDGARD ONCE THIS WAR IS OVER. THAT LAND COULD YIELD INCALCULABLE WEALTH FOR OUR PEOPLE.
THAT WEALTH IS ALL THAT MATTERS.

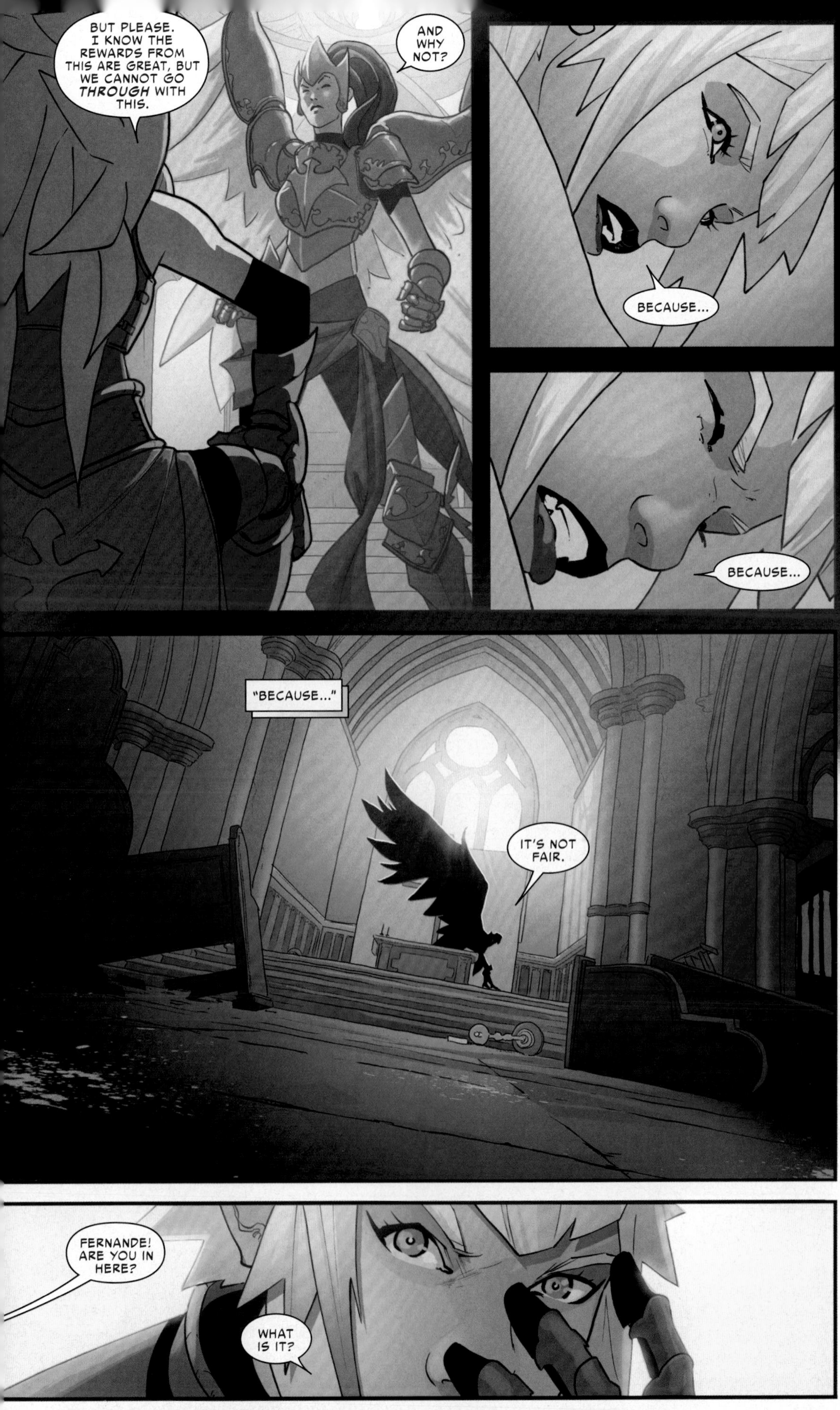
BUT PLEASE. I KNOW THE REWARDS FROM THIS ARE GREAT, BUT WE CANNOT GO THROUGH WITH THIS.
AND WHY NOT?
BECAUSE...
BECAUSE...
"BECAUSE..."
IT'S NOT FAIR.
FERNANDE! ARE YOU IN HERE?
WHAT IS IT?

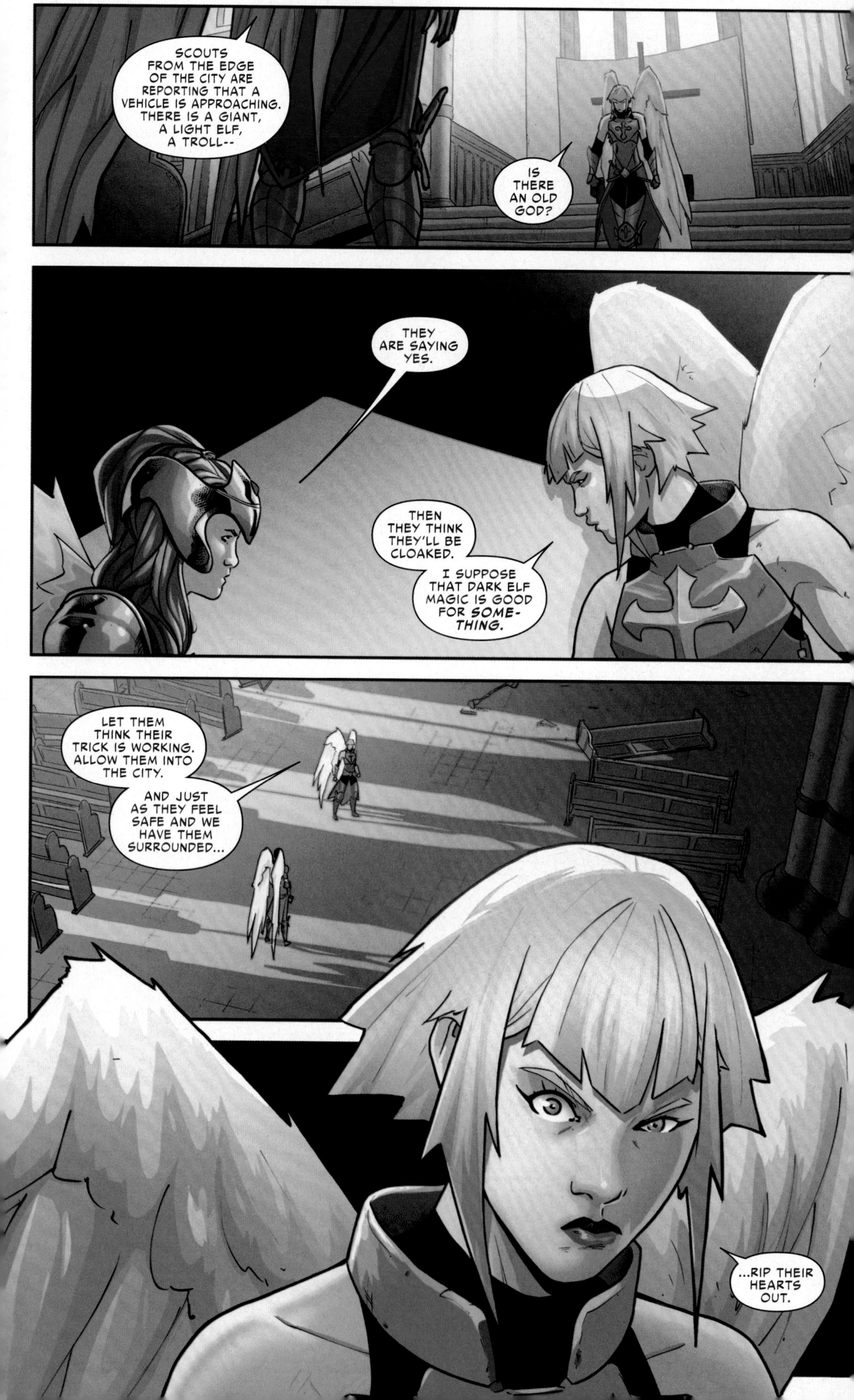
SCOUTS FROM THE EDGE OF THE CITY ARE REPORTING THAT A VEHICLE IS APPROACHING. THERE IS A GIANT, A LIGHT ELF, A TROLL--
IS THERE AN OLD GOD?
THEY ARE SAYING YES.
THEN THEY THINK THEY'LL BE CLOAKED.
I SUPPOSE THAT DARK ELF MAGIC IS GOOD FOR SOME-THING.
LET THEM THINK THEIR TRICK IS WORKING. ALLOW THEM INTO THE CITY.
AND JUST AS THEY FEEL SAFE AND WE HAVE THEM SURROUNDED...
...RIP THEIR HEARTS OUT.

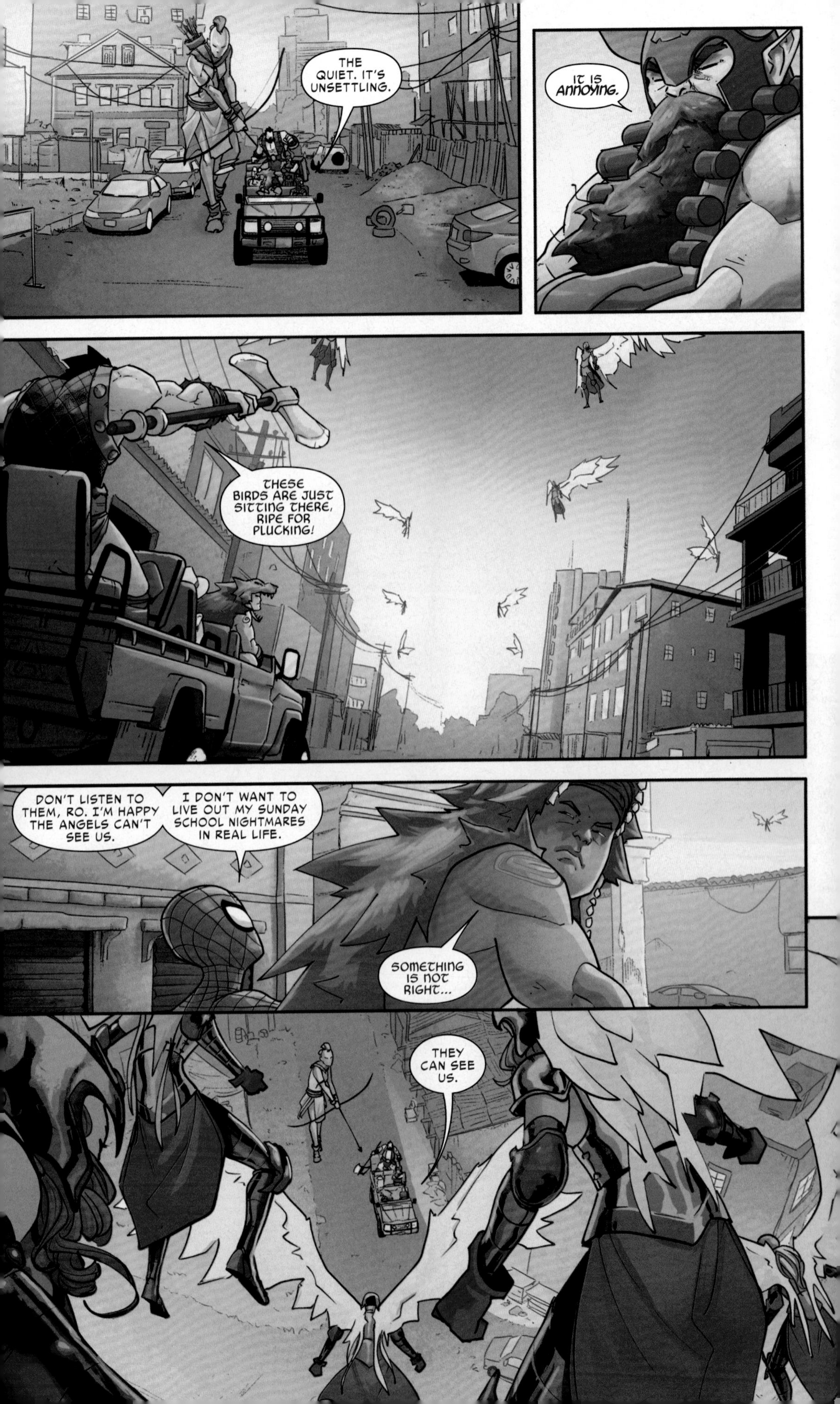

THE QUIET. IT'S UNSETTLING.
IT IS ANNOYING.
THESE BIRDS ARE JUST SITTING THERE, RIPE FOR PLUCKING!
DON'T LISTEN TO THEM, RO. I'M HAPPY THE ANGELS CAN'T SEE US.
I DON'T WANT TO LIVE OUT MY SUNDAY SCHOOL NIGHTMARES IN REAL LIFE.
SOMETHING IS NOT RIGHT...
THEY CAN SEE US.

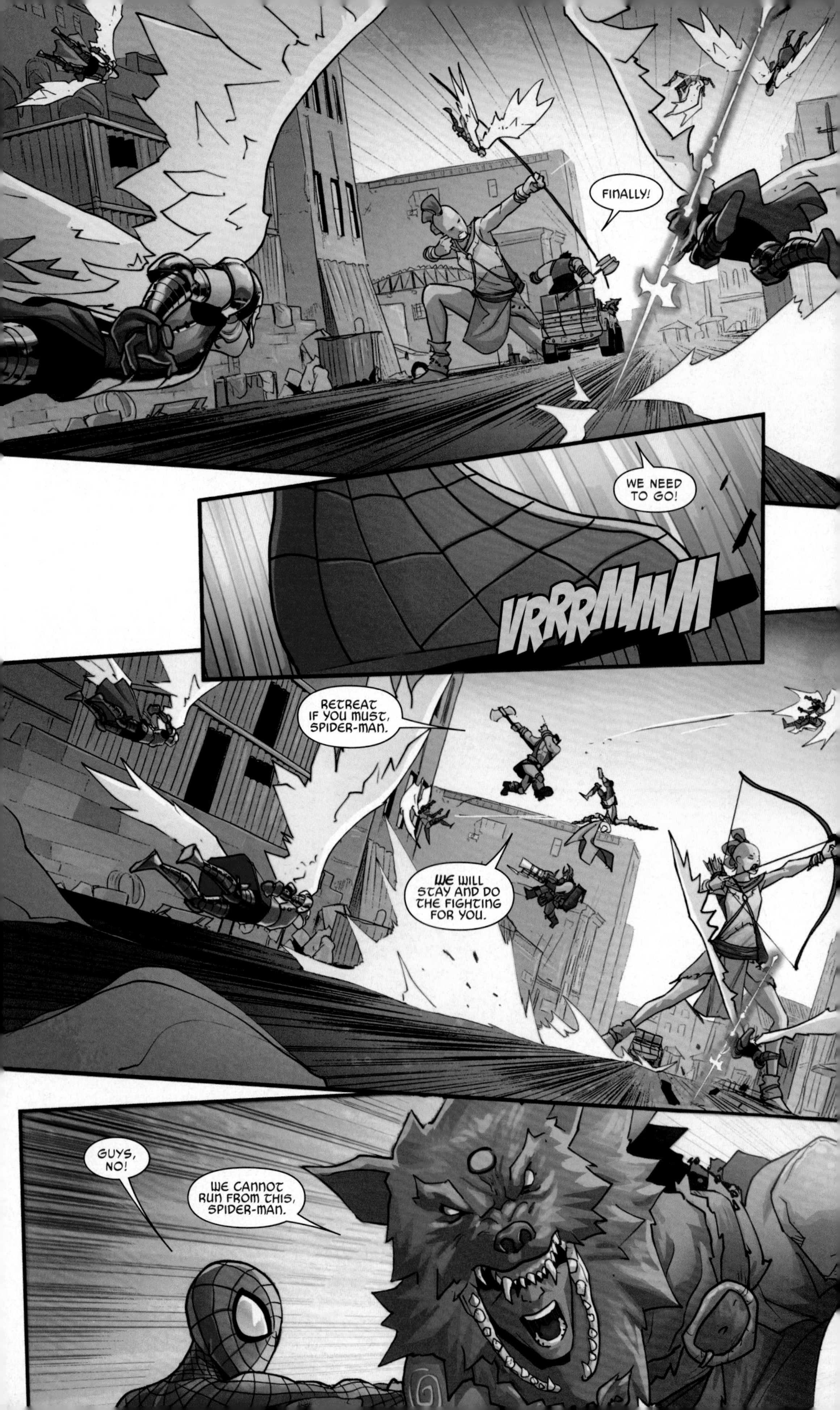
FINALLY!
WE NEED TO GO!
VRRRMMMM
RETREAT IF YOU MUST, SPIDER-MAN.
WE WILL STAY AND DO THE FIGHTING FOR YOU.
GUYS, NO!
WE CANNOT RUN FROM THIS, SPIDER-MAN.

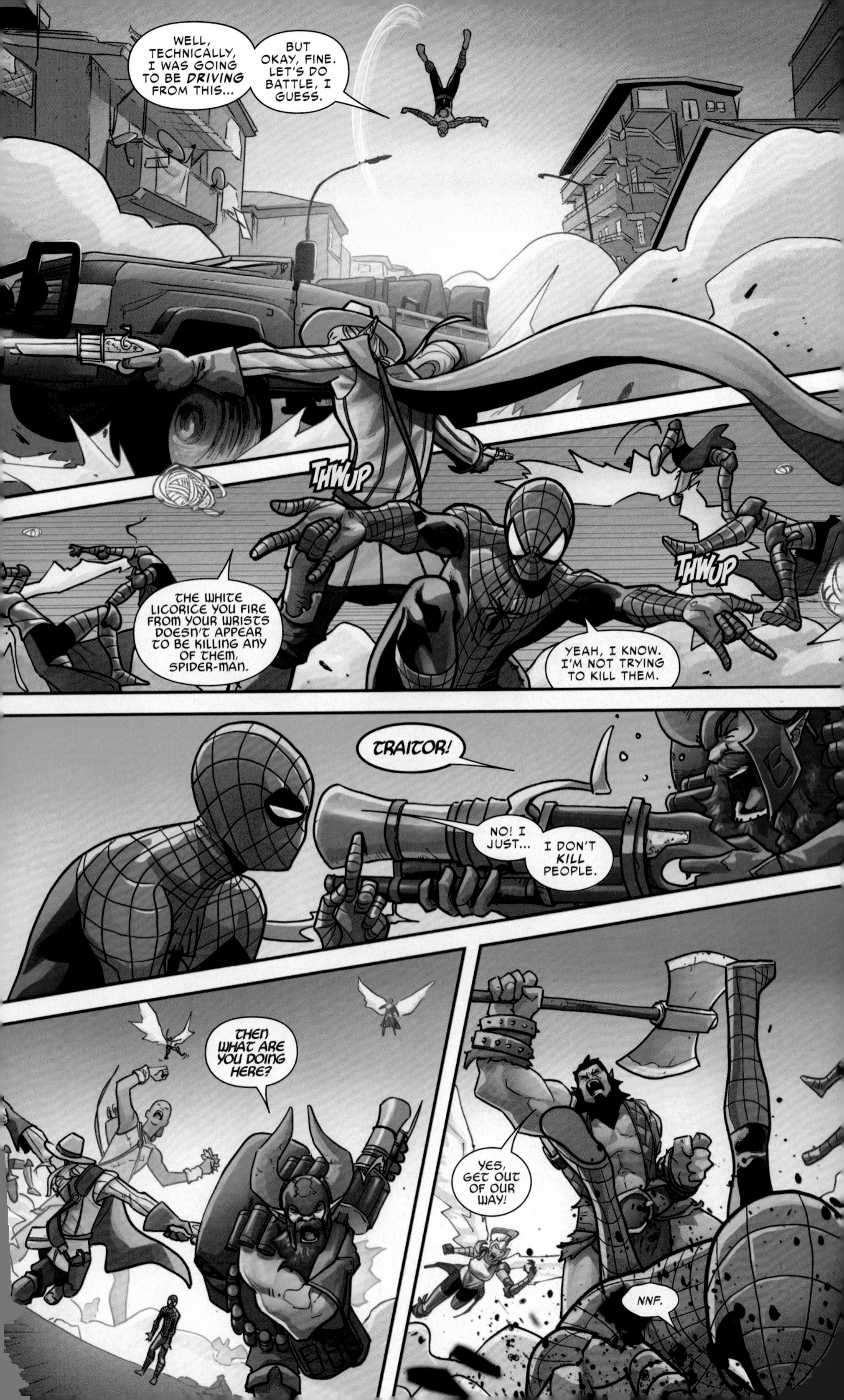

WELL, TECHNICALLY, I WAS GOING TO BE DRIVING FROM THIS...
BUT OKAY, FINE. LET'S DO BATTLE, I GUESS.
THWUP
THWUP
THE WHITE LICORICE YOU FIRE FROM YOUR WRISTS DOESN'T APPEAR TO BE KILLING ANY OF THEM, SPIDER-MAN.
YEAH, I KNOW. I'M NOT TRYING TO KILL THEM.
TRAITOR!
NO! I JUST...
I DON'T KILL PEOPLE.
THEN WHAT ARE YOU DOING HERE?
YES, GET OUT OF OUR WAY!
NNF.

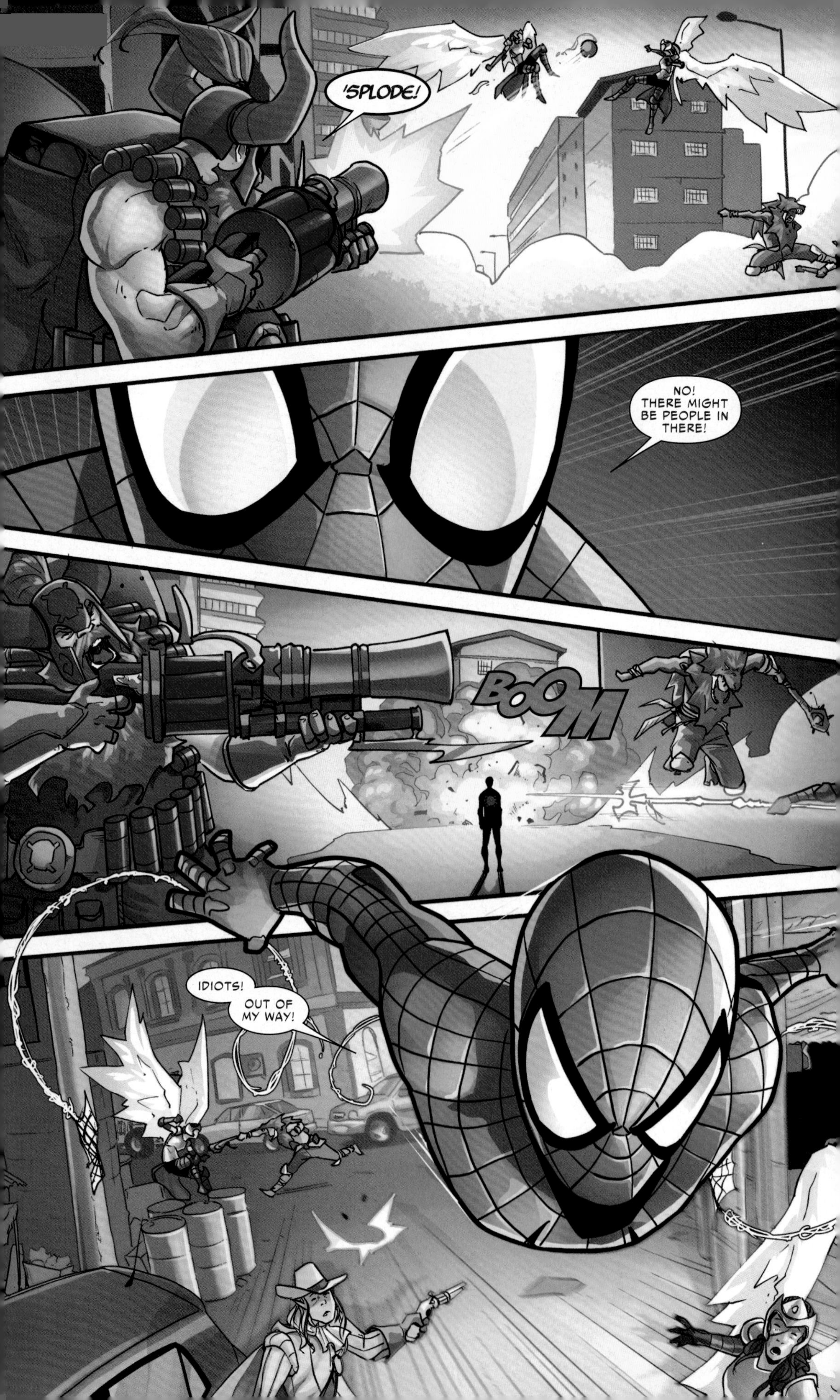
'SPLODE!
NO! THERE MIGHT BE PEOPLE IN THERE!
BOOM
IDIOTS!
OUT OF MY WAY!

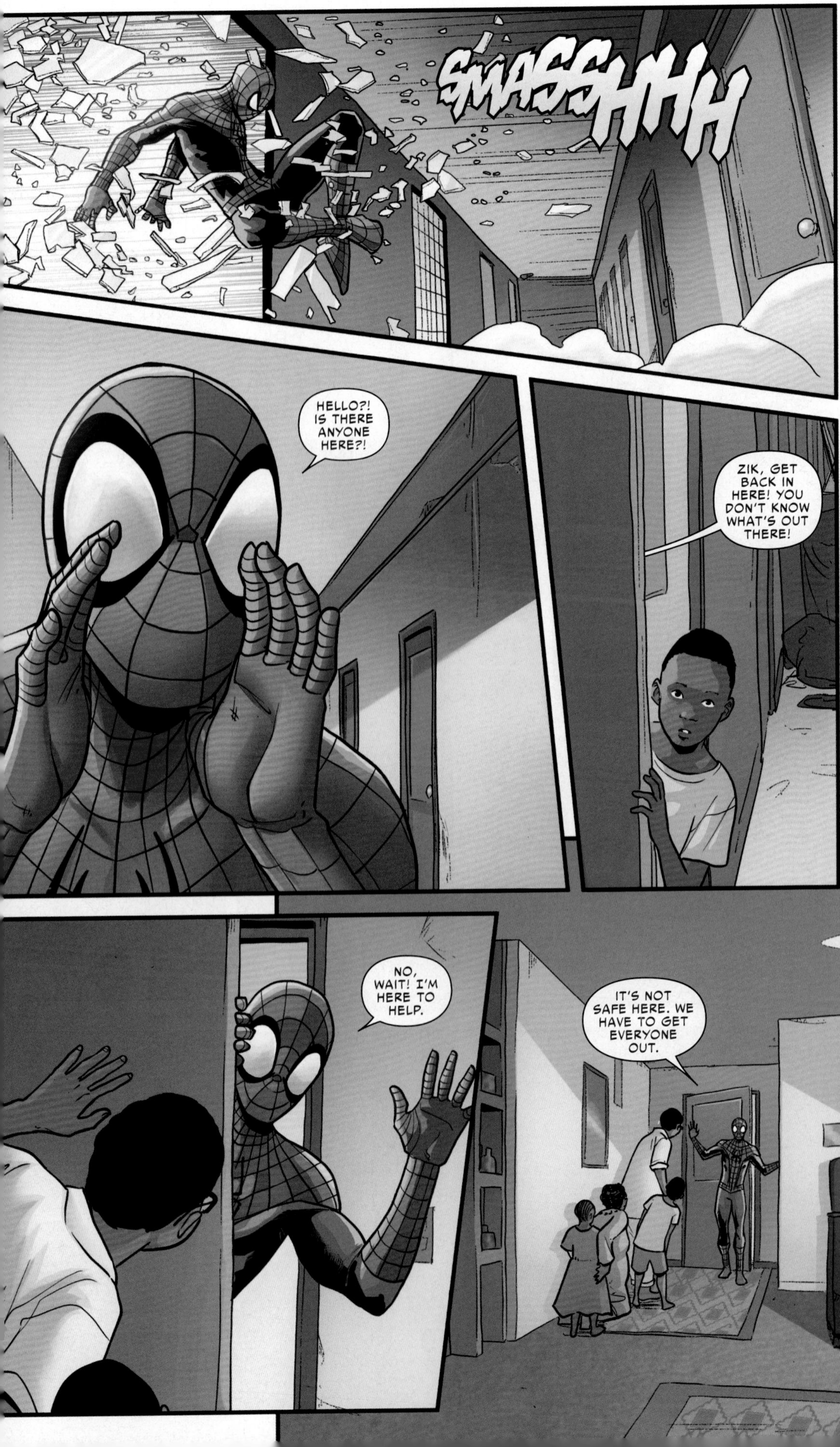
SMASSHHH
HELLO?! IS THERE ANYONE HERE?!
ZIK, GET BACK IN HERE! YOU DON'T KNOW WHAT'S OUT THERE!
NO, WAIT! I'M HERE TO HELP.
IT'S NOT SAFE HERE. WE HAVE TO GET EVERYONE OUT.

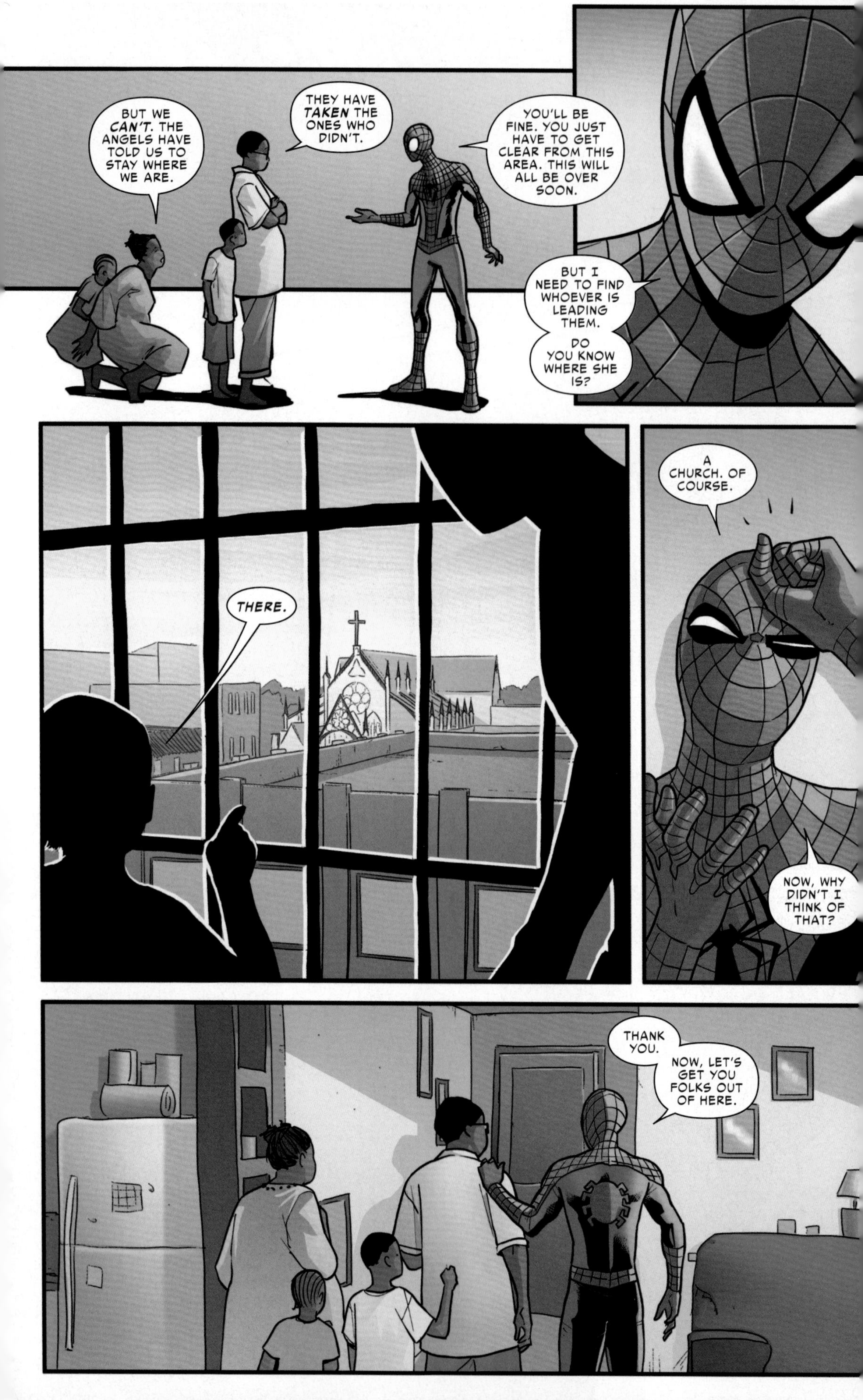
BUT WE *CAN'T*. THE ANGELS HAVE TOLD US TO STAY WHERE WE ARE.
THEY HAVE *TAKEN* THE ONES WHO DIDN'T.
YOU'LL BE FINE. YOU JUST HAVE TO GET CLEAR FROM THIS AREA. THIS WILL ALL BE OVER SOON.
BUT I NEED TO FIND WHOEVER IS LEADING THEM.
DO YOU KNOW WHERE SHE IS?
THERE.
A CHURCH. OF COURSE.
NOW, WHY DIDN'T I THINK OF THAT?
THANK YOU.
NOW, LET'S GET YOU FOLKS OUT OF HERE.

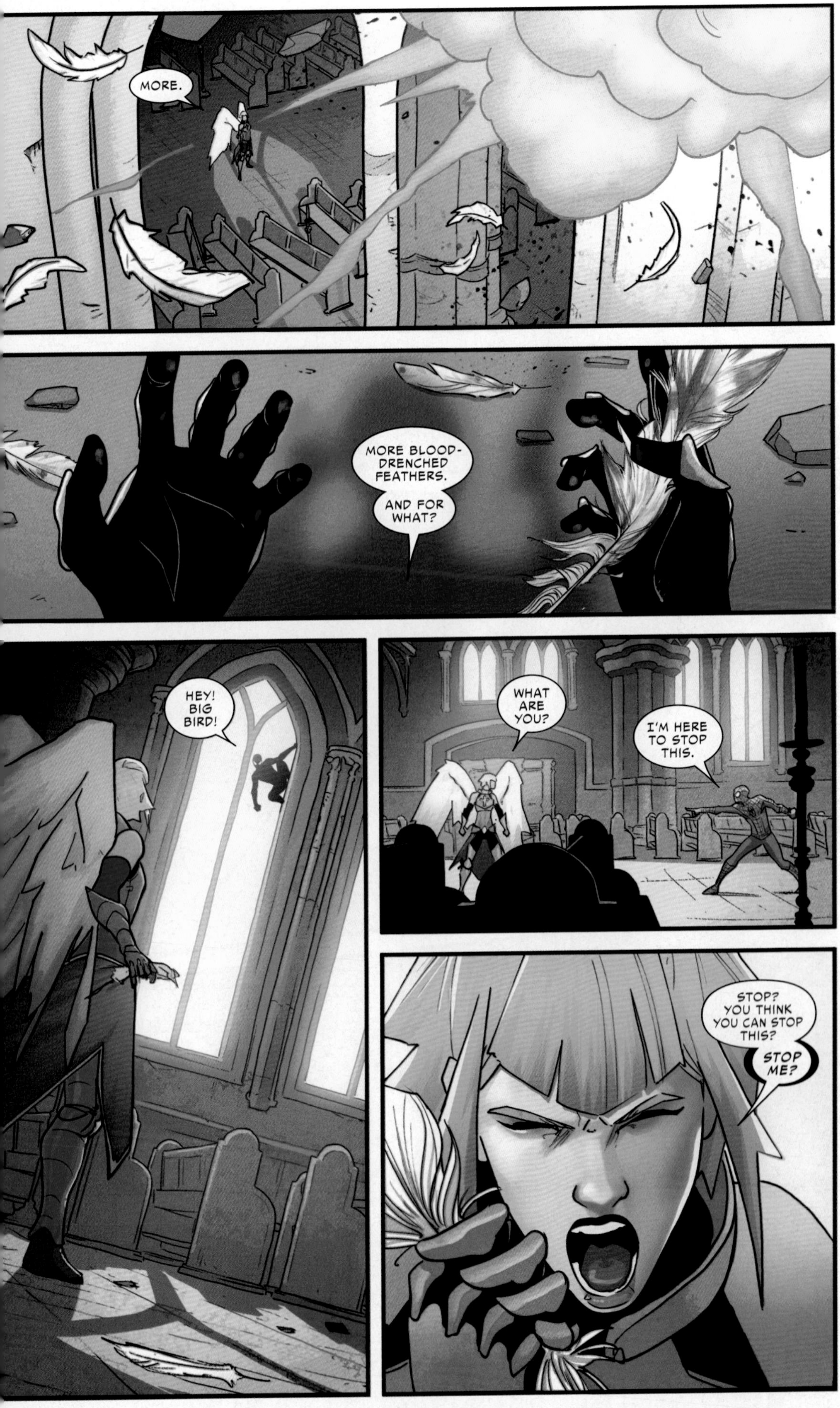
MORE.
MORE BLOOD-DRENCHED FEATHERS.
AND FOR WHAT?
HEY! BIG BIRD!
WHAT ARE YOU?
I'M HERE TO STOP THIS.
STOP? YOU THINK YOU CAN STOP THIS?
STOP ME?

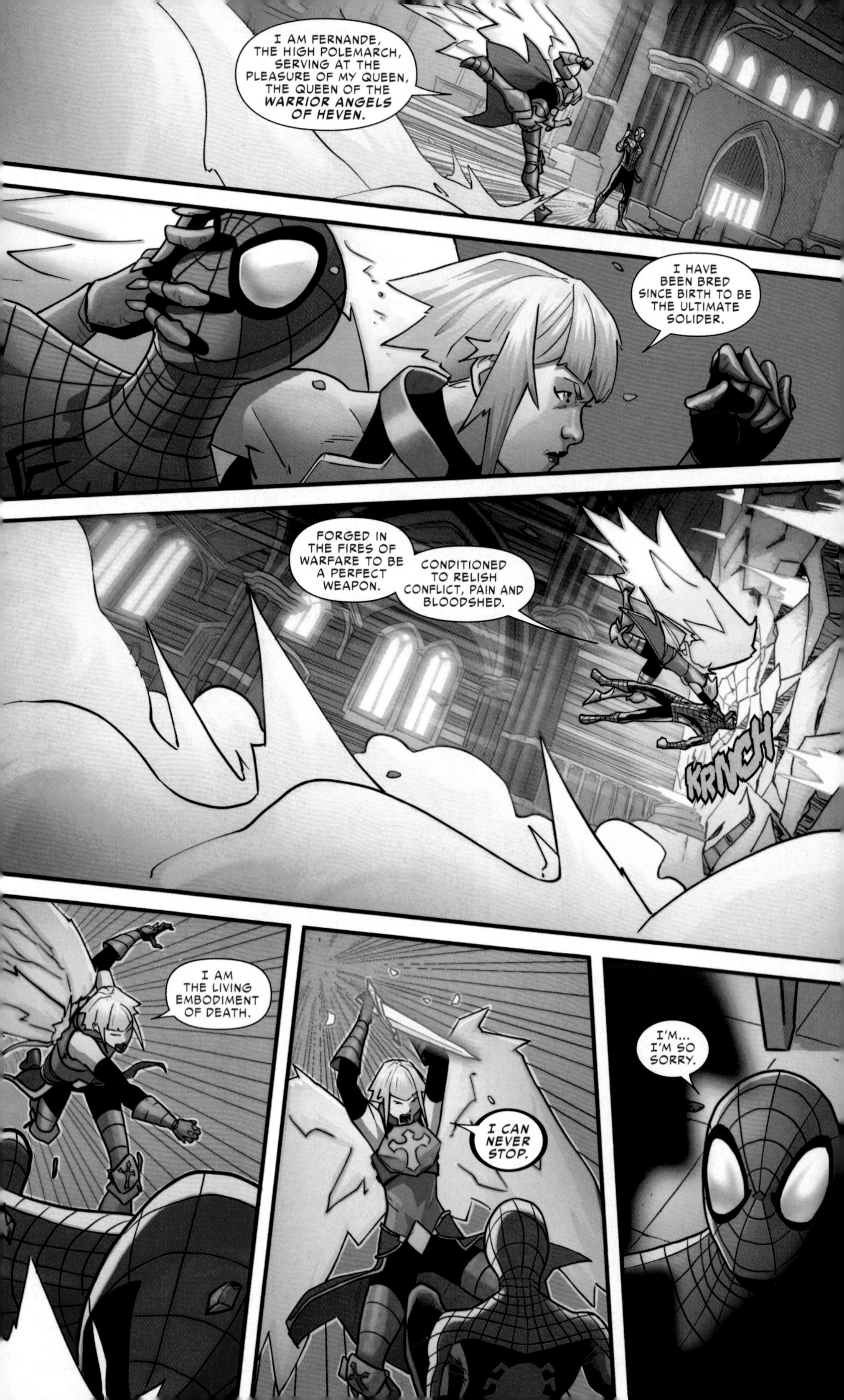

I AM FERNANDE, THE HIGH POLEMARCH, SERVING AT THE PLEASURE OF MY QUEEN, THE QUEEN OF THE *WARRIOR ANGELS OF HEVEN.*
I HAVE BEEN BRED SINCE BIRTH TO BE THE ULTIMATE SOLIDER.
FORGED IN THE FIRES OF WARFARE TO BE A PERFECT WEAPON.
CONDITIONED TO RELISH CONFLICT, PAIN AND BLOODSHED.
KRNCH
I AM THE LIVING EMBODIMENT OF DEATH.
I CAN NEVER STOP.
I'M... I'M SO SORRY.

WHAT?

I'M SORRY. THAT ALL SOUNDS HORRIBLE.

DON'T YOU EVER WISH YOU COULD STOP? I KNOW I DO.

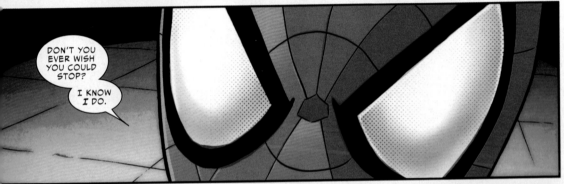

HOW?

WELL, THE FIRST STEP IS, YOU COULD HELP ME UP.

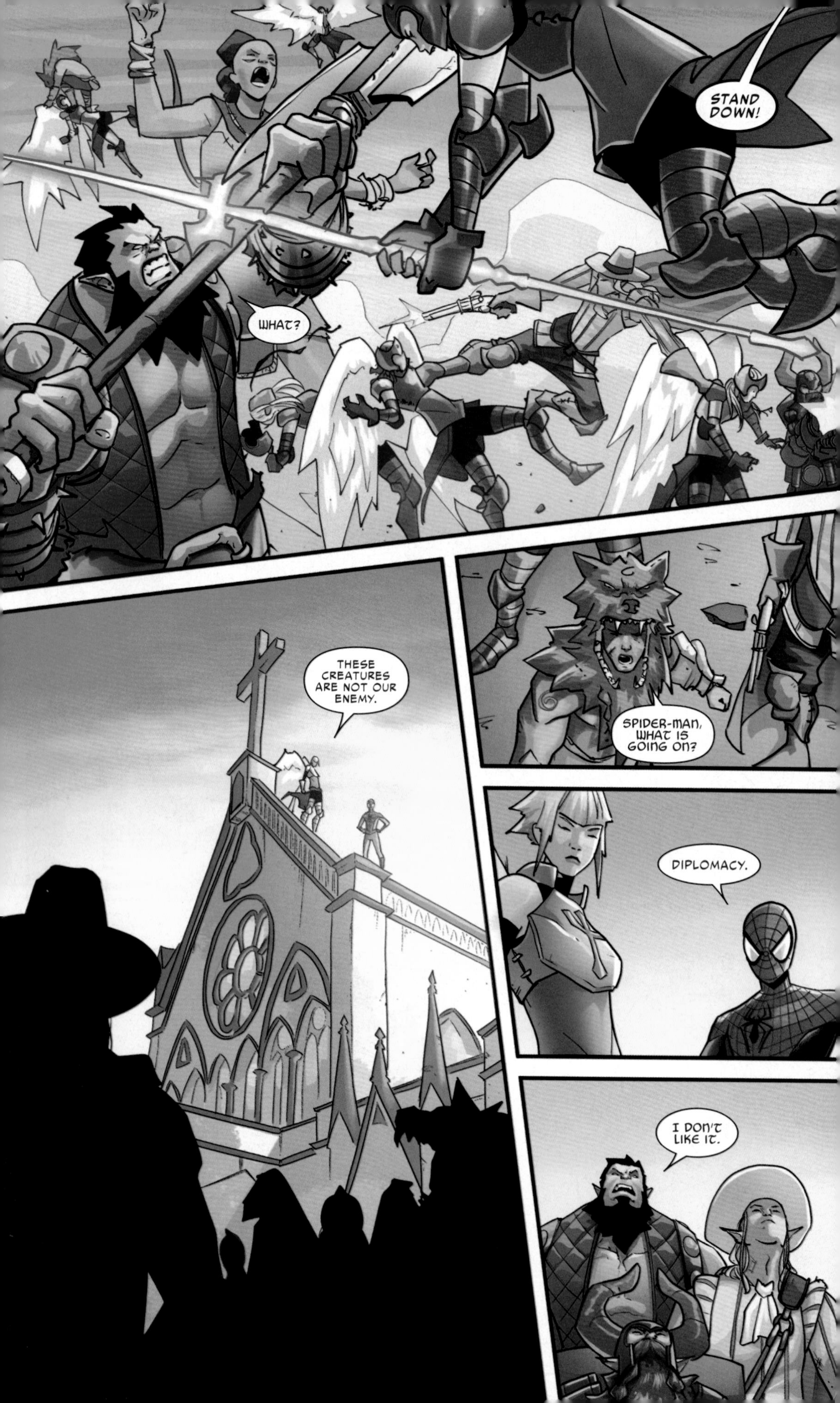
STAND DOWN!
WHAT?
THESE CREATURES ARE NOT OUR ENEMY.
SPIDER-MAN, WHAT IS GOING ON?
DIPLOMACY.
I DON'T LIKE IT.

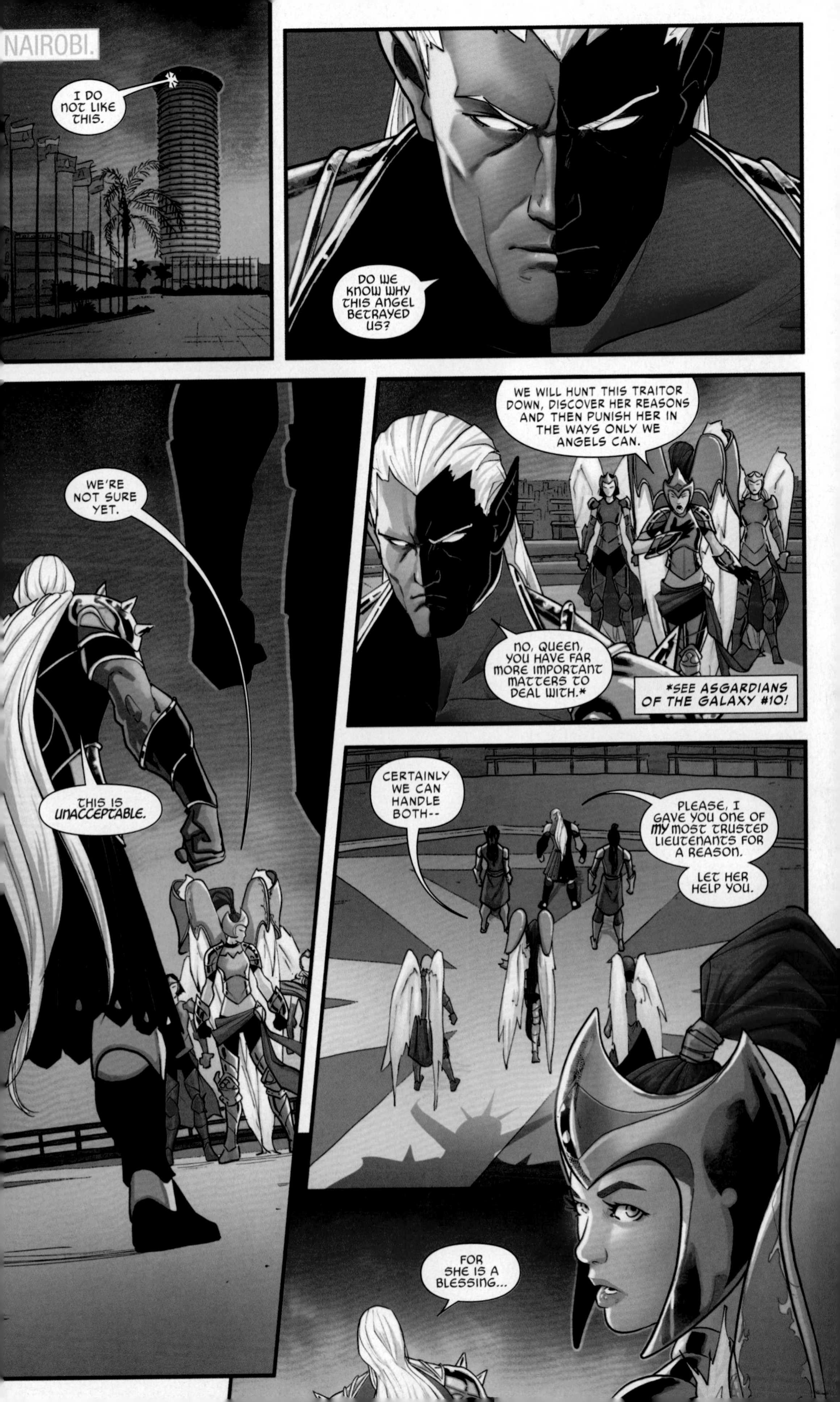
NAIROBI.
I DO NOT LIKE THIS.
DO WE KNOW WHY THIS ANGEL BETRAYED US?
WE'RE NOT SURE YET.
THIS IS UNACCEPTABLE.
WE WILL HUNT THIS TRAITOR DOWN, DISCOVER HER REASONS AND THEN PUNISH HER IN THE WAYS ONLY WE ANGELS CAN.
NO, QUEEN, YOU HAVE FAR MORE IMPORTANT MATTERS TO DEAL WITH.*
*SEE ASGARDIANS OF THE GALAXY #10!
CERTAINLY WE CAN HANDLE BOTH--
PLEASE, I GAVE YOU ONE OF MY MOST TRUSTED LIEUTENANTS FOR A REASON.
LET HER HELP YOU.
FOR SHE IS A BLESSING...

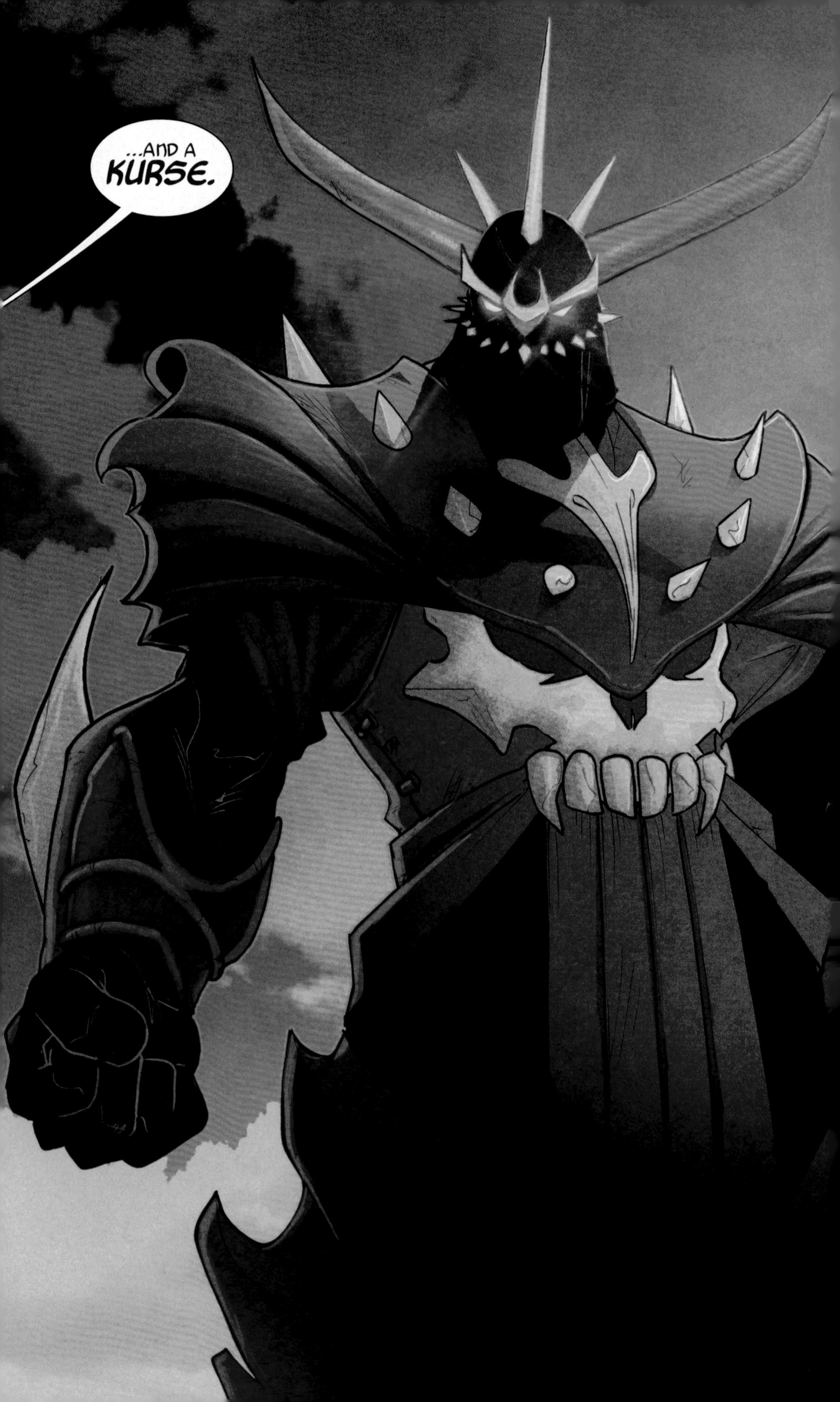
...AND A KURSE.

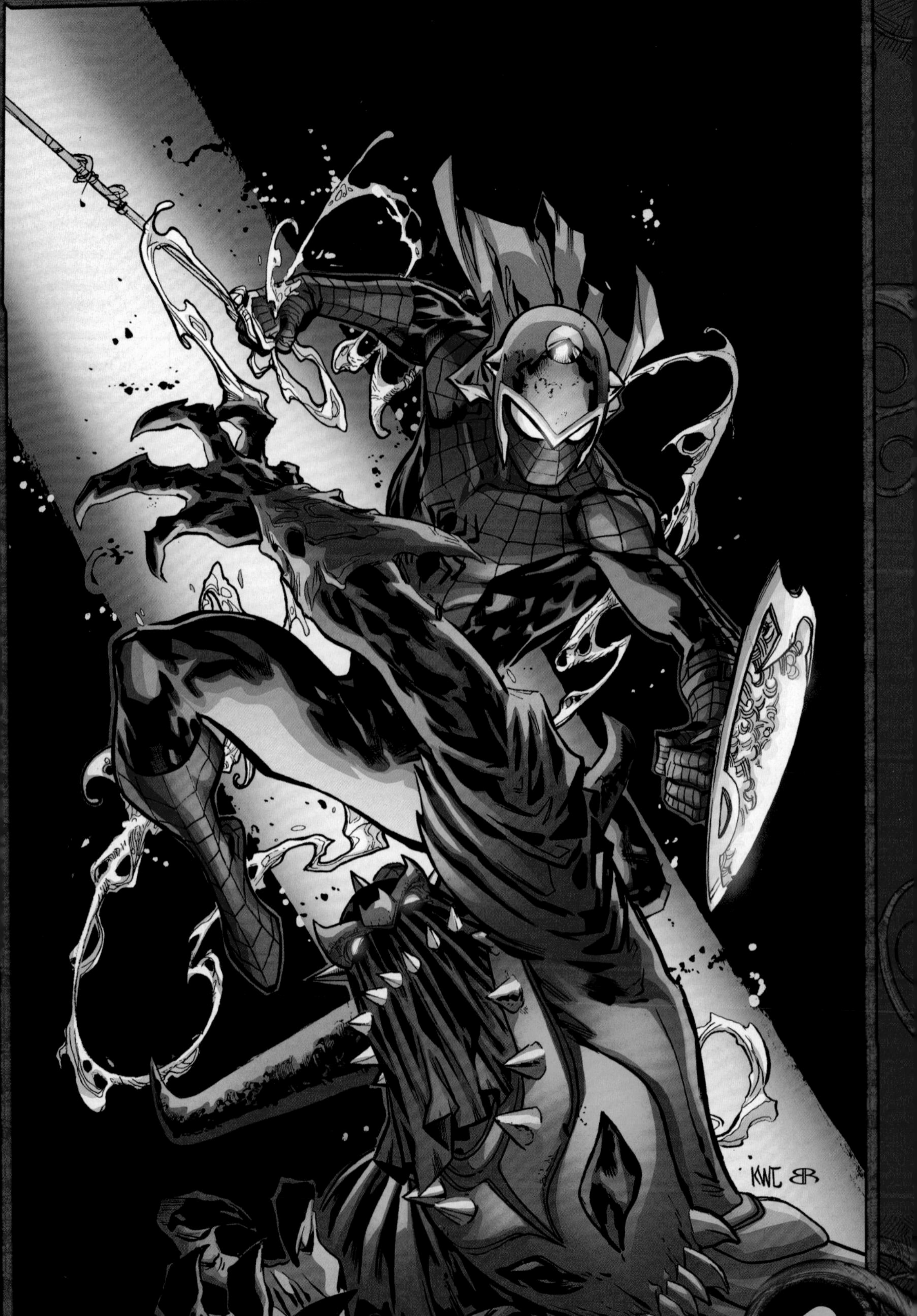
#2

Spider-Man & the League of Realms

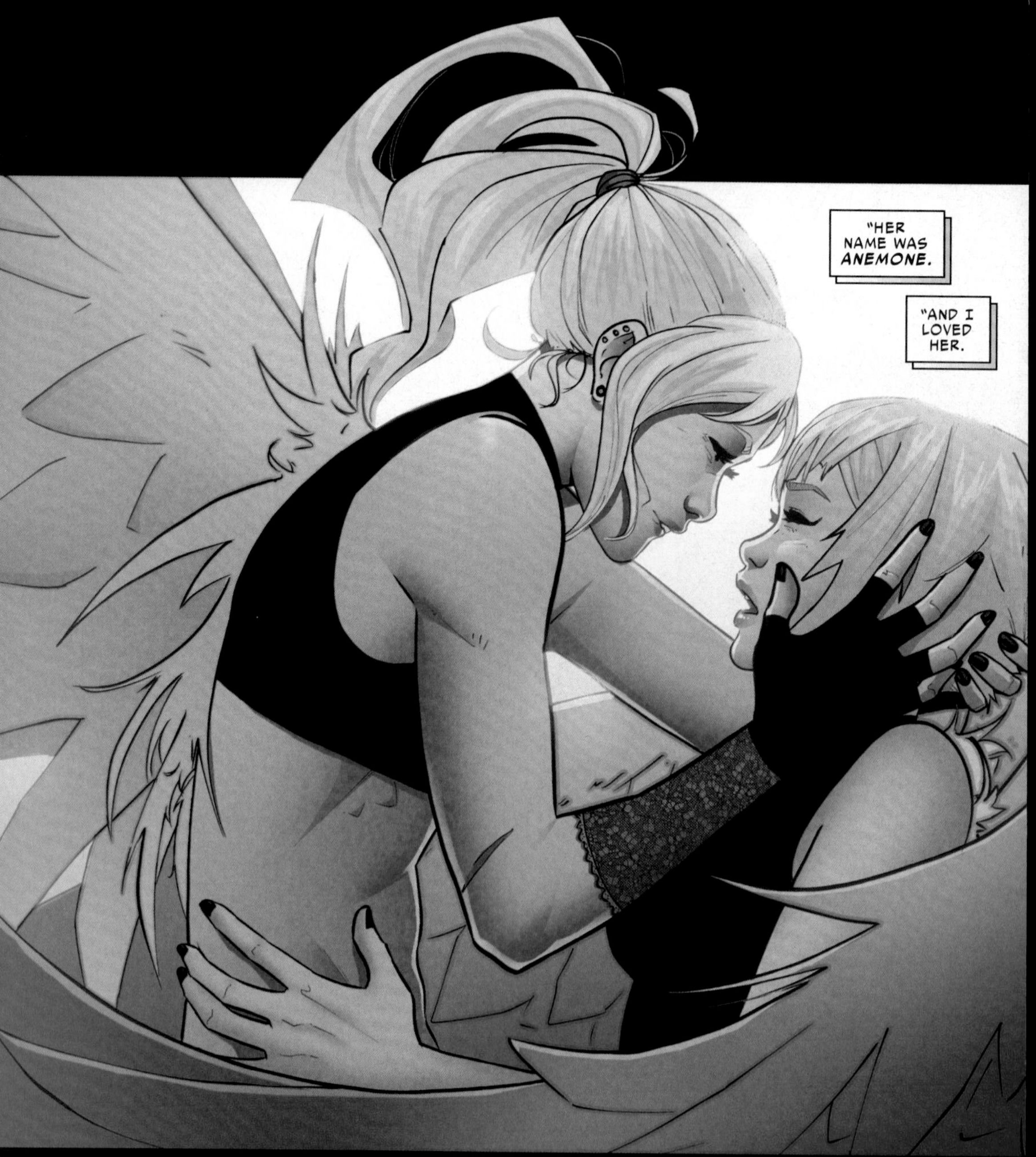
"HER NAME WAS ANEMONE.
"AND I LOVED HER.

Spider-Man and the League of Realms:
"WHY WE FIGHT"
Part 2 of 3

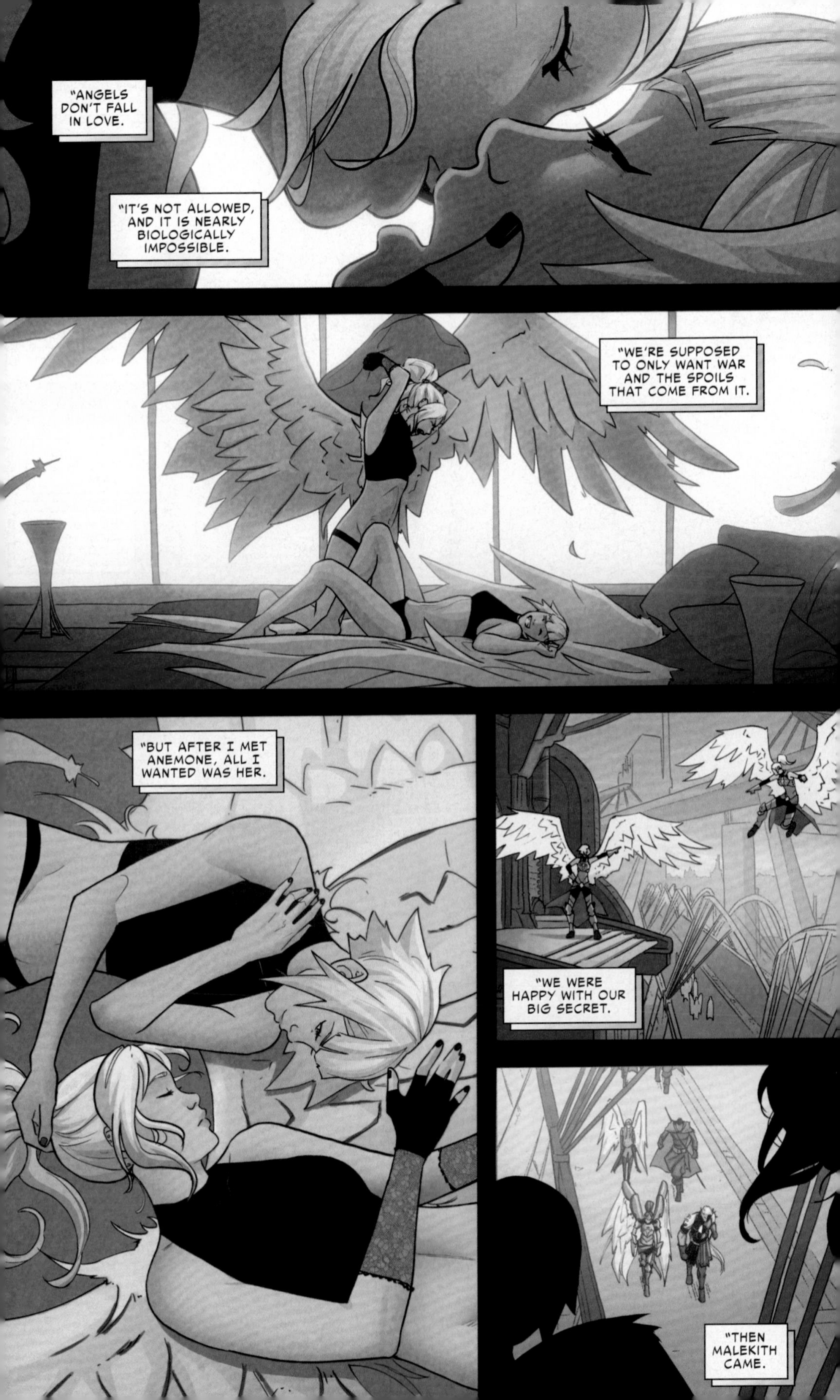
"ANGELS DON'T FALL IN LOVE.
"IT'S NOT ALLOWED, AND IT IS NEARLY BIOLOGICALLY IMPOSSIBLE.
"WE'RE SUPPOSED TO ONLY WANT WAR AND THE SPOILS THAT COME FROM IT.
"BUT AFTER I MET ANEMONE, ALL I WANTED WAS HER.
"WE WERE HAPPY WITH OUR BIG SECRET.
"THEN MALEKITH CAME.

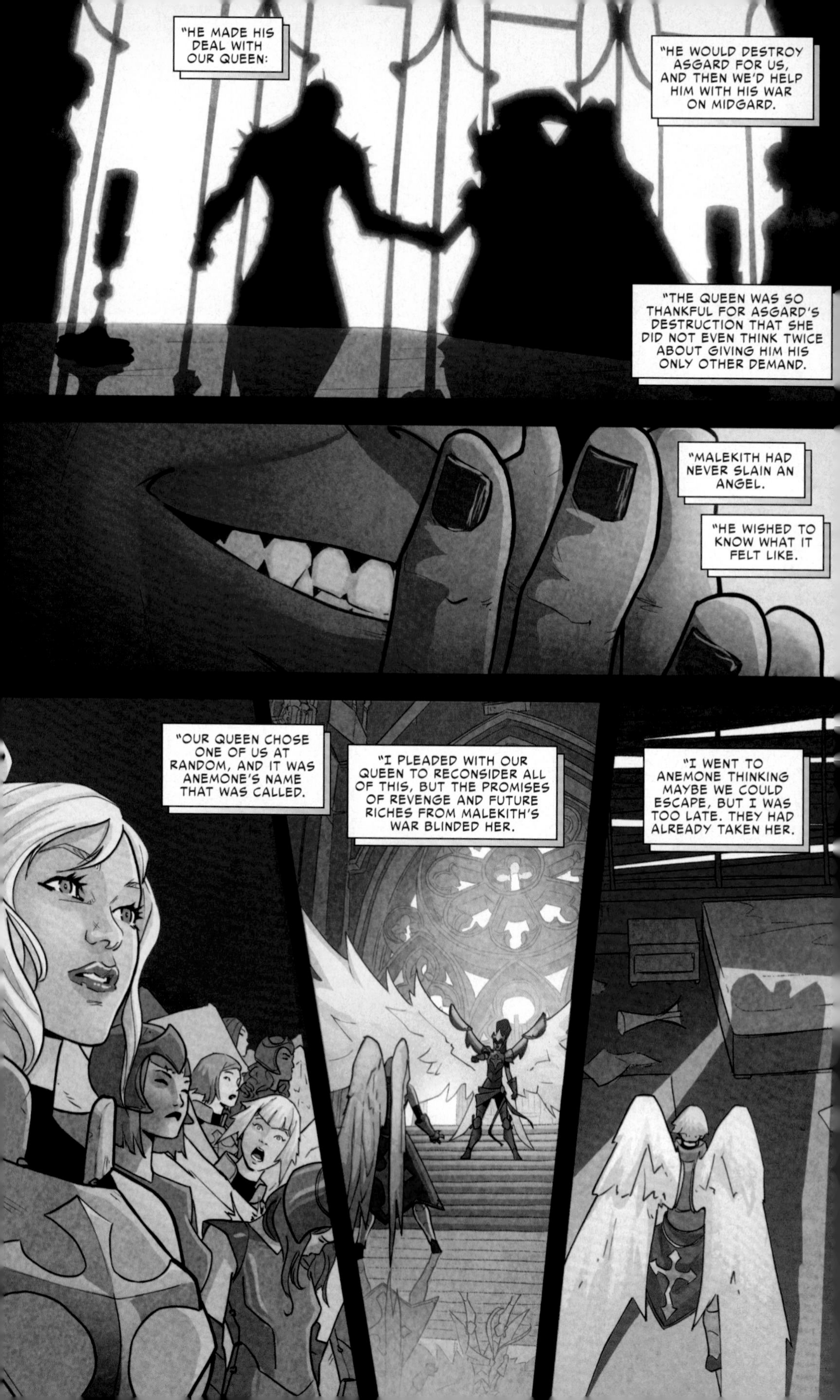
"HE MADE HIS DEAL WITH OUR QUEEN:
"HE WOULD DESTROY ASGARD FOR US, AND THEN WE'D HELP HIM WITH HIS WAR ON MIDGARD.
"THE QUEEN WAS SO THANKFUL FOR ASGARD'S DESTRUCTION THAT SHE DID NOT EVEN THINK TWICE ABOUT GIVING HIM HIS ONLY OTHER DEMAND.
"MALEKITH HAD NEVER SLAIN AN ANGEL.
"HE WISHED TO KNOW WHAT IT FELT LIKE.
"OUR QUEEN CHOSE ONE OF US AT RANDOM, AND IT WAS ANEMONE'S NAME THAT WAS CALLED.
"I PLEADED WITH OUR QUEEN TO RECONSIDER ALL OF THIS, BUT THE PROMISES OF REVENGE AND FUTURE RICHES FROM MALEKITH'S WAR BLINDED HER.
"I WENT TO ANEMONE THINKING MAYBE WE COULD ESCAPE, BUT I WAS TOO LATE. THEY HAD ALREADY TAKEN HER.

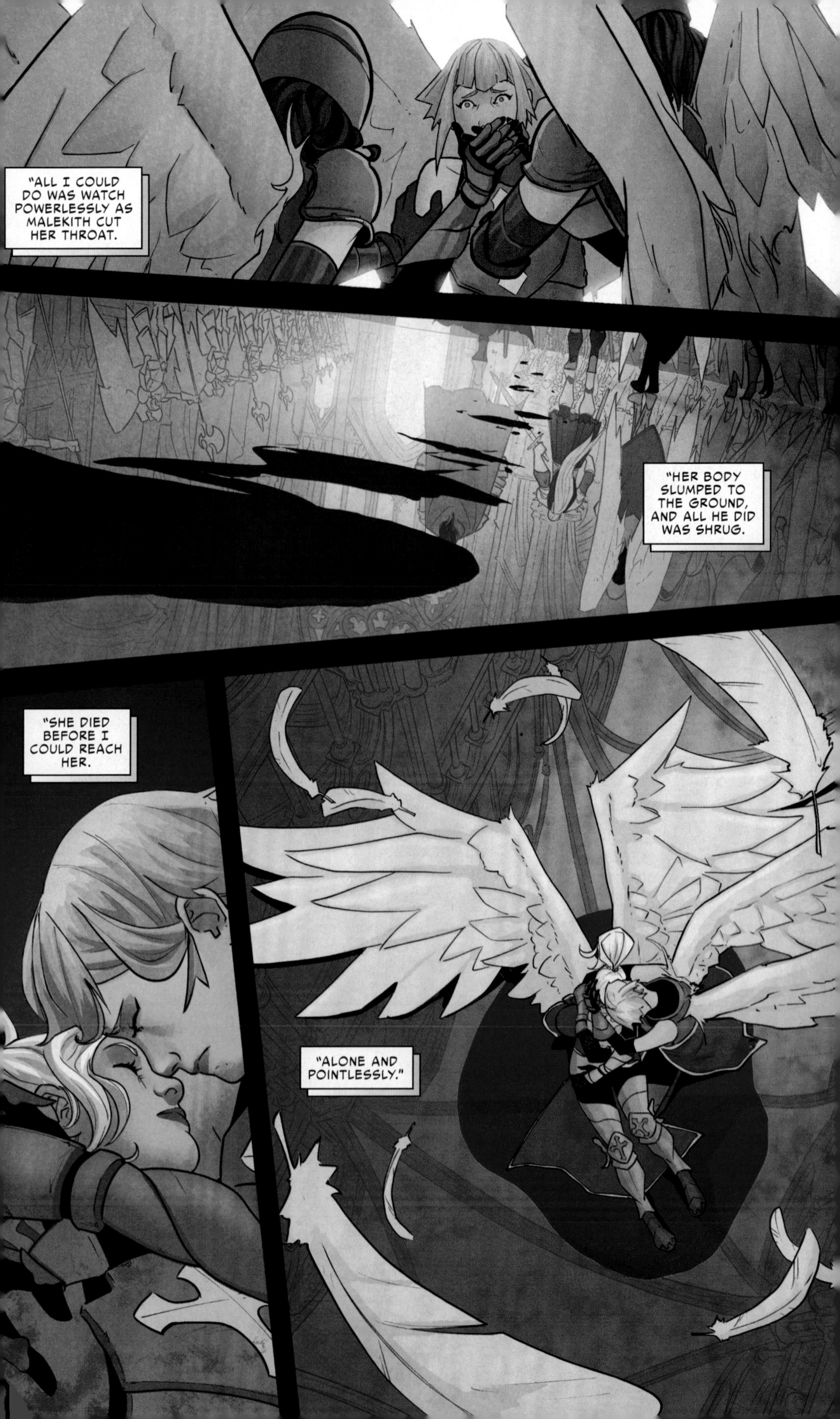
"ALL I COULD DO WAS WATCH POWERLESSLY AS MALEKITH CUT HER THROAT.
"HER BODY SLUMPED TO THE GROUND, AND ALL HE DID WAS SHRUG.
"SHE DIED BEFORE I COULD REACH HER.
"ALONE AND POINTLESSLY."

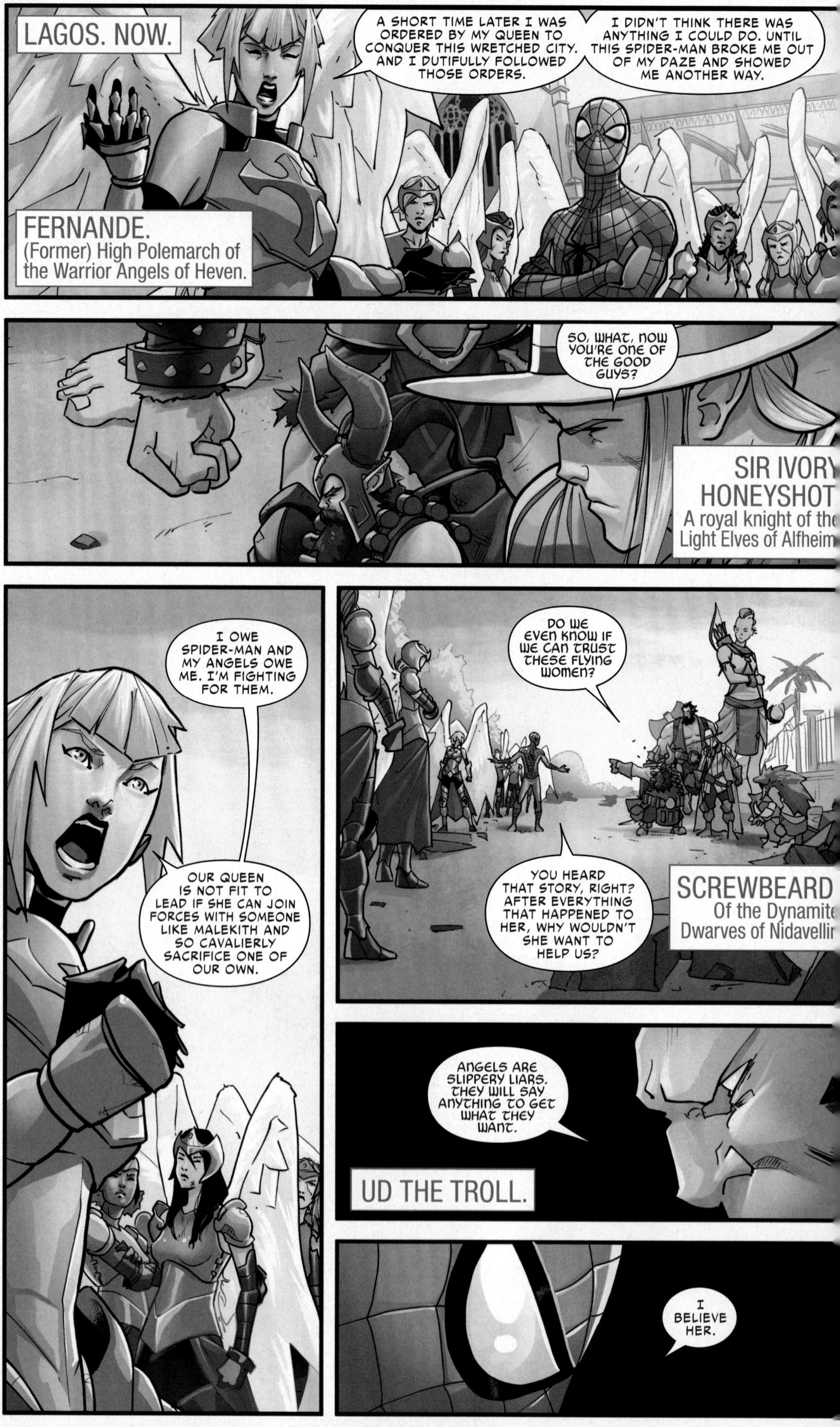

LAGOS. NOW.
A SHORT TIME LATER I WAS ORDERED BY MY QUEEN TO CONQUER THIS WRETCHED CITY. AND I DUTIFULLY FOLLOWED THOSE ORDERS.
I DIDN'T THINK THERE WAS ANYTHING I COULD DO. UNTIL THIS SPIDER-MAN BROKE ME OUT OF MY DAZE AND SHOWED ME ANOTHER WAY.
FERNANDE. (Former) High Polemarch of the Warrior Angels of Heven.
SO, WHAT, NOW YOU'RE ONE OF THE GOOD GUYS?
SIR IVORY HONEYSHOT A royal knight of the Light Elves of Alfheim
I OWE SPIDER-MAN AND MY ANGELS OWE ME. I'M FIGHTING FOR THEM.
OUR QUEEN IS NOT FIT TO LEAD IF SHE CAN JOIN FORCES WITH SOMEONE LIKE MALEKITH AND SO CAVALIERLY SACRIFICE ONE OF OUR OWN.
DO WE EVEN KNOW IF WE CAN TRUST THESE FLYING WOMEN?
YOU HEARD THAT STORY, RIGHT? AFTER EVERYTHING THAT HAPPENED TO HER, WHY WOULDN'T SHE WANT TO HELP US?
SCREWBEARD Of the Dynamite Dwarves of Nidavellir
ANGELS ARE SLIPPERY LIARS. THEY WILL SAY ANYTHING TO GET WHAT THEY WANT.
UD THE TROLL.
I BELIEVE HER.

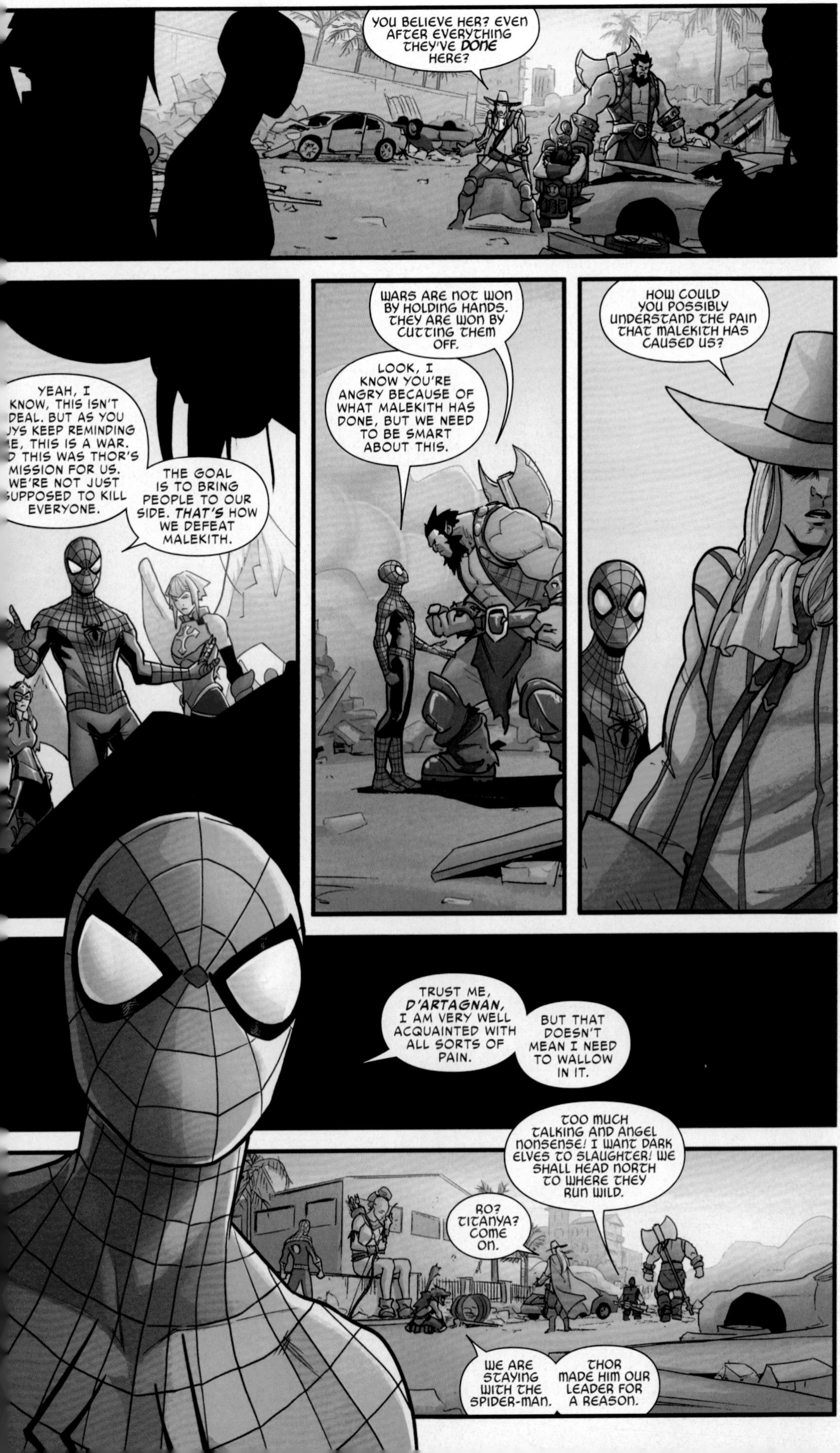

YOU BELIEVE HER? EVEN AFTER EVERYTHING THEY'VE DONE HERE?
YEAH, I KNOW, THIS ISN'T DEAL. BUT AS YOU UYS KEEP REMINDING E, THIS IS A WAR. D THIS WAS THOR'S MISSION FOR US. WE'RE NOT JUST SUPPOSED TO KILL EVERYONE.
THE GOAL IS TO BRING PEOPLE TO OUR SIDE. THAT'S HOW WE DEFEAT MALEKITH.
WARS ARE NOT WON BY HOLDING HANDS. THEY ARE WON BY CUTTING THEM OFF.
LOOK, I KNOW YOU'RE ANGRY BECAUSE OF WHAT MALEKITH HAS DONE, BUT WE NEED TO BE SMART ABOUT THIS.
HOW COULD YOU POSSIBLY UNDERSTAND THE PAIN THAT MALEKITH HAS CAUSED US?
TRUST ME, D'ARTAGNAN, I AM VERY WELL ACQUAINTED WITH ALL SORTS OF PAIN.
BUT THAT DOESN'T MEAN I NEED TO WALLOW IN IT.
TOO MUCH TALKING AND ANGEL NONSENSE! I WANT DARK ELVES TO SLAUGHTER! WE SHALL HEAD NORTH TO WHERE THEY RUN WILD.
RO? TITANYA? COME ON.
WE ARE STAYING WITH THE SPIDER-MAN.
THOR MADE HIM OUR LEADER FOR A REASON.

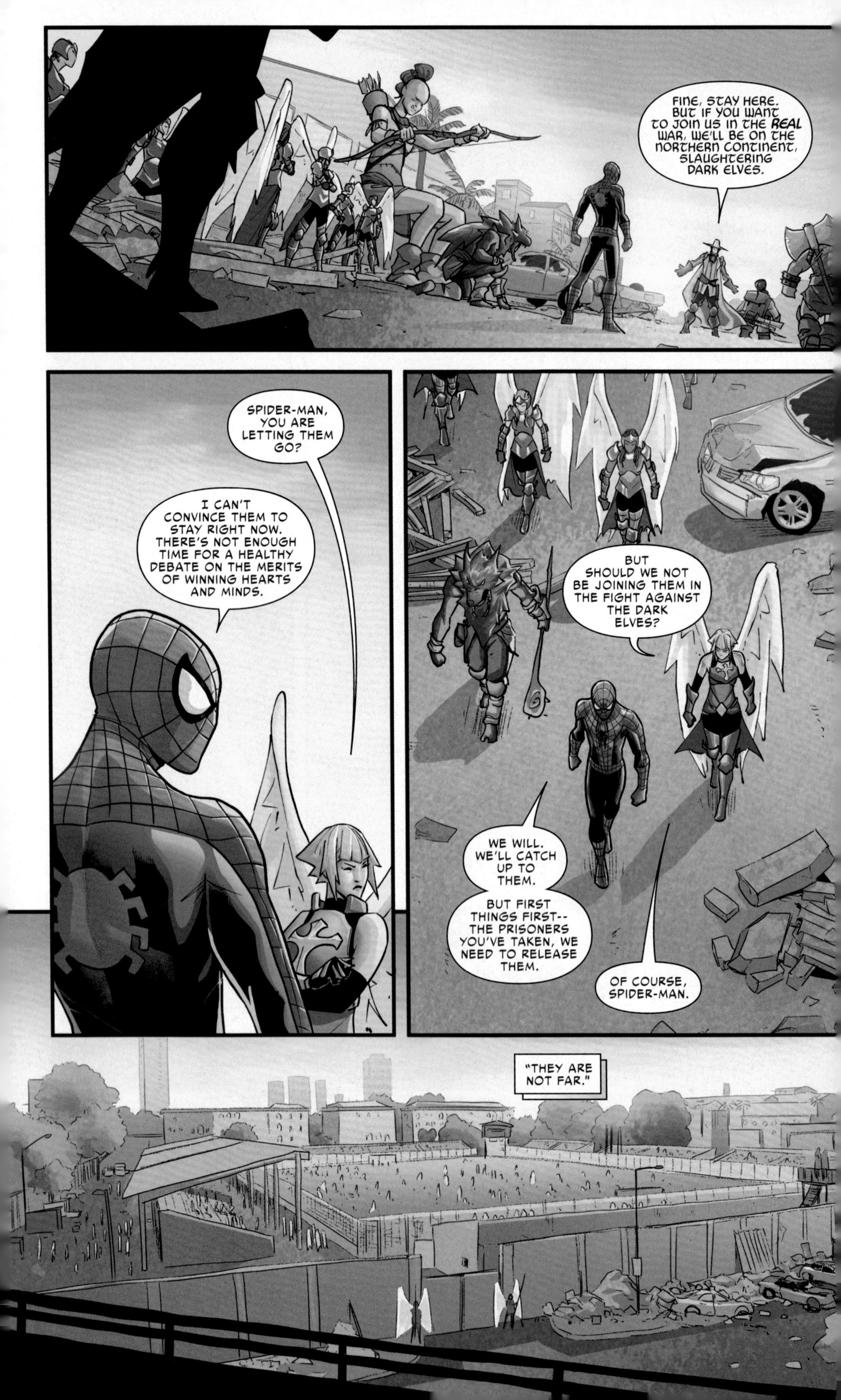

FINE, STAY HERE. BUT IF YOU WANT TO JOIN US IN THE **REAL** WAR, WE'LL BE ON THE NORTHERN CONTINENT, SLAUGHTERING DARK ELVES.
SPIDER-MAN, YOU ARE LETTING THEM GO?
I CAN'T CONVINCE THEM TO STAY RIGHT NOW. THERE'S NOT ENOUGH TIME FOR A HEALTHY DEBATE ON THE MERITS OF WINNING HEARTS AND MINDS.
BUT SHOULD WE NOT BE JOINING THEM IN THE FIGHT AGAINST THE DARK ELVES?
WE WILL. WE'LL CATCH UP TO THEM.
BUT FIRST THINGS FIRST-- THE PRISONERS YOU'VE TAKEN, WE NEED TO RELEASE THEM.
OF COURSE, SPIDER-MAN.
"THEY ARE NOT FAR."

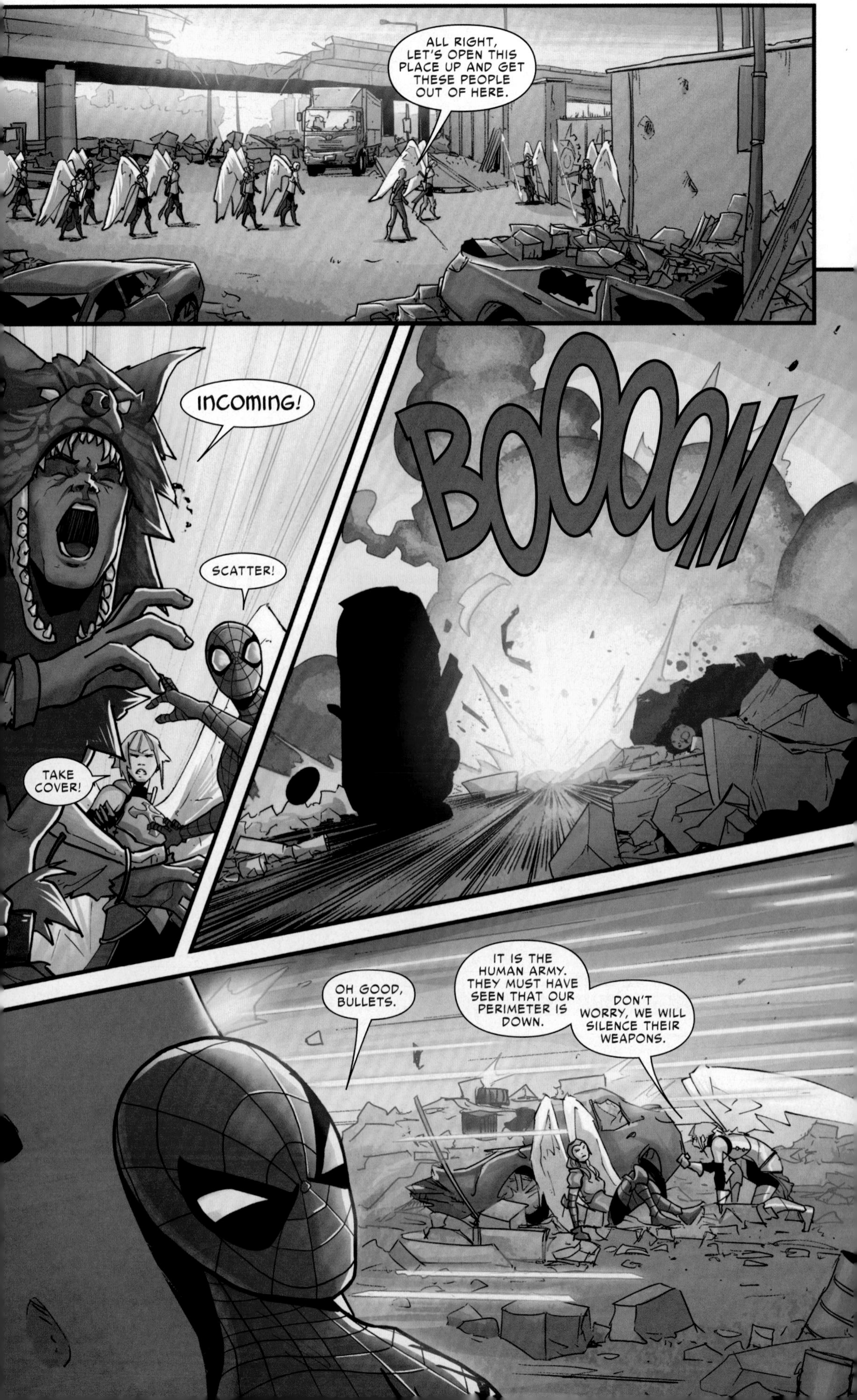
ALL RIGHT, LET'S OPEN THIS PLACE UP AND GET THESE PEOPLE OUT OF HERE.
INCOMING!
SCATTER!
TAKE COVER!
BOOOOM
OH GOOD, BULLETS.
IT IS THE HUMAN ARMY. THEY MUST HAVE SEEN THAT OUR PERIMETER IS DOWN.
DON'T WORRY, WE WILL SILENCE THEIR WEAPONS.

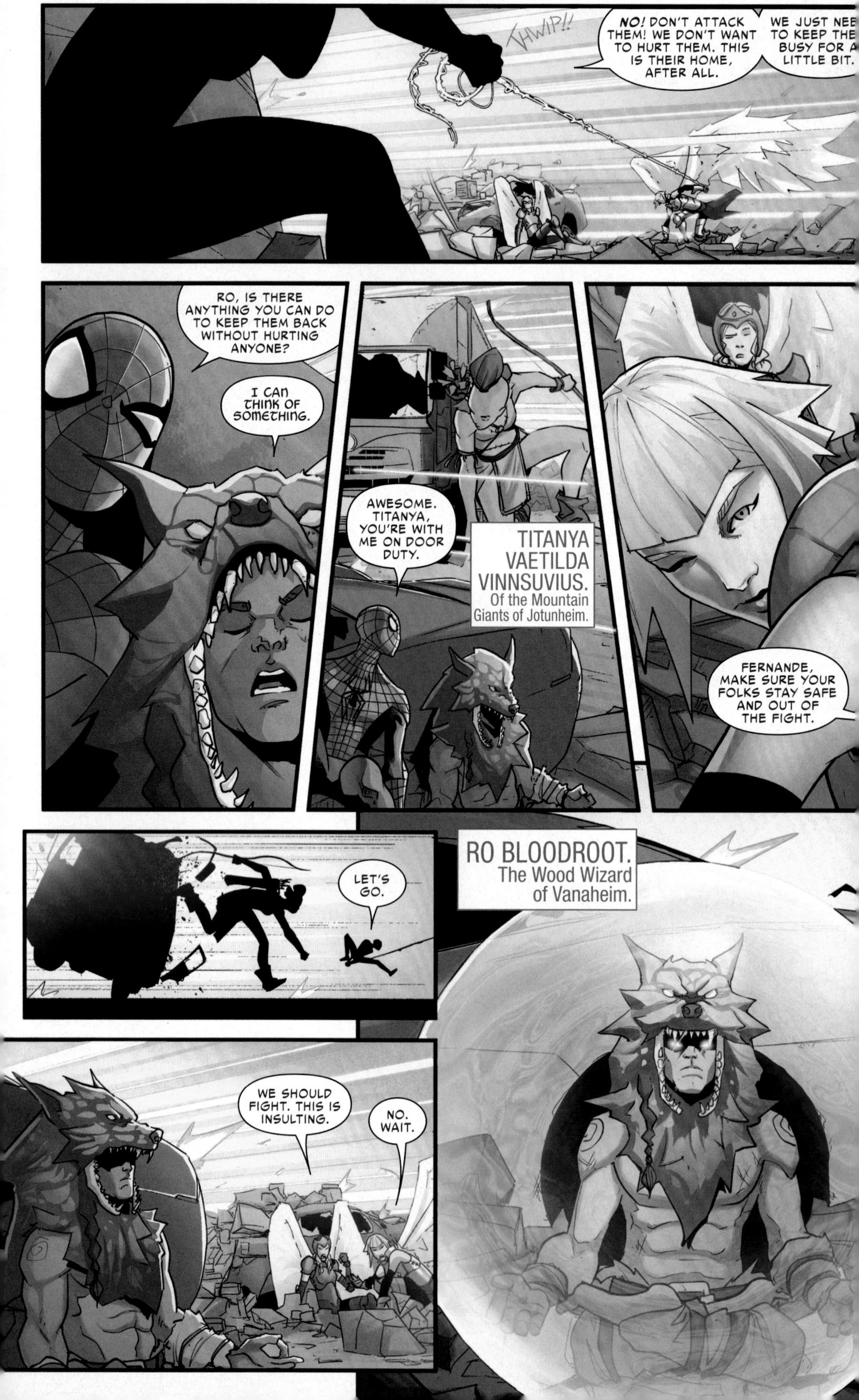
THWIP!!
NO! DON'T ATTACK THEM! WE DON'T WANT TO HURT THEM. THIS IS THEIR HOME, AFTER ALL.
WE JUST NEE TO KEEP THE BUSY FOR A LITTLE BIT.
RO, IS THERE ANYTHING YOU CAN DO TO KEEP THEM BACK WITHOUT HURTING ANYONE?
I CAN THINK OF SOMETHING.
AWESOME. TITANYA, YOU'RE WITH ME ON DOOR DUTY.
TITANYA VAETILDA VINNSUVIUS. Of the Mountain Giants of Jotunheim.
FERNANDE, MAKE SURE YOUR FOLKS STAY SAFE AND OUT OF THE FIGHT.
LET'S GO.
RO BLOODROOT. The Wood Wizard of Vanaheim.
WE SHOULD FIGHT. THIS IS INSULTING.
NO. WAIT.

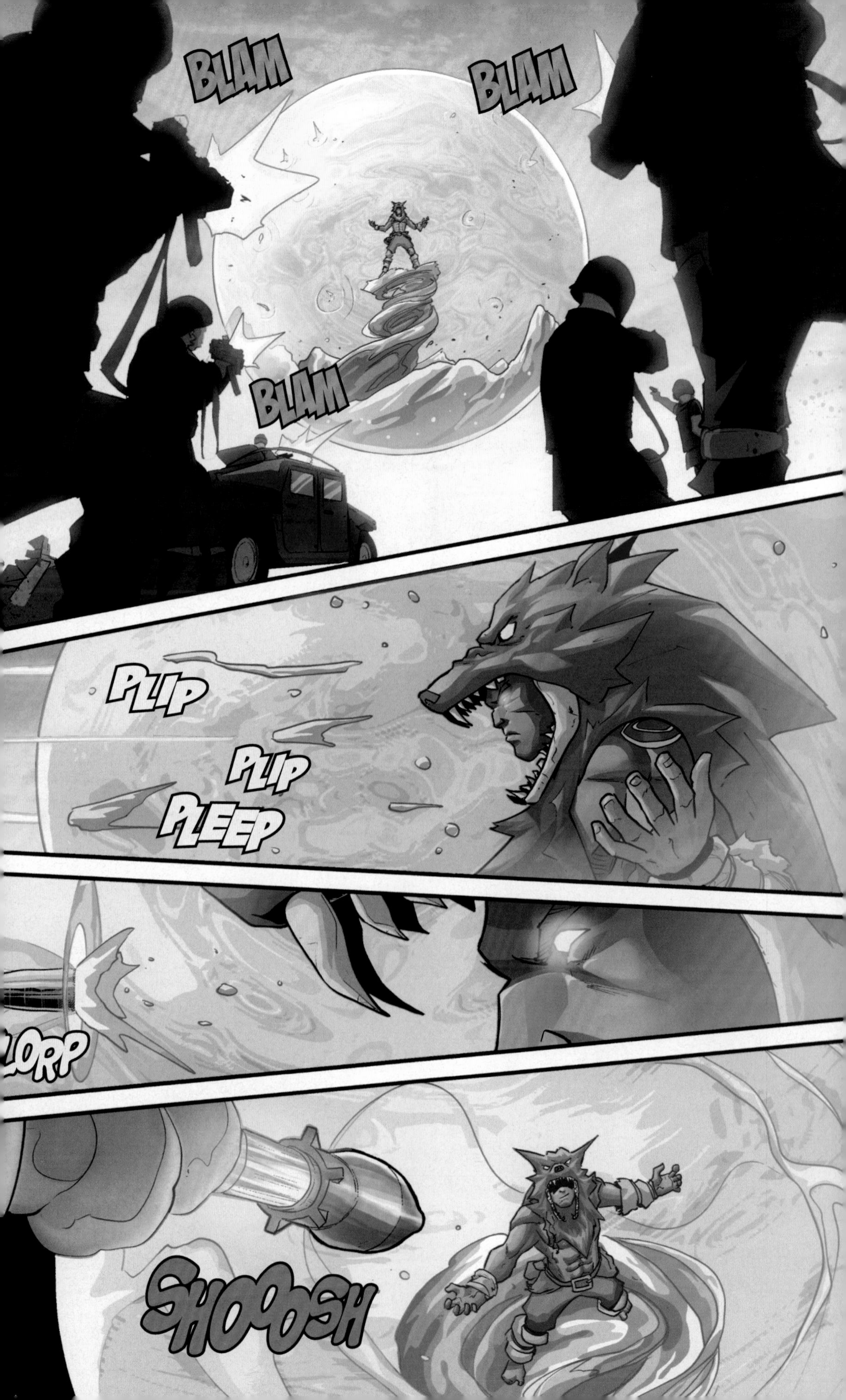
BLAM
BLAM
BLAM
PLIP
PLIP
PLEEP
LORP
SHOOOSH

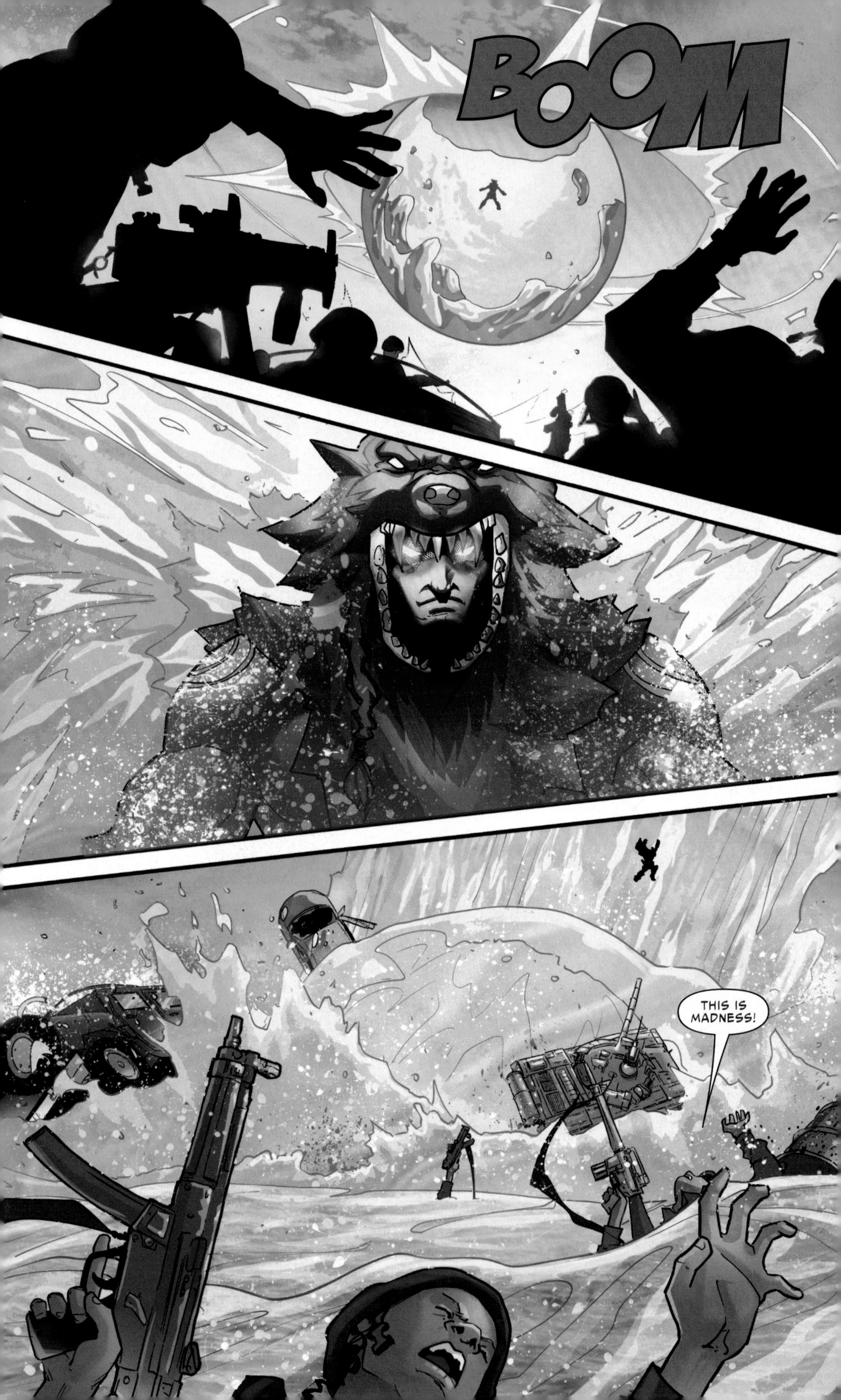
BOOM
THIS IS MADNESS!

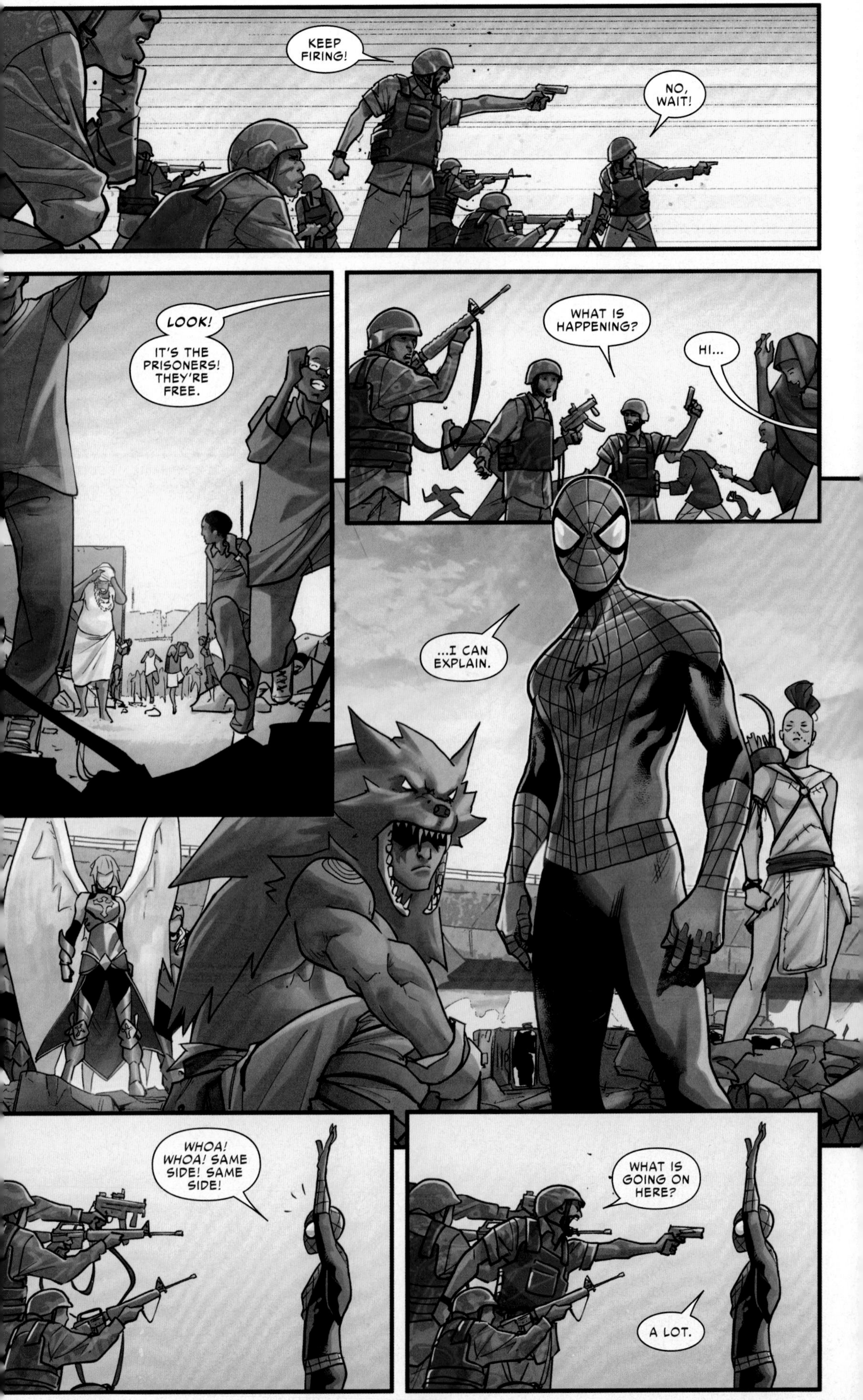
KEEP FIRING!
NO, WAIT!
LOOK!
IT'S THE PRISONERS! THEY'RE FREE.
WHAT IS HAPPENING?
HI...
...I CAN EXPLAIN.
WHOA! WHOA! SAME SIDE! SAME SIDE!
WHAT IS GOING ON HERE?
A LOT.

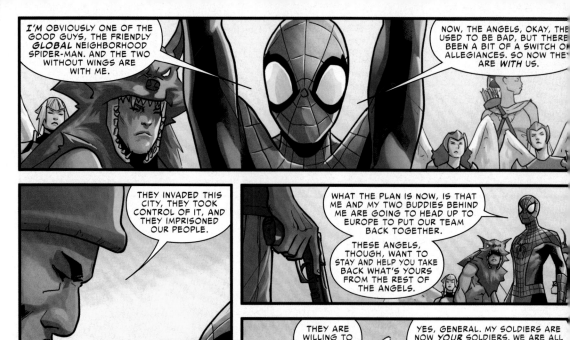

I'M OBVIOUSLY ONE OF THE GOOD GUYS, THE FRIENDLY *GLOBAL* NEIGHBORHOOD SPIDER-MAN. AND THE TWO WITHOUT WINGS ARE WITH ME.

NOW, THE ANGELS, OKAY, THE USED TO BE BAD, BUT THERE BEEN A BIT OF A SWITCH OF ALLEGIANCES. SO NOW THE ARE *WITH* US.

THEY INVADED THIS CITY, THEY TOOK CONTROL OF IT, AND THEY IMPRISONED OUR PEOPLE.

RIGHT, I KNOW. THIS IS ALL SUPER CONFUSING. I DON'T EVEN REALLY KNOW WHAT'S GOING ON.

BUT ONE THING THAT IS CERTAINLY CLEAR IS THAT WE'VE FREED ALL THE PRISONERS.

WHAT THE PLAN IS NOW, IS THAT ME AND MY TWO BUDDIES BEHIND ME ARE GOING TO HEAD UP TO EUROPE TO PUT OUR TEAM BACK TOGETHER.

THESE ANGELS, THOUGH, WANT TO STAY AND HELP YOU TAKE BACK WHAT'S YOURS FROM THE REST OF THE ANGELS.

THEY ARE WILLING TO FIGHT WITH US?

YES, GENERAL. MY SOLDIERS ARE NOW *YOUR* SOLDIERS. WE ARE ALL FIGHTING FOR THE SAME THING. THEY WILL HELP YOU TAKE BACK YOUR LANDS WHILE I TRAVEL WITH SPIDER-MAN TO HELP HIM.

IT IS THE LEAST I CAN DO.

WOW, FERNANDE, ARE YOU SURE ABOUT THAT?

YOU'D FIGHT YOUR OWN PEOPLE?

YES, SPIDER-MAN. I THINK IT IS IMPORTANT THAT I AM SEEN FIGHTING ALONGSIDE YOU.

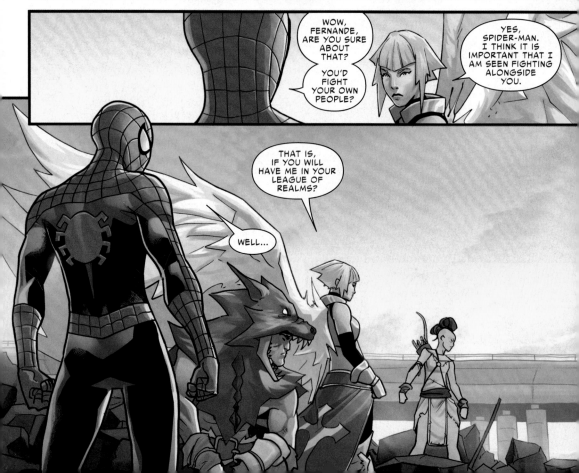

THAT IS, IF YOU WILL HAVE ME IN YOUR LEAGUE OF REALMS?

WELL...

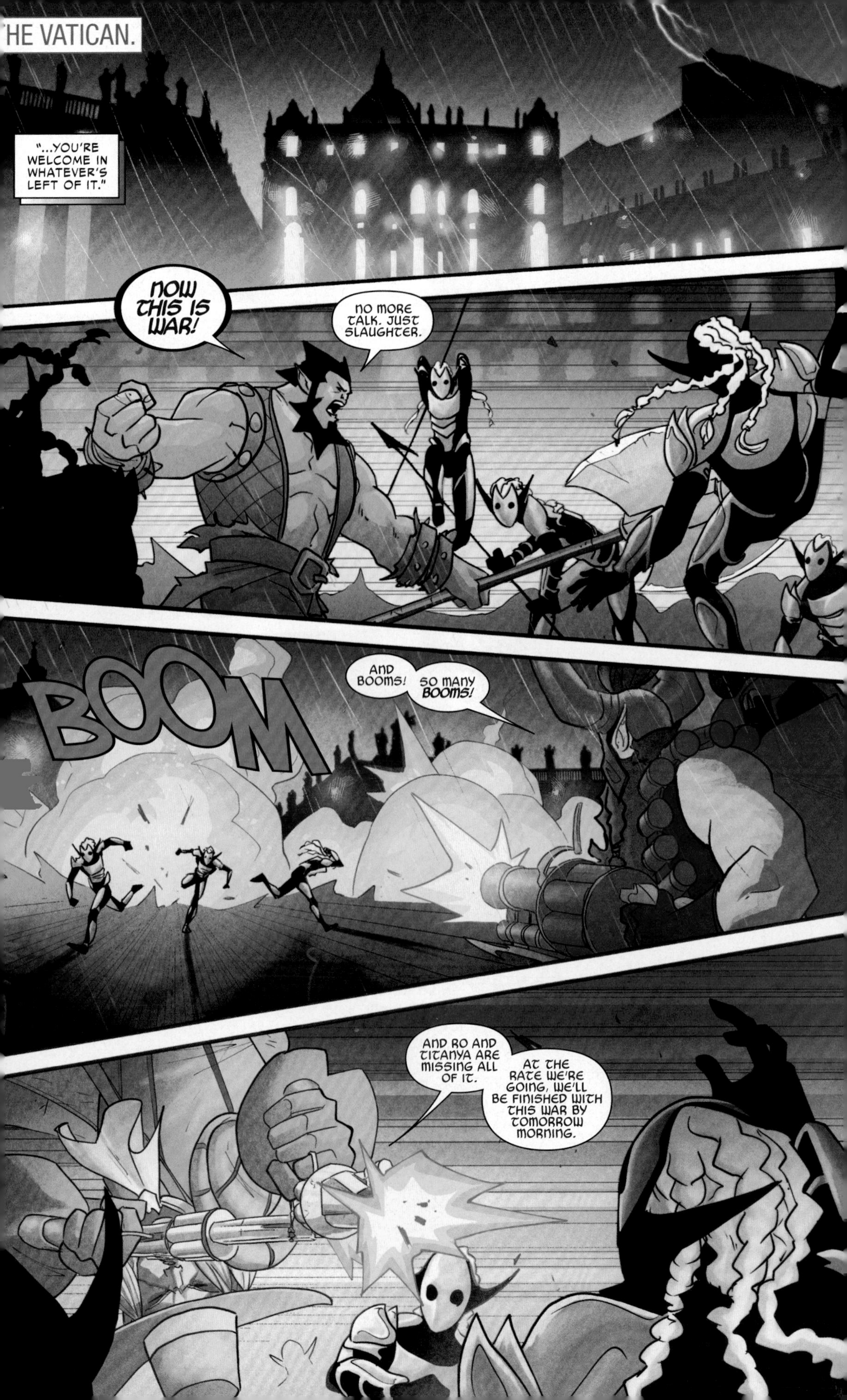
HE VATICAN.
"...YOU'RE WELCOME IN WHATEVER'S LEFT OF IT."
NOW THIS IS WAR!
NO MORE TALK. JUST SLAUGHTER.
BOOM
AND BOOMS!
SO MANY BOOMS!
AND RO AND TITANYA ARE MISSING ALL OF IT.
AT THE RATE WE'RE GOING, WE'LL BE FINISHED WITH THIS WAR BY TOMORROW MORNING.

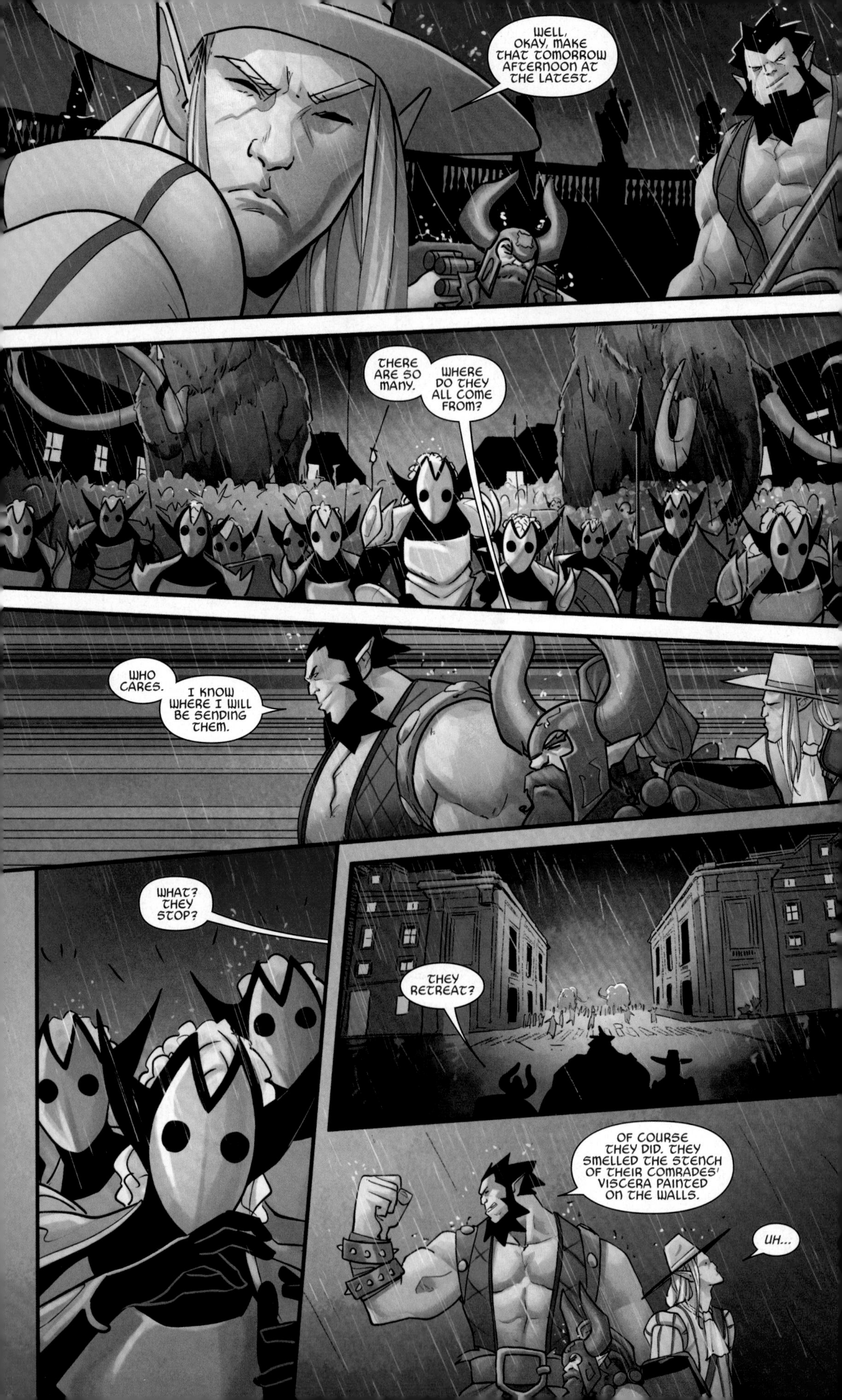
WELL, OKAY, MAKE THAT TOMORROW AFTERNOON AT THE LATEST.
THERE ARE SO MANY.
WHERE DO THEY ALL COME FROM?
WHO CARES.
I KNOW WHERE I WILL BE SENDING THEM.
WHAT? THEY STOP?
THEY RETREAT?
OF COURSE THEY DID. THEY SMELLED THE STENCH OF THEIR COMRADES' VISCERA PAINTED ON THE WALLS.
UH...

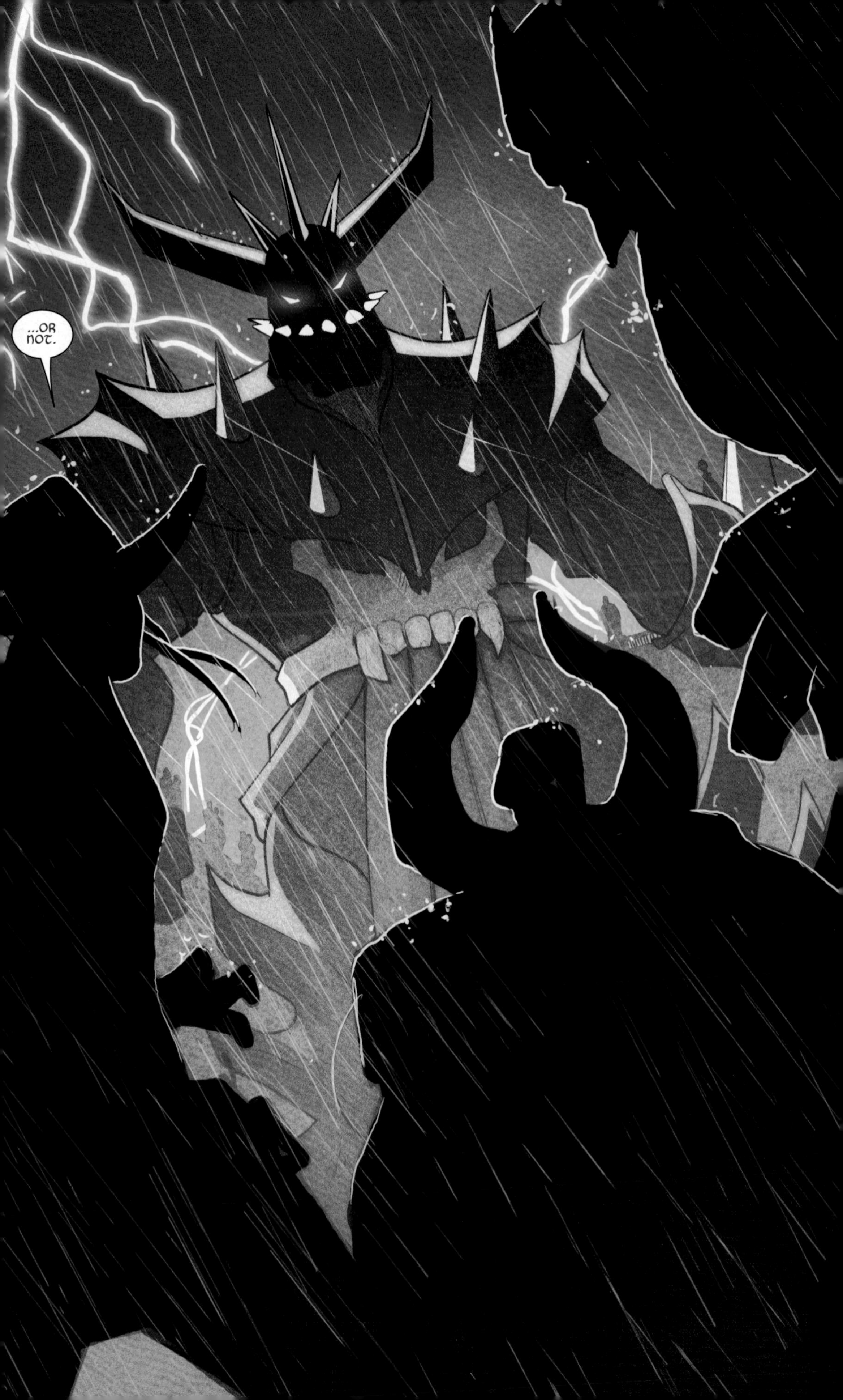
...OR NOT.

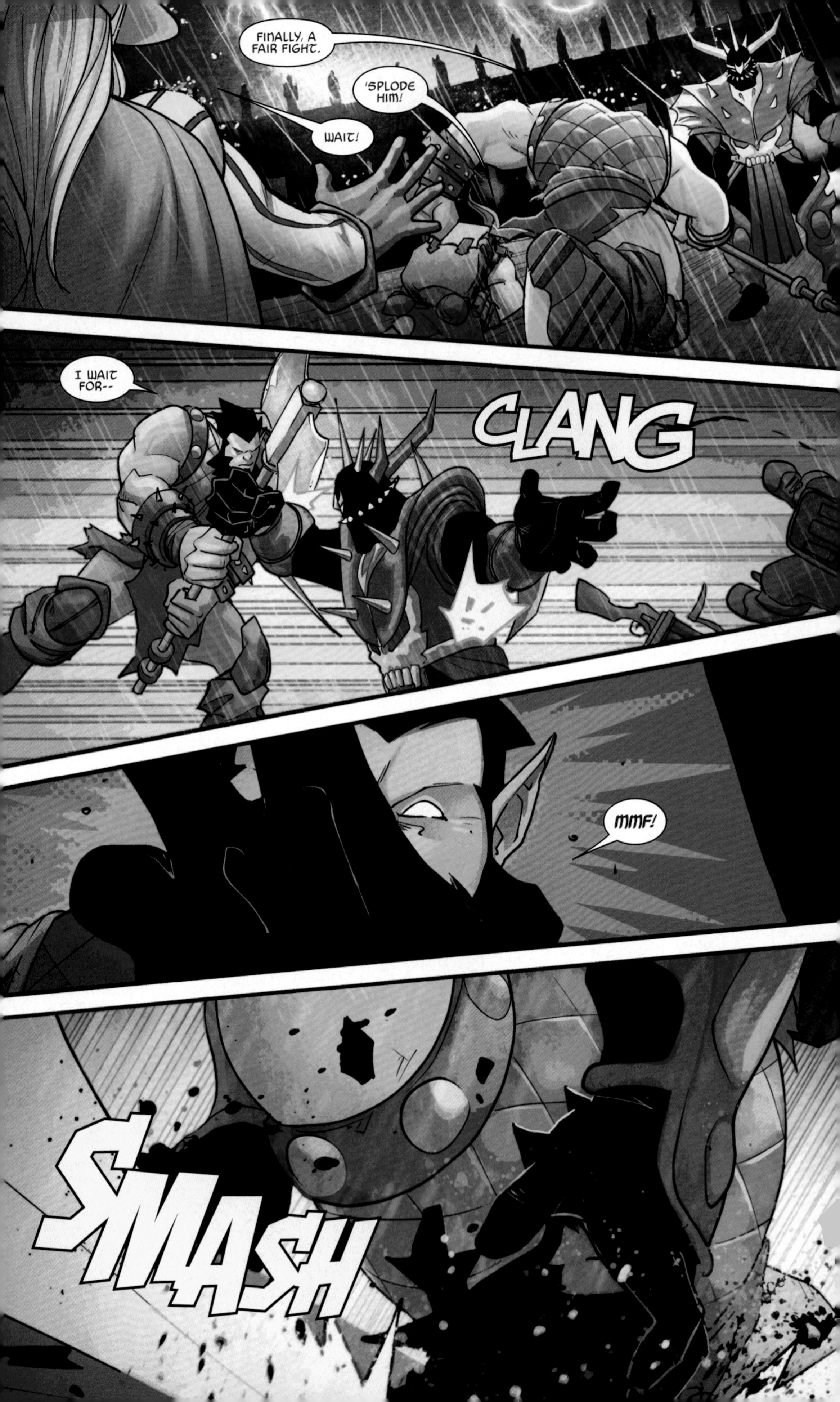
FINALLY, A FAIR FIGHT.
'SPLODE HIM!
WAIT!
I WAIT FOR--
CLANG
MMF!
SMASH

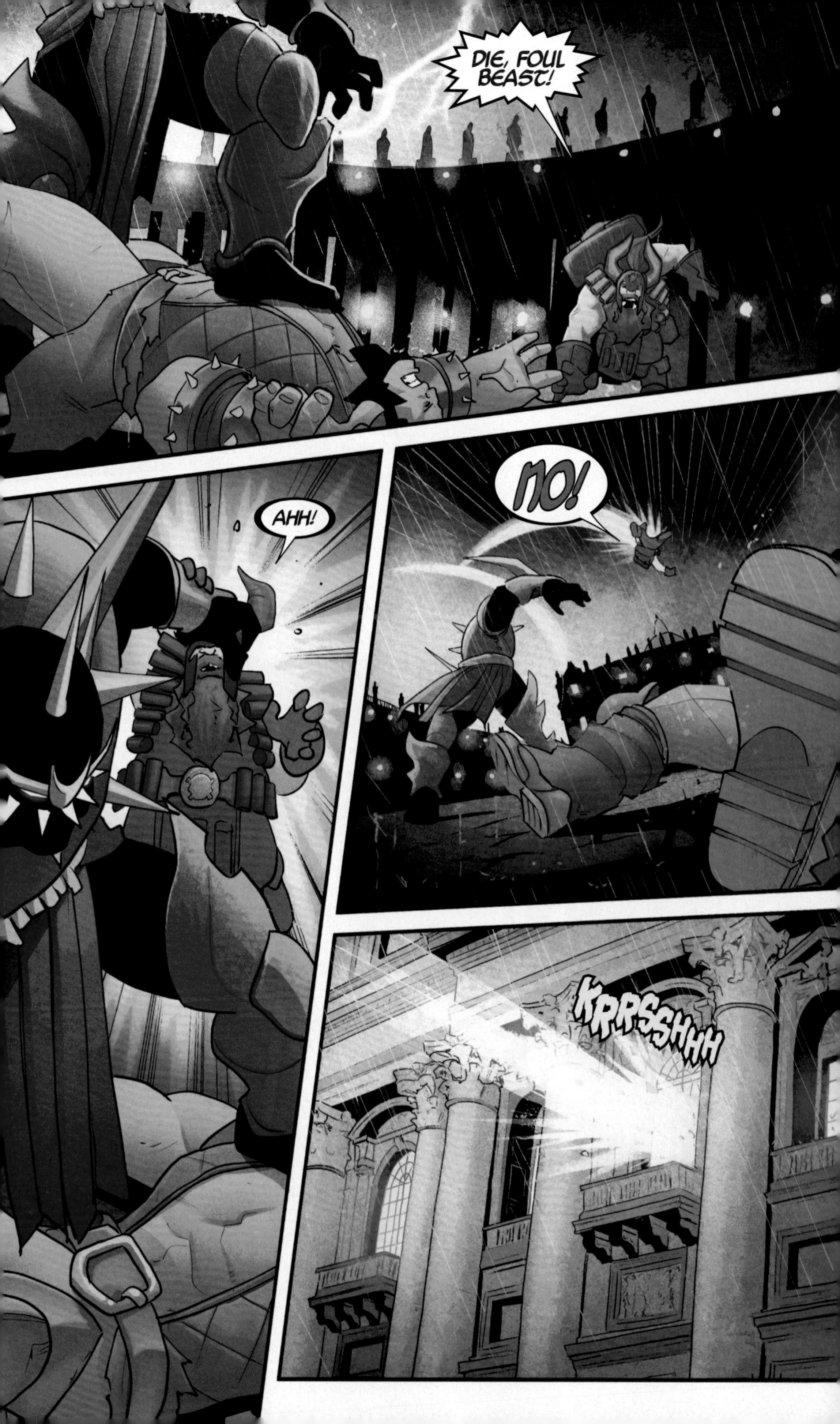
DIE, FOUL BEAST!
AHH!
NO!
KRRSSHHH

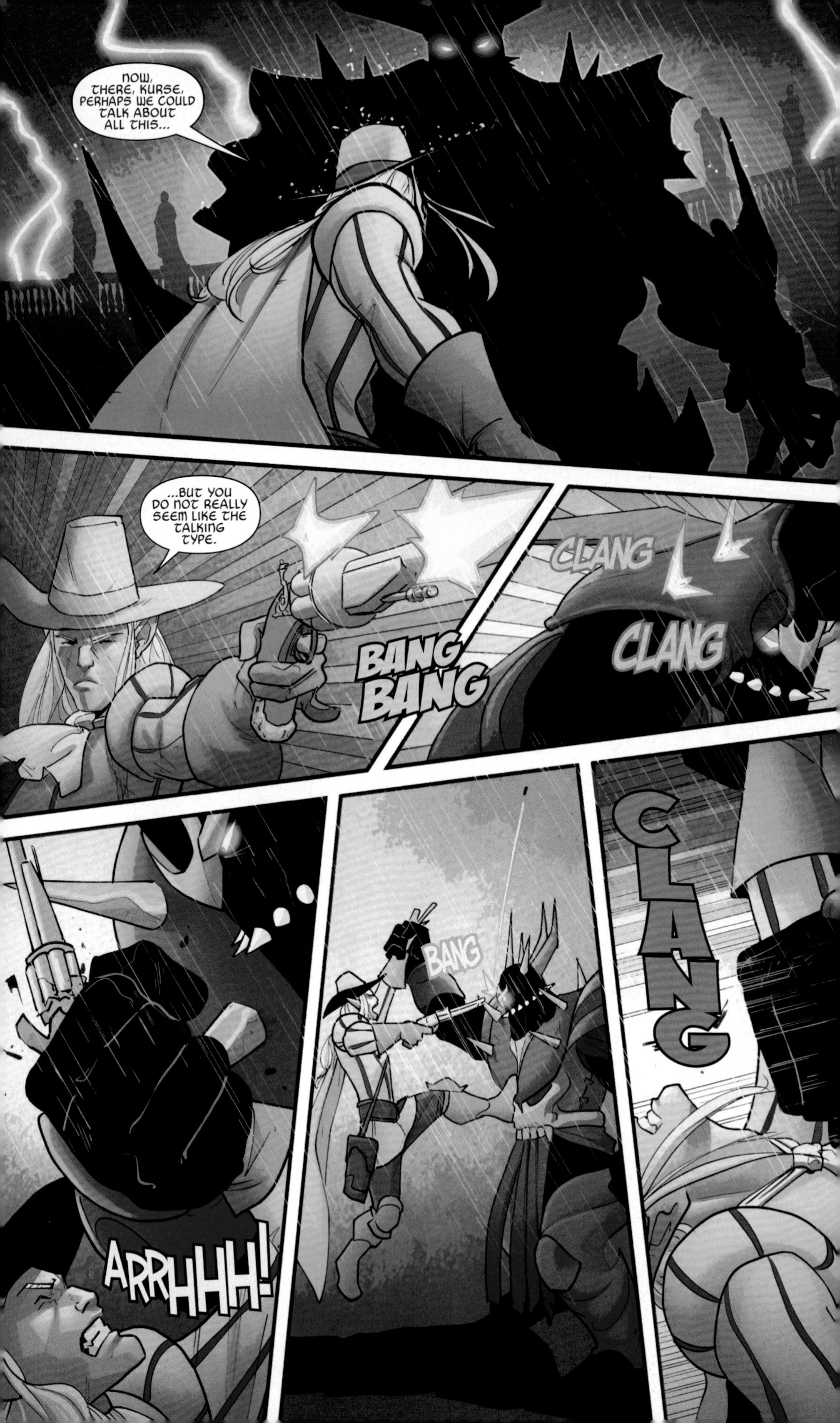
NOW, THERE, KURSE, PERHAPS WE COULD TALK ABOUT ALL THIS...
...BUT YOU DO NOT REALLY SEEM LIKE THE TALKING TYPE.
BANG BANG
CLANG
CLANG
ARRHHH!
BANG
CLANG

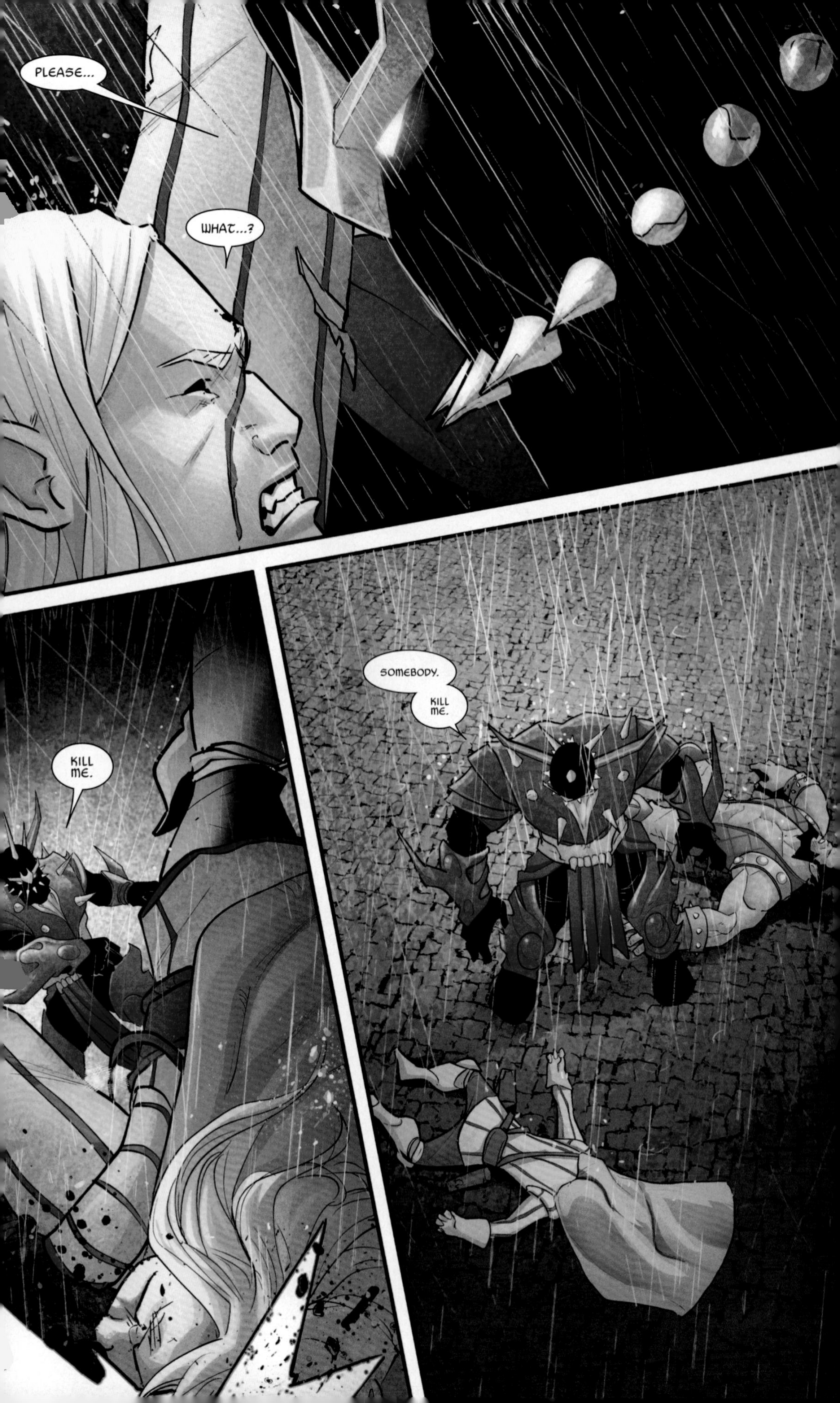
PLEASE...
WHAT...?
KILL ME.
SOMEBODY.
KILL ME.

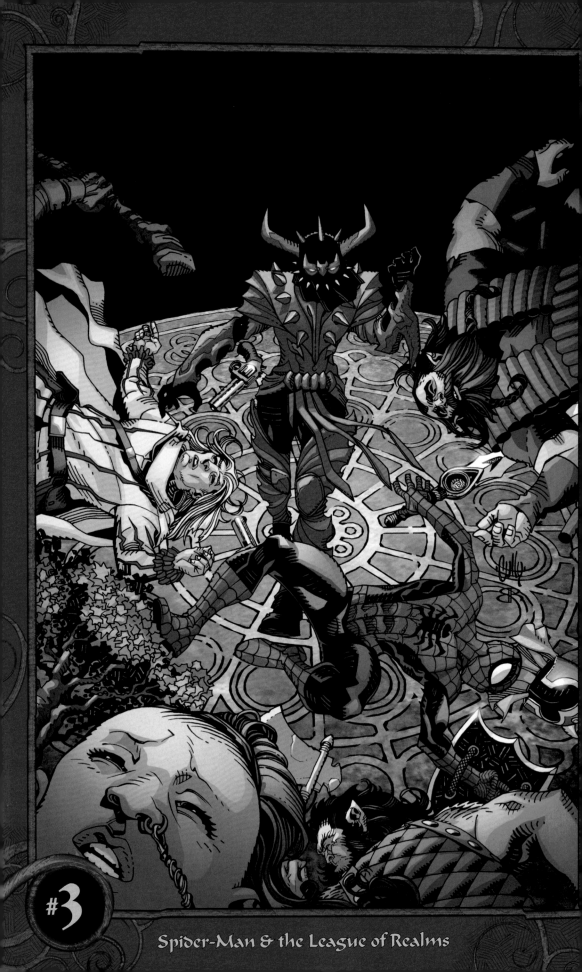

#3

Spider-Man & the League of Realms

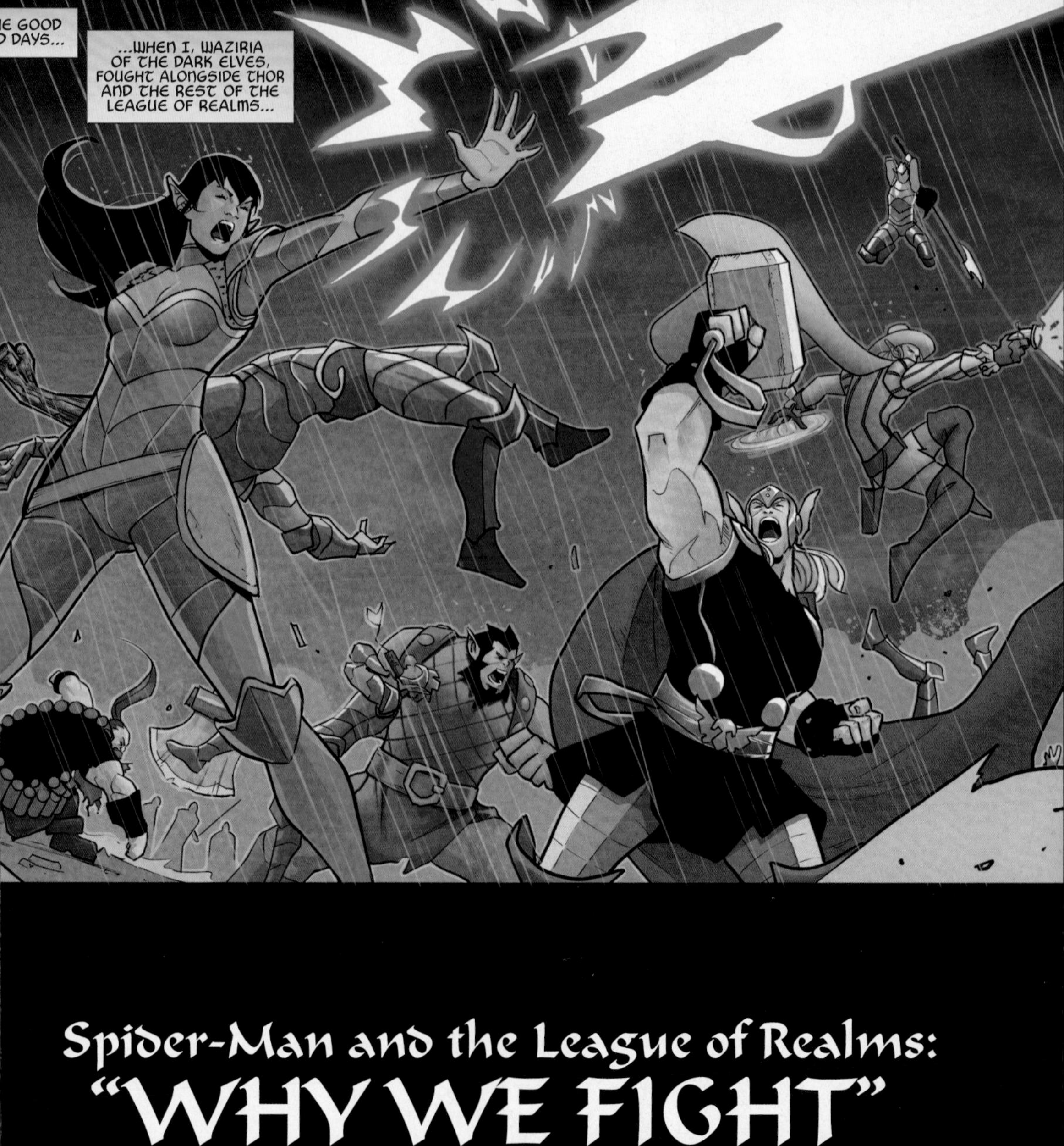
...WHEN I, WAZIRIA OF THE DARK ELVES, FOUGHT ALONGSIDE THOR AND THE REST OF THE LEAGUE OF REALMS...

Spider-Man and the League of Realms: "WHY WE FIGHT"

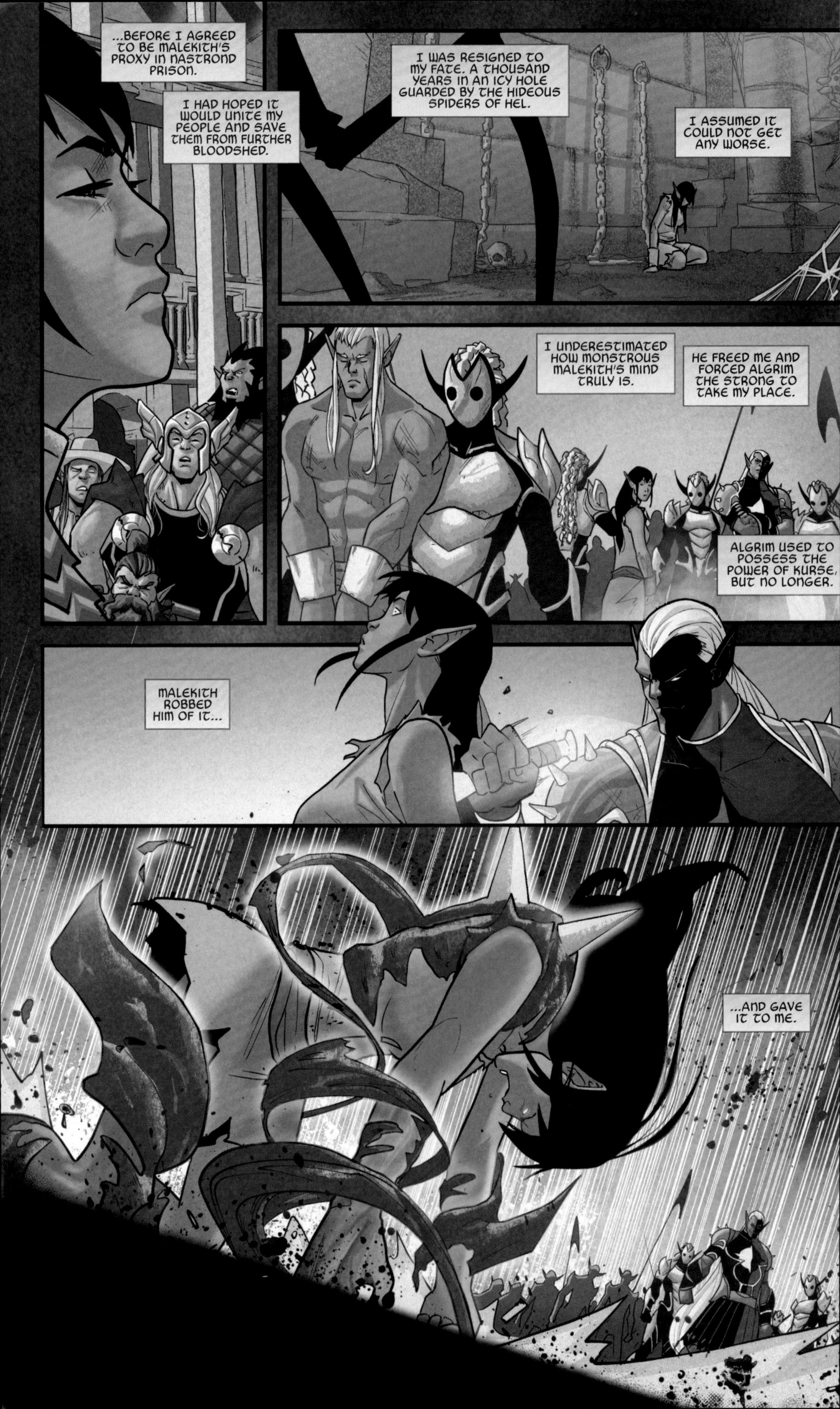
...BEFORE I AGREED TO BE MALEKITH'S PROXY IN NASTROND PRISON.
I HAD HOPED IT WOULD UNITE MY PEOPLE AND SAVE THEM FROM FURTHER BLOODSHED.
I WAS RESIGNED TO MY FATE. A THOUSAND YEARS IN AN ICY HOLE GUARDED BY THE HIDEOUS SPIDERS OF HEL.
I ASSUMED IT COULD NOT GET ANY WORSE.
I UNDERESTIMATED HOW MONSTROUS MALEKITH'S MIND TRULY IS.
HE FREED ME AND FORCED ALGRIM THE STRONG TO TAKE MY PLACE.
ALGRIM USED TO POSSESS THE POWER OF KURSE, BUT NO LONGER.
MALEKITH ROBBED HIM OF IT...
...AND GAVE IT TO ME.

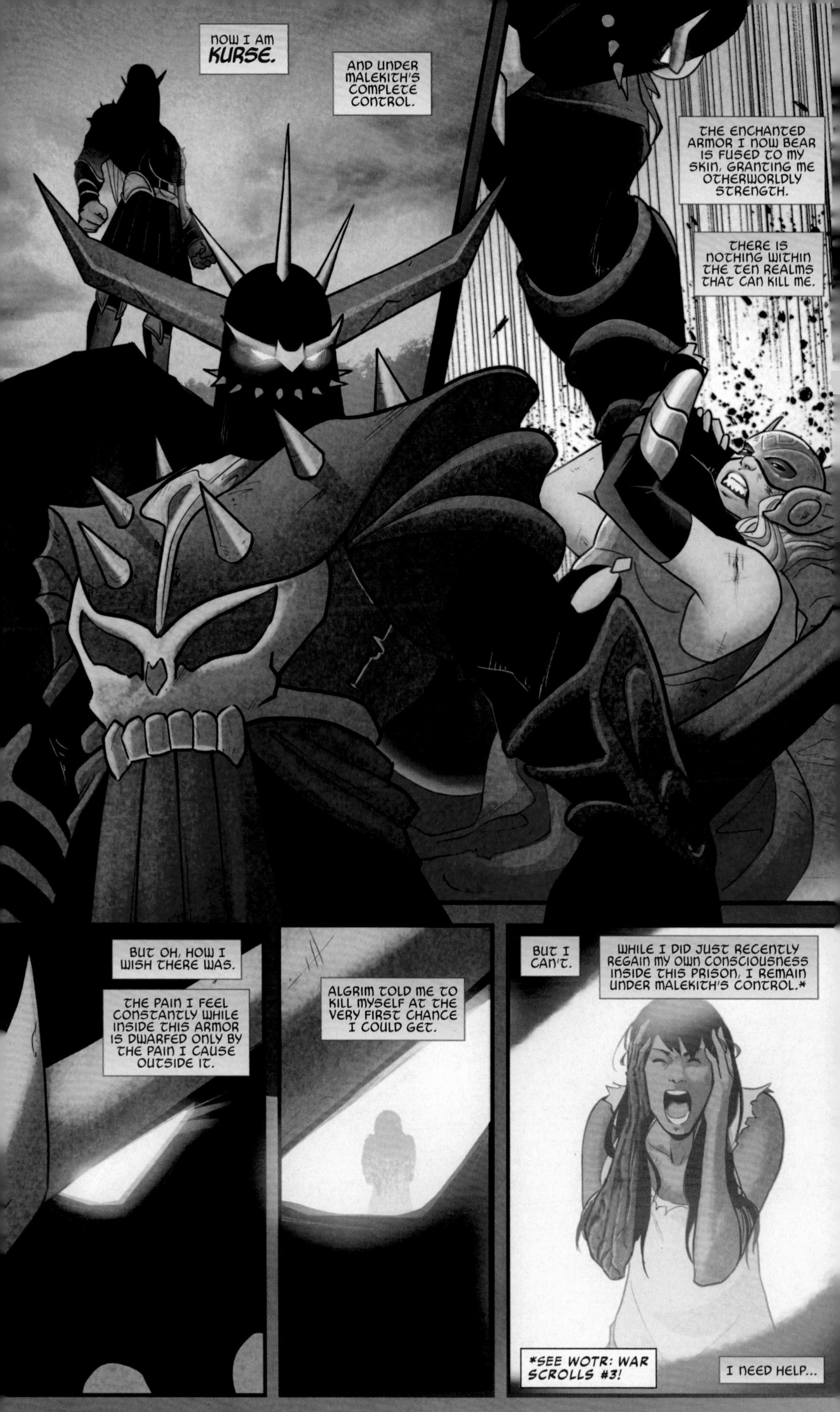
NOW I AM KURSE.
AND UNDER MALEKITH'S COMPLETE CONTROL.
THE ENCHANTED ARMOR I NOW BEAR IS FUSED TO MY SKIN, GRANTING ME OTHERWORLDLY STRENGTH.
THERE IS NOTHING WITHIN THE TEN REALMS THAT CAN KILL ME.
BUT OH, HOW I WISH THERE WAS.
THE PAIN I FEEL CONSTANTLY WHILE INSIDE THIS ARMOR IS DWARFED ONLY BY THE PAIN I CAUSE OUTSIDE IT.
ALGRIM TOLD ME TO KILL MYSELF AT THE VERY FIRST CHANCE I COULD GET.
BUT I CAN'T.
WHILE I DID JUST RECENTLY REGAIN MY OWN CONSCIOUSNESS INSIDE THIS PRISON, I REMAIN UNDER MALEKITH'S CONTROL.*
*SEE WOTR: WAR SCROLLS #3!
I NEED HELP...

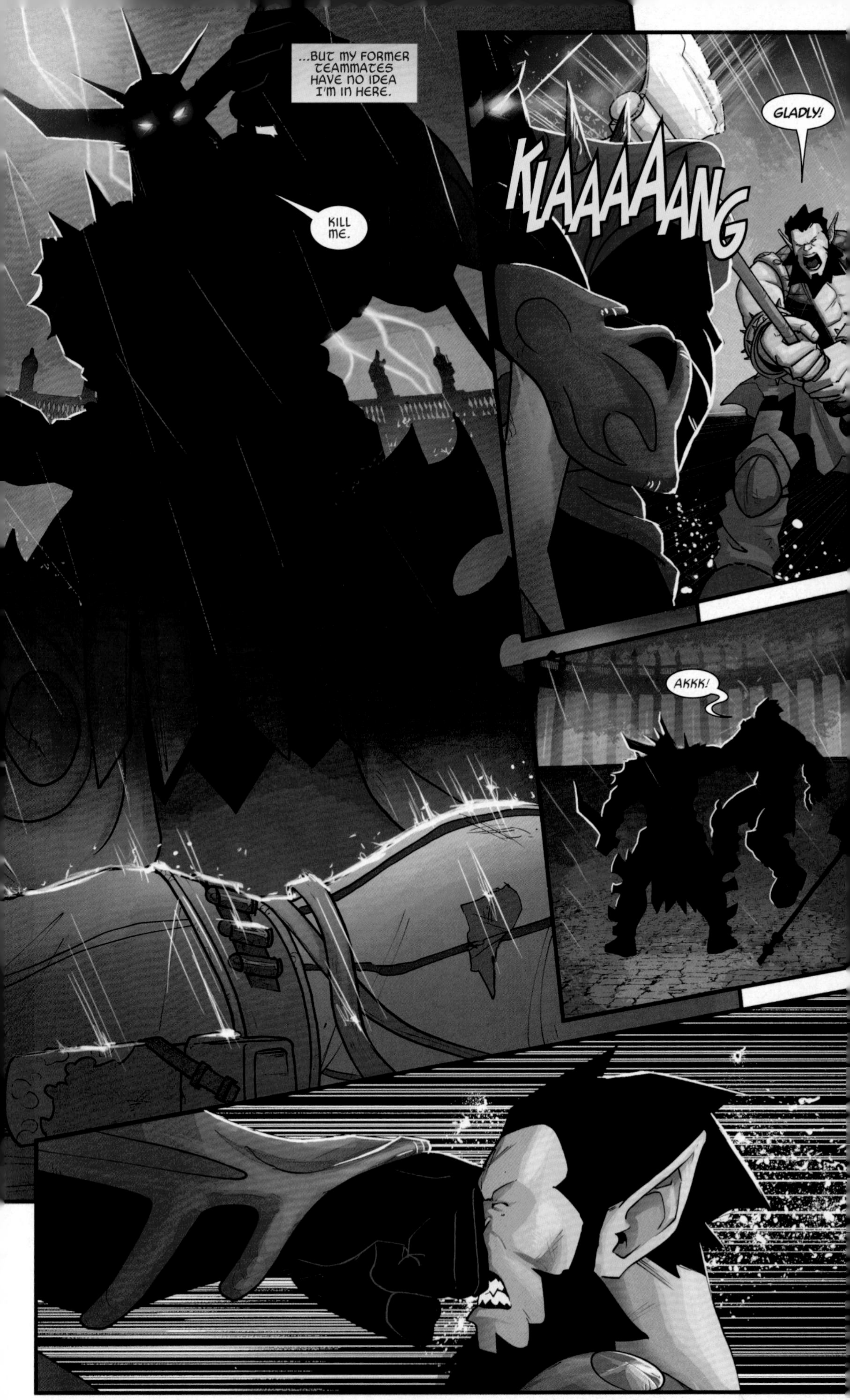
...BUT MY FORMER TEAMMATES HAVE NO IDEA I'M IN HERE.
KILL ME.
KLAAAAAANG
GLADLY!
AKKK!

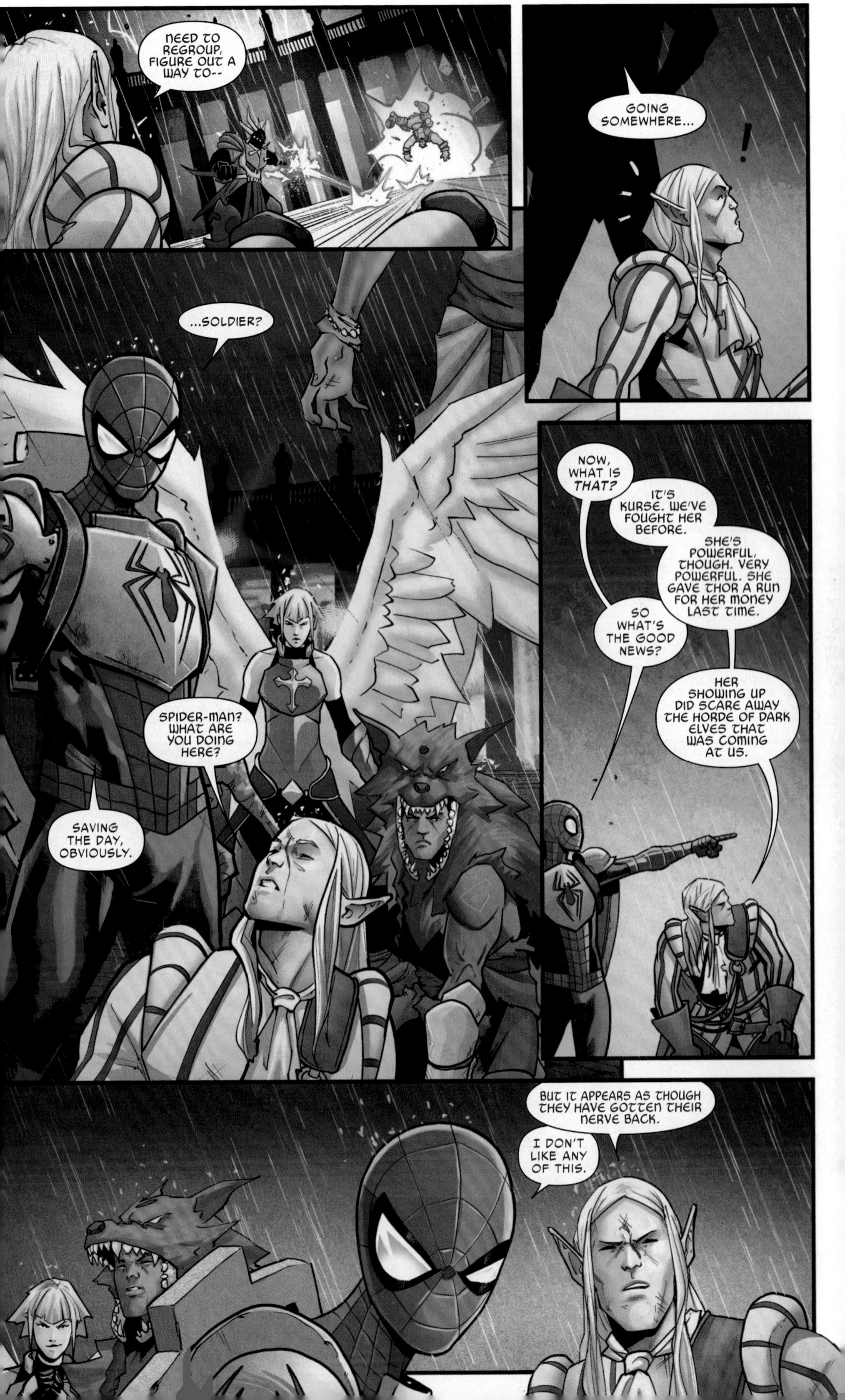
NEED TO REGROUP, FIGURE OUT A WAY TO--
GOING SOMEWHERE...
!
...SOLDIER?
NOW, WHAT IS THAT?
IT'S KURSE. WE'VE FOUGHT HER BEFORE.
SHE'S POWERFUL, THOUGH. VERY POWERFUL. SHE GAVE THOR A RUN FOR HER MONEY LAST TIME.
SO WHAT'S THE GOOD NEWS?
HER SHOWING UP DID SCARE AWAY THE HORDE OF DARK ELVES THAT WAS COMING AT US.
SPIDER-MAN? WHAT ARE YOU DOING HERE?
SAVING THE DAY, OBVIOUSLY.
BUT IT APPEARS AS THOUGH THEY HAVE GOTTEN THEIR NERVE BACK.
I DON'T LIKE ANY OF THIS.

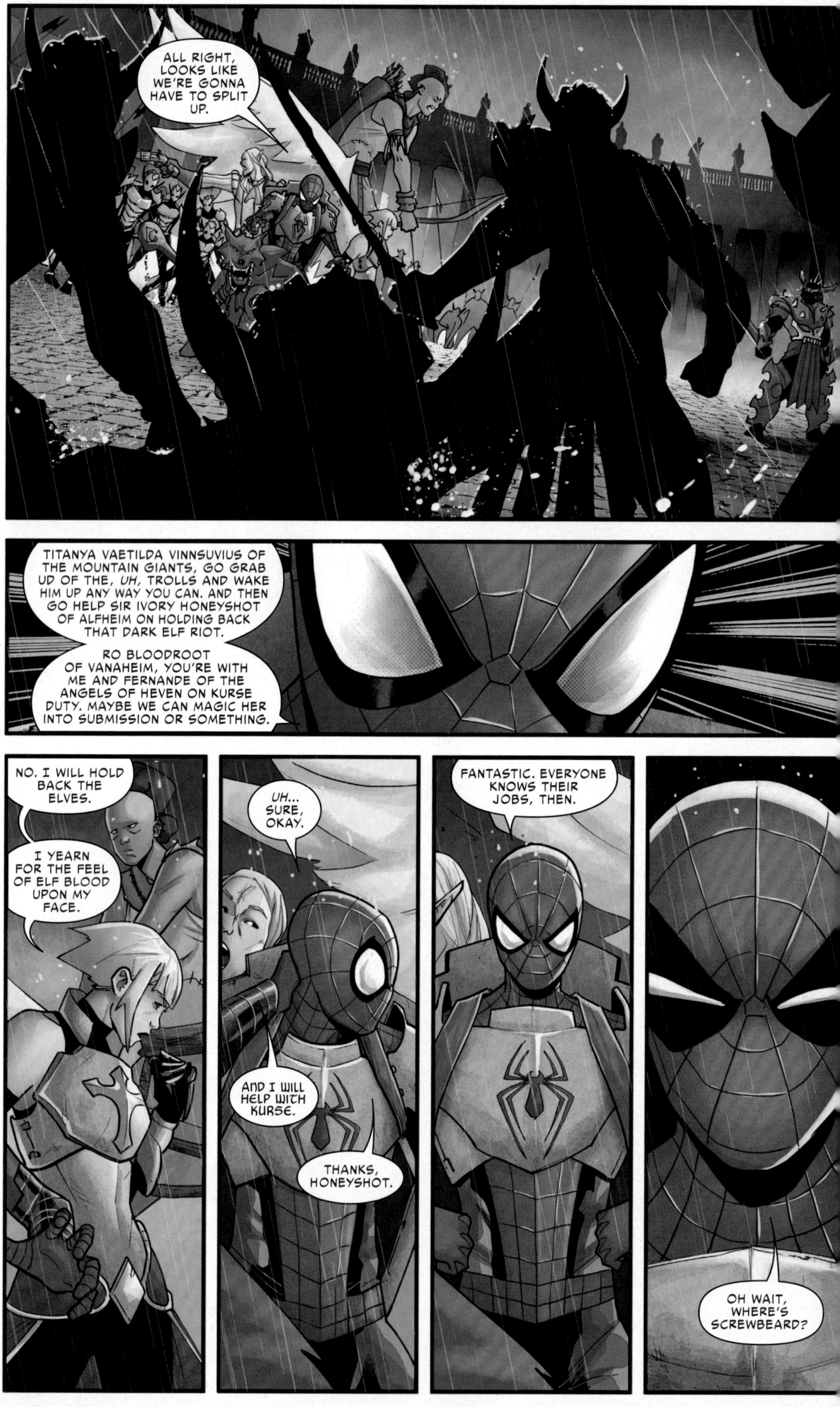
ALL RIGHT, LOOKS LIKE WE'RE GONNA HAVE TO SPLIT UP.
TITANYA VAETILDA VINNSUVIUS OF THE MOUNTAIN GIANTS, GO GRAB UD OF THE, UH, TROLLS AND WAKE HIM UP ANY WAY YOU CAN. AND THEN GO HELP SIR IVORY HONEYSHOT OF ALFHEIM ON HOLDING BACK THAT DARK ELF RIOT.
RO BLOODROOT OF VANAHEIM, YOU'RE WITH ME AND FERNANDE OF THE ANGELS OF HEVEN ON KURSE DUTY. MAYBE WE CAN MAGIC HER INTO SUBMISSION OR SOMETHING.
NO. I WILL HOLD BACK THE ELVES.
I YEARN FOR THE FEEL OF ELF BLOOD UPON MY FACE.
UH... SURE, OKAY.
AND I WILL HELP WITH KURSE.
THANKS, HONEYSHOT.
FANTASTIC. EVERYONE KNOWS THEIR JOBS, THEN.
OH WAIT, WHERE'S SCREWBEARD?

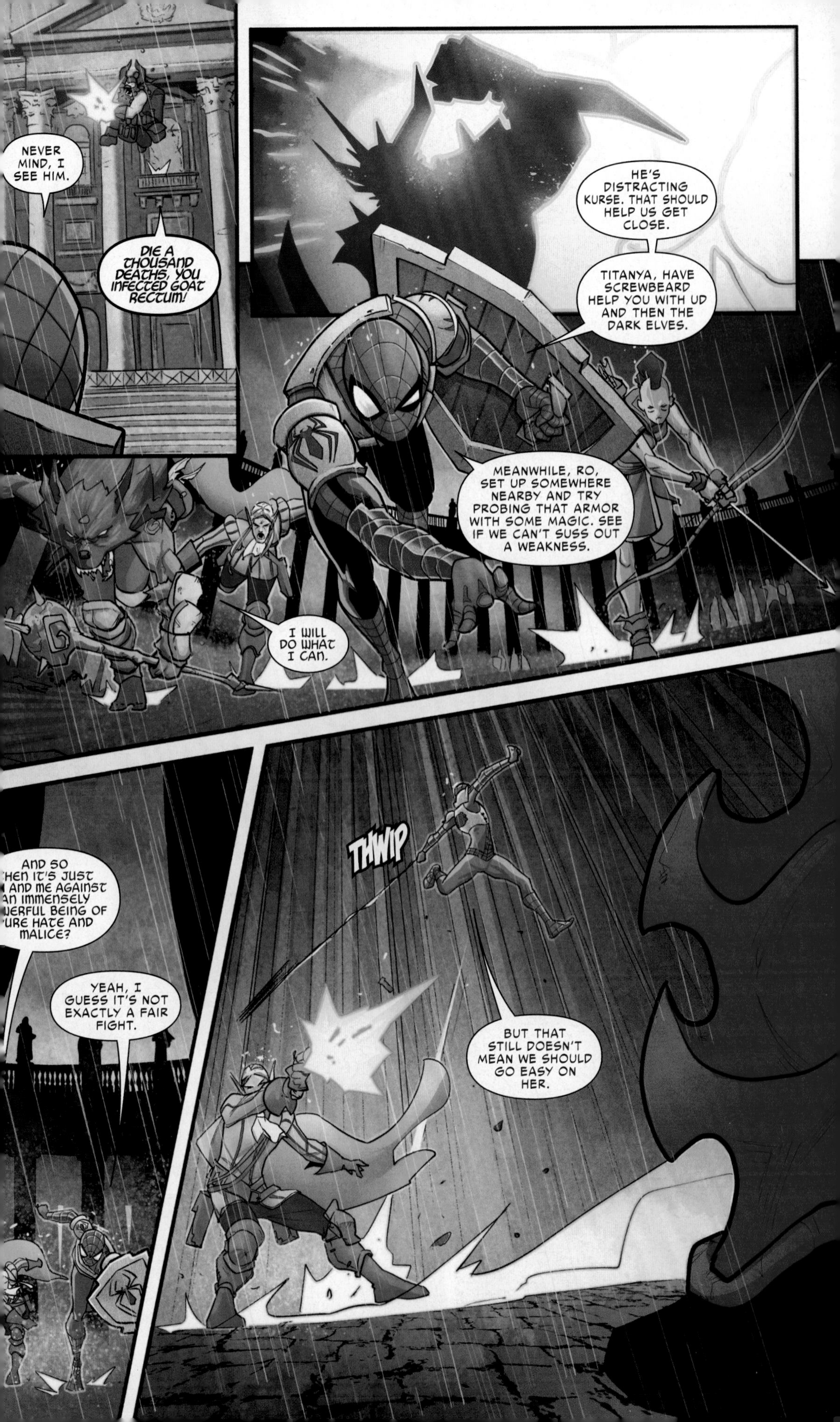
NEVER MIND, I SEE HIM.
DIE A THOUSAND DEATHS, YOU INFECTED GOAT RECTUM!
HE'S DISTRACTING KURSE. THAT SHOULD HELP US GET CLOSE.
TITANYA, HAVE SCREWBEARD HELP YOU WITH UD AND THEN THE DARK ELVES.
MEANWHILE, RO, SET UP SOMEWHERE NEARBY AND TRY PROBING THAT ARMOR WITH SOME MAGIC. SEE IF WE CAN'T SUSS OUT A WEAKNESS.
I WILL DO WHAT I CAN.
THWIP
YEAH, I GUESS IT'S NOT EXACTLY A FAIR FIGHT.
BUT THAT STILL DOESN'T MEAN WE SHOULD GO EASY ON HER.

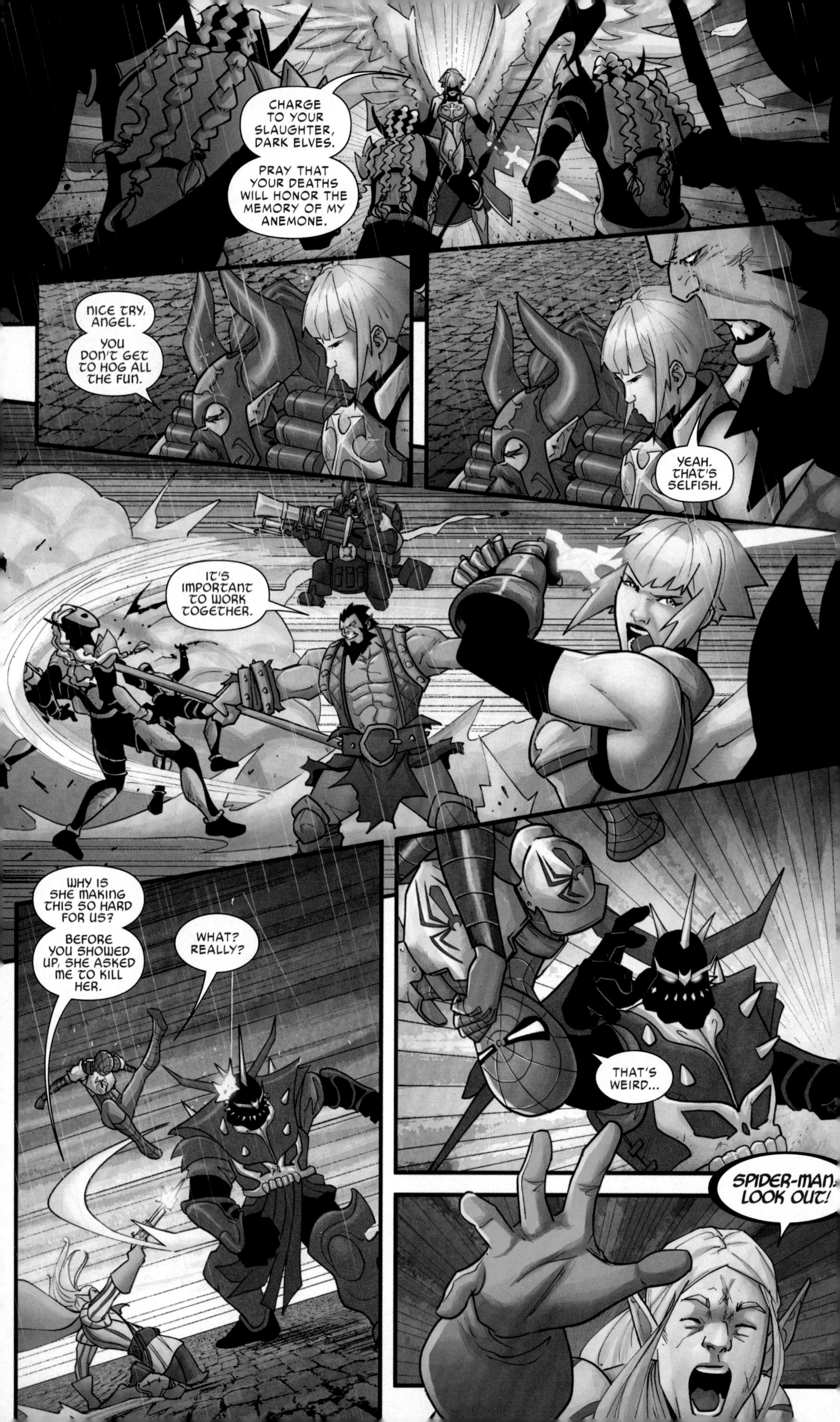
CHARGE TO YOUR SLAUGHTER, DARK ELVES.
PRAY THAT YOUR DEATHS WILL HONOR THE MEMORY OF MY ANEMONE.
NICE TRY, ANGEL.
YOU DON'T GET TO HOG ALL THE FUN.
YEAH. THAT'S SELFISH.
IT'S IMPORTANT TO WORK TOGETHER.
WHY IS SHE MAKING THIS SO HARD FOR US?
BEFORE YOU SHOWED UP, SHE ASKED ME TO KILL HER.
WHAT? REALLY?
THAT'S WEIRD...
SPIDER-MAN. LOOK OUT!

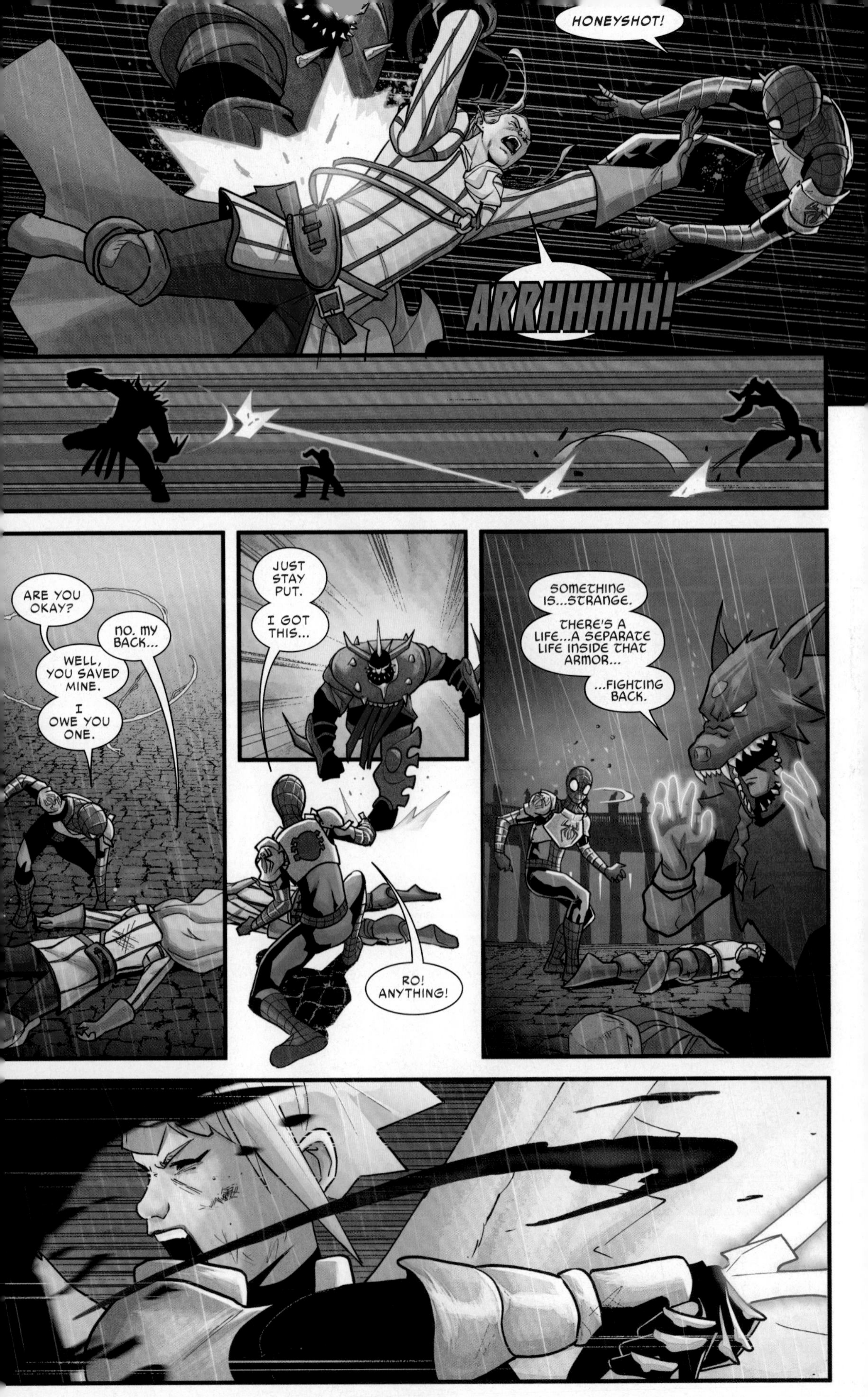

HONEYSHOT!
ARRHHHHH!
ARE YOU OKAY?
NO. MY BACK...
WELL, YOU SAVED MINE.
I OWE YOU ONE.
JUST STAY PUT.
I GOT THIS...
RO! ANYTHING!
SOMETHING IS...STRANGE.
THERE'S A LIFE...A SEPARATE LIFE INSIDE THAT ARMOR...
...FIGHTING BACK.

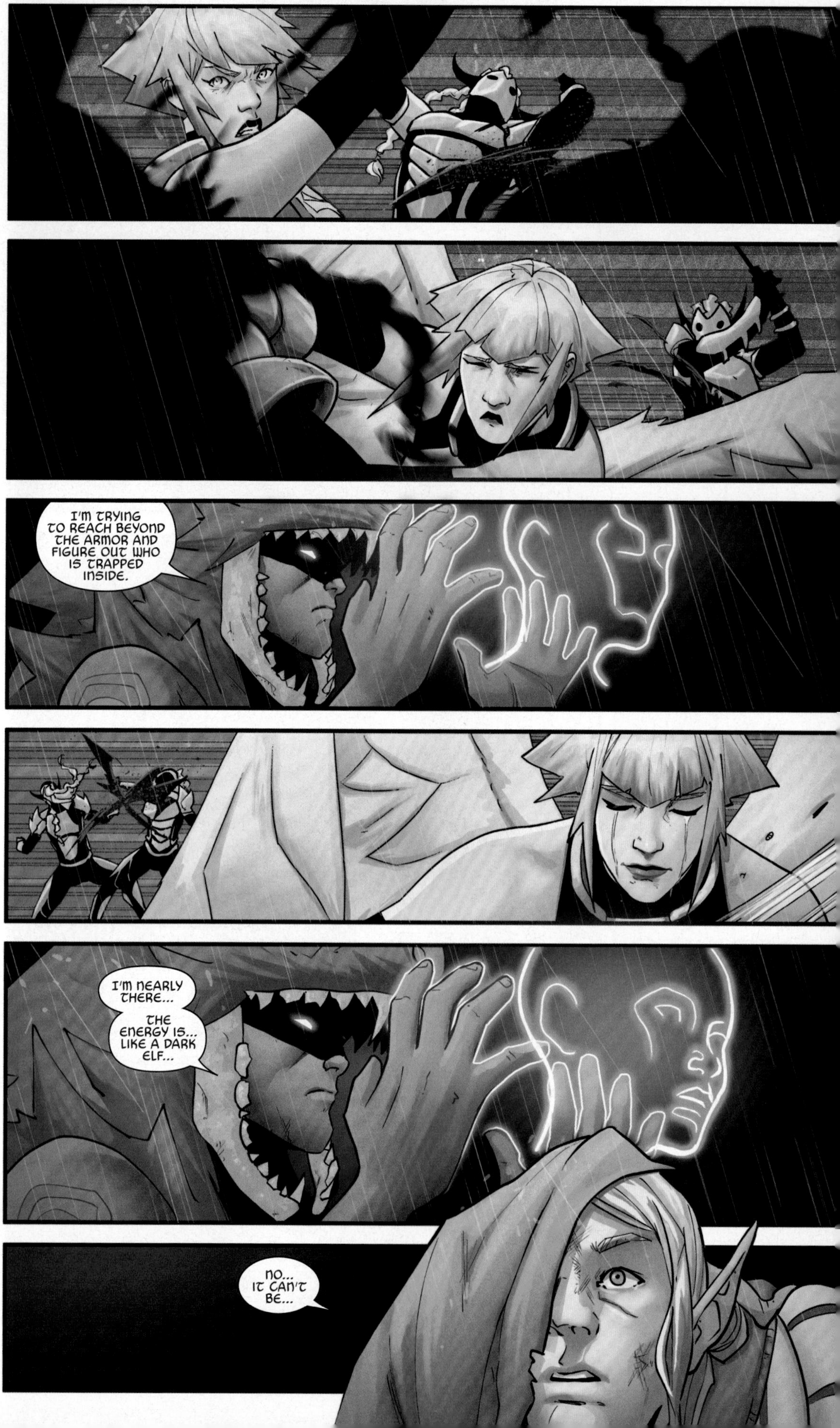
I'M TRYING TO REACH BEYOND THE ARMOR AND FIGURE OUT WHO IS TRAPPED INSIDE.
I'M NEARLY THERE...
THE ENERGY IS... LIKE A DARK ELF...
NO... IT CAN'T BE...

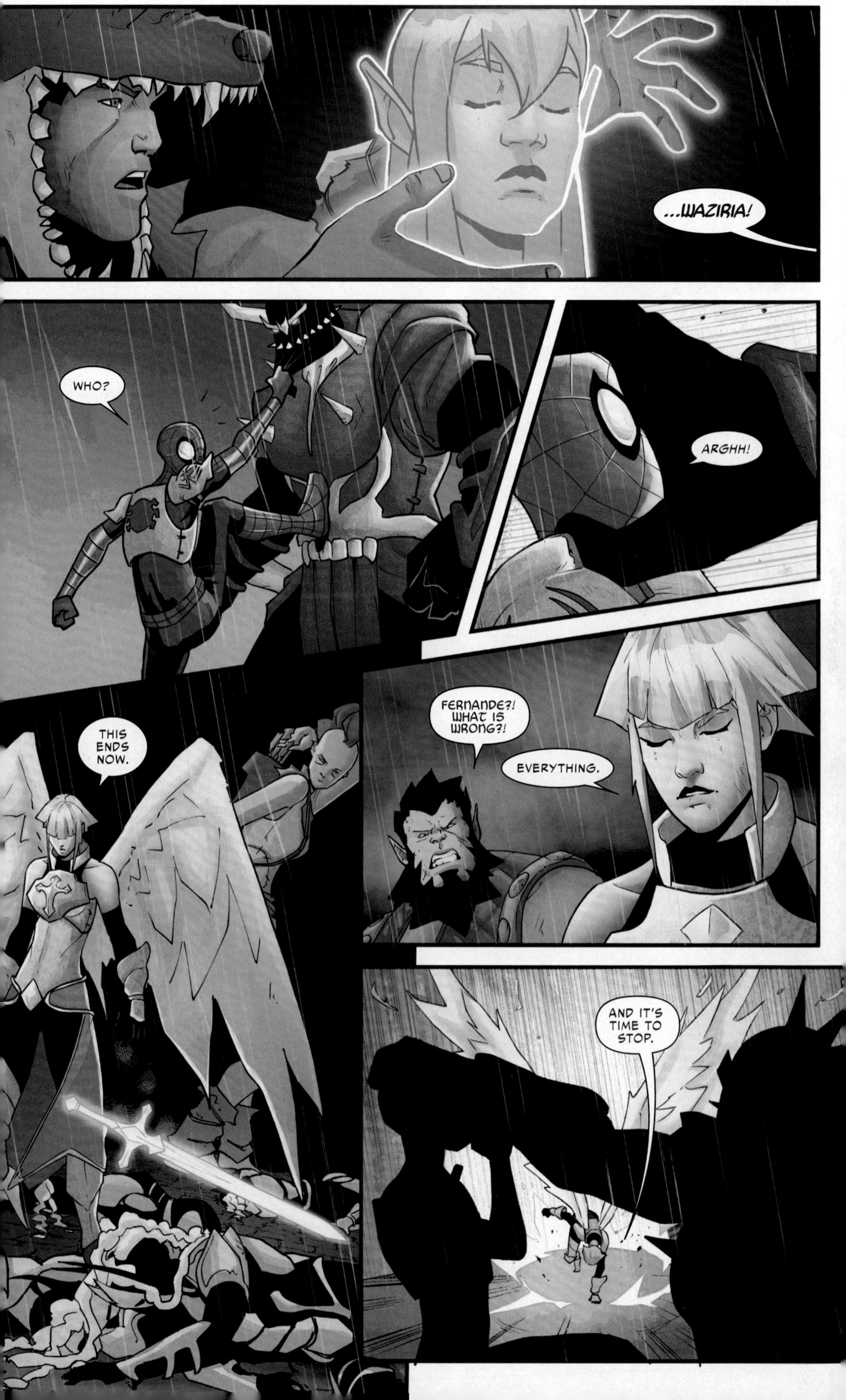
...WAZIRIA!
WHO?
ARGHH!
THIS ENDS NOW.
FERNANDE?! WHAT IS WRONG?!
EVERYTHING.
AND IT'S TIME TO STOP.

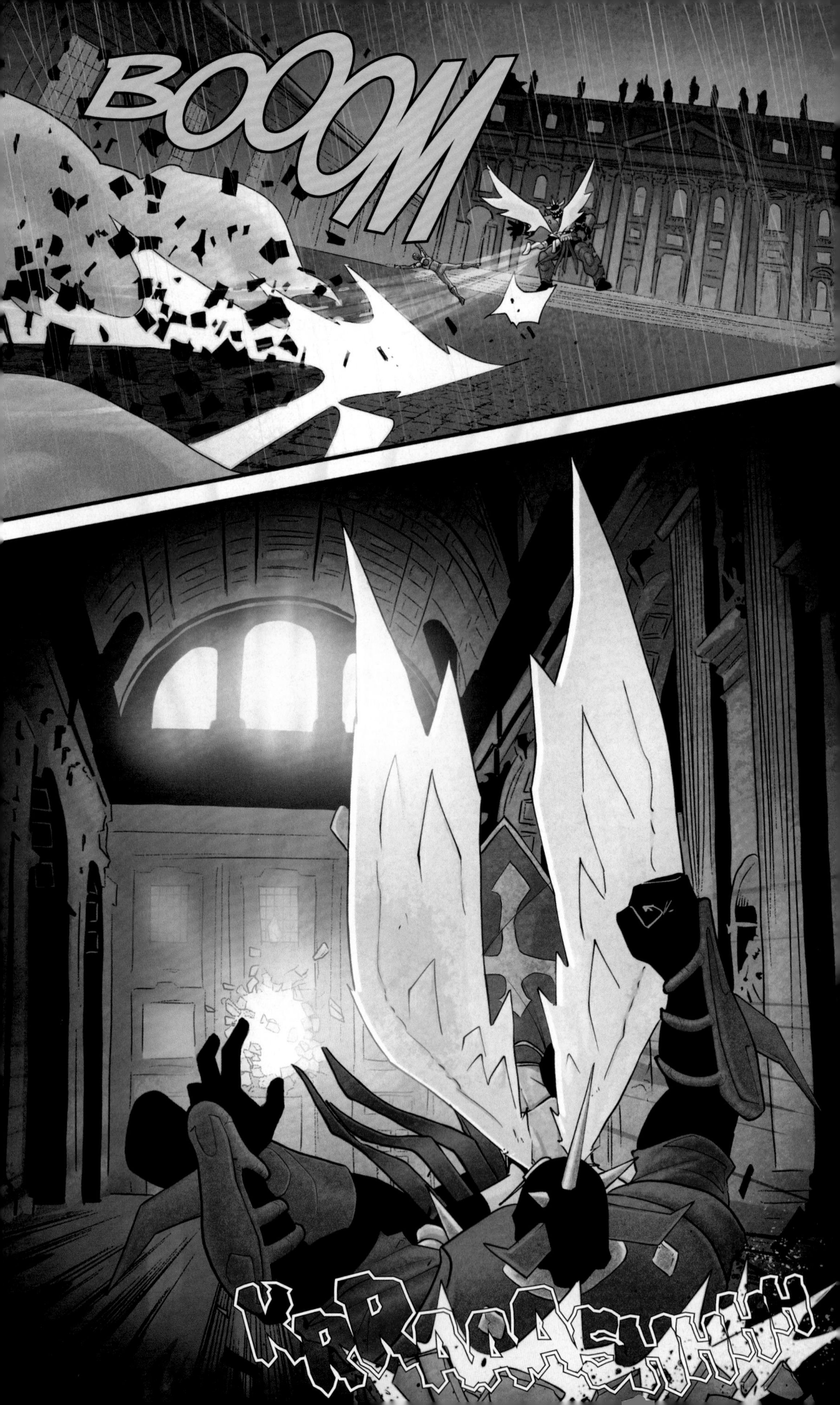
BOOOM
KRAACKSHHH

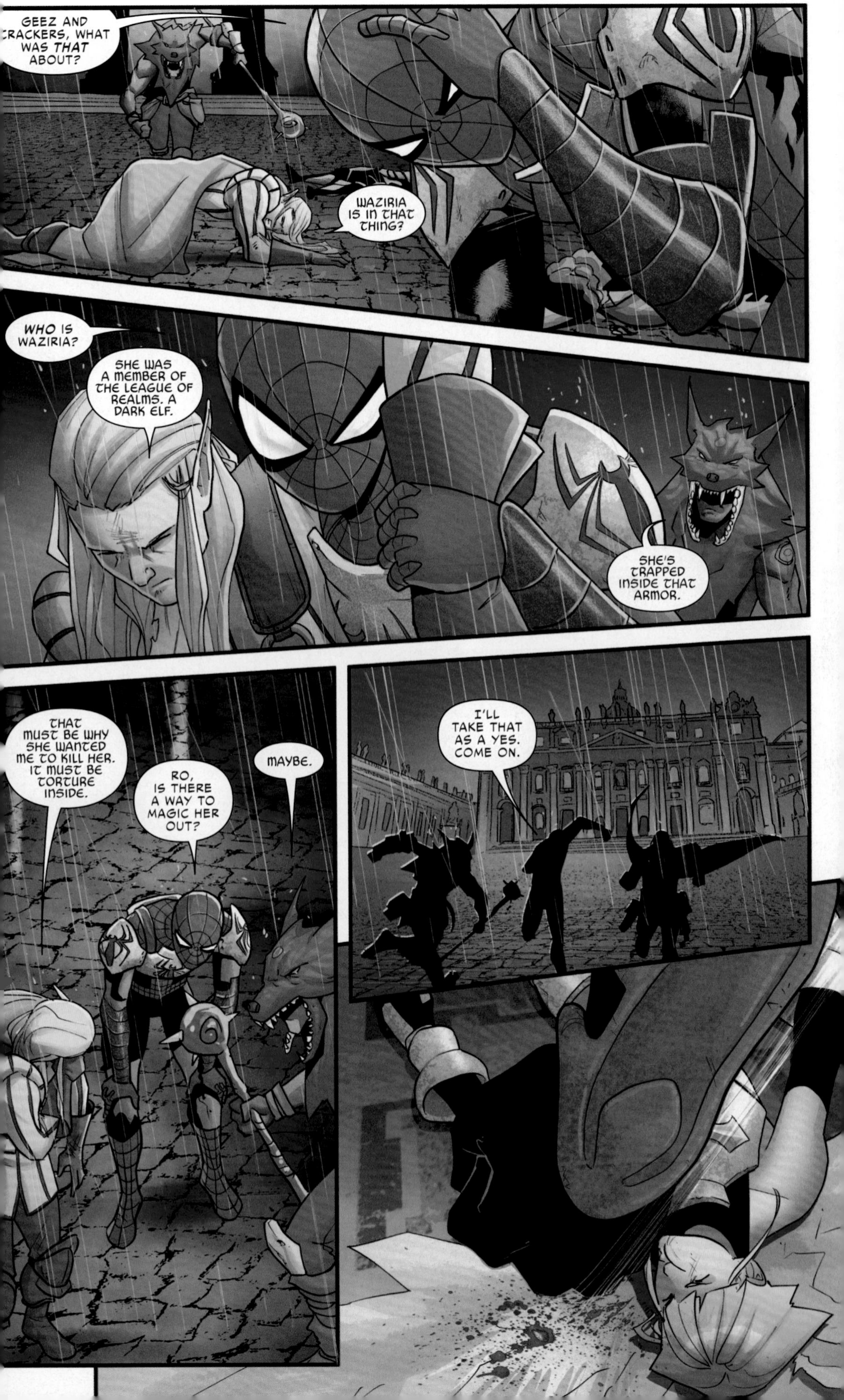
GEEZ AND CRACKERS, WHAT WAS *THAT* ABOUT?
WAZIRIA IS IN THAT THING?
WHO IS WAZIRIA?
SHE WAS A MEMBER OF THE LEAGUE OF REALMS. A DARK ELF.
SHE'S TRAPPED INSIDE THAT ARMOR.
THAT MUST BE WHY SHE WANTED ME TO KILL HER. IT MUST BE TORTURE INSIDE.
RO, IS THERE A WAY TO MAGIC HER OUT?
MAYBE.
I'LL TAKE THAT AS A YES. COME ON.

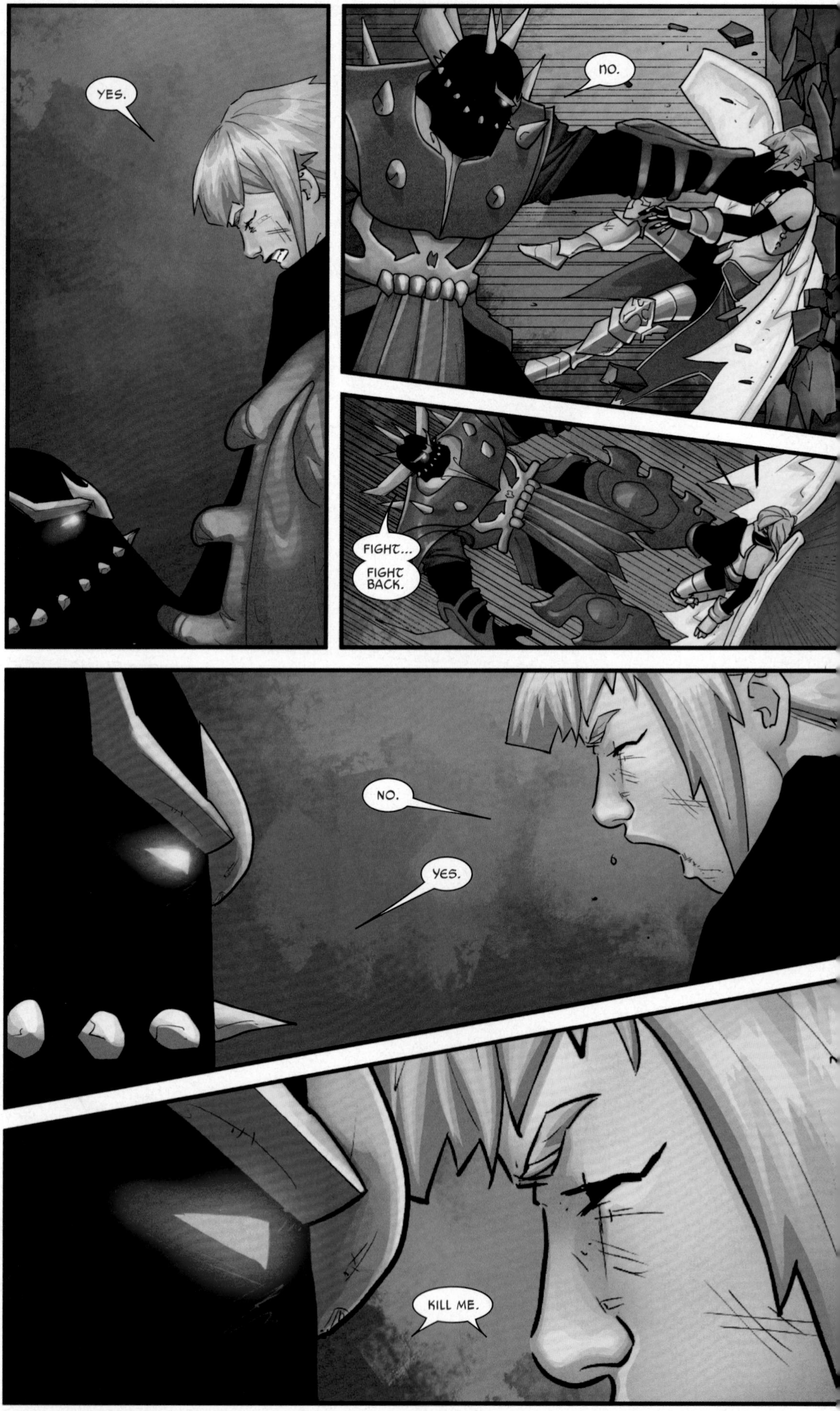
YES.
no.
FIGHT...
FIGHT BACK.
NO.
YES.
KILL ME.

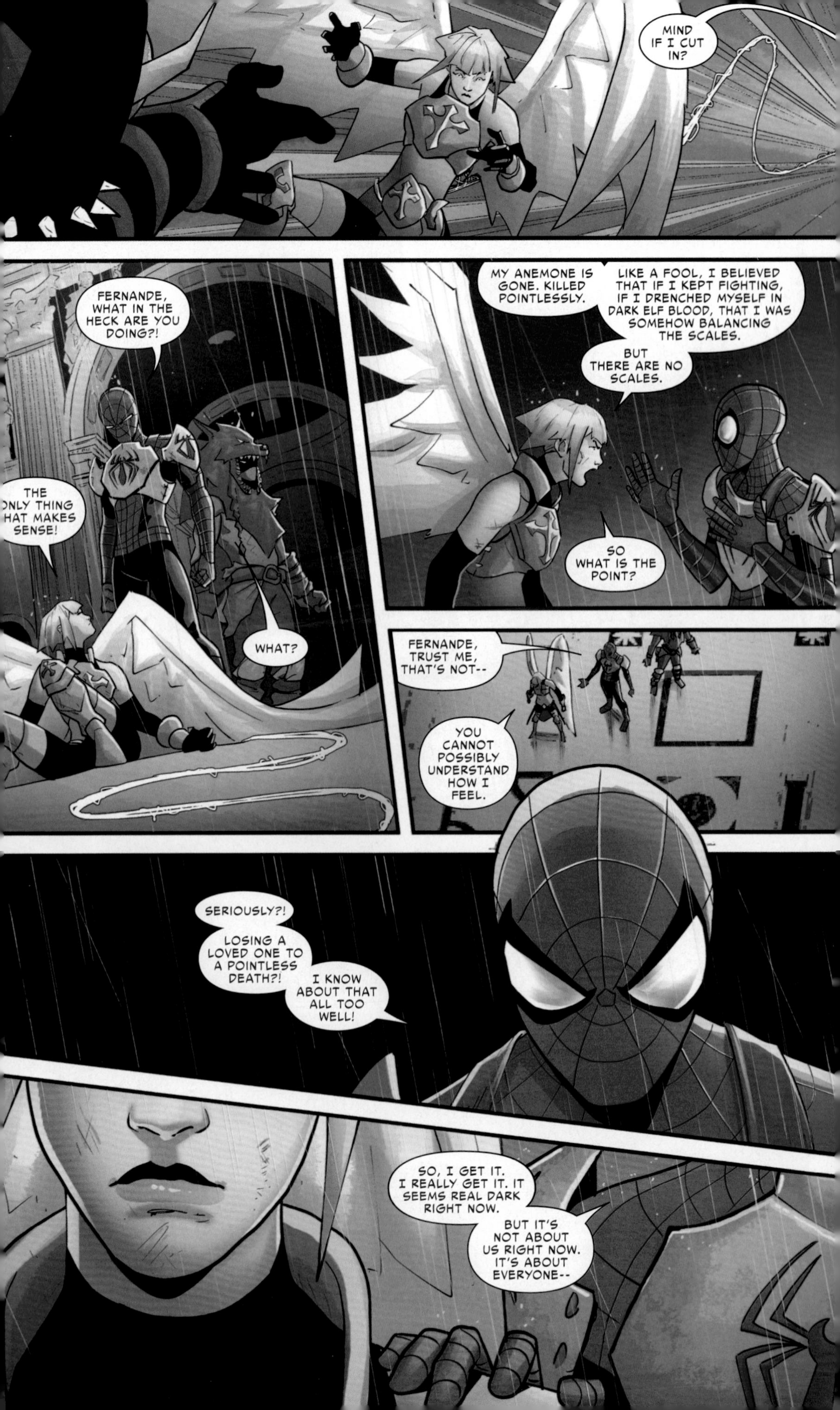
MIND IF I CUT IN?
FERNANDE, WHAT IN THE HECK ARE YOU DOING?!
THE ONLY THING THAT MAKES SENSE!
WHAT?
MY ANEMONE IS GONE. KILLED POINTLESSLY.
LIKE A FOOL, I BELIEVED THAT IF I KEPT FIGHTING, IF I DRENCHED MYSELF IN DARK ELF BLOOD, THAT I WAS SOMEHOW BALANCING THE SCALES.
BUT THERE ARE NO SCALES.
SO WHAT IS THE POINT?
FERNANDE, TRUST ME, THAT'S NOT--
YOU CANNOT POSSIBLY UNDERSTAND HOW I FEEL.
SERIOUSLY?!
LOSING A LOVED ONE TO A POINTLESS DEATH?!
I KNOW ABOUT THAT ALL TOO WELL!
SO, I GET IT. I REALLY GET IT. IT SEEMS REAL DARK RIGHT NOW.
BUT IT'S NOT ABOUT US RIGHT NOW. IT'S ABOUT EVERYONE--

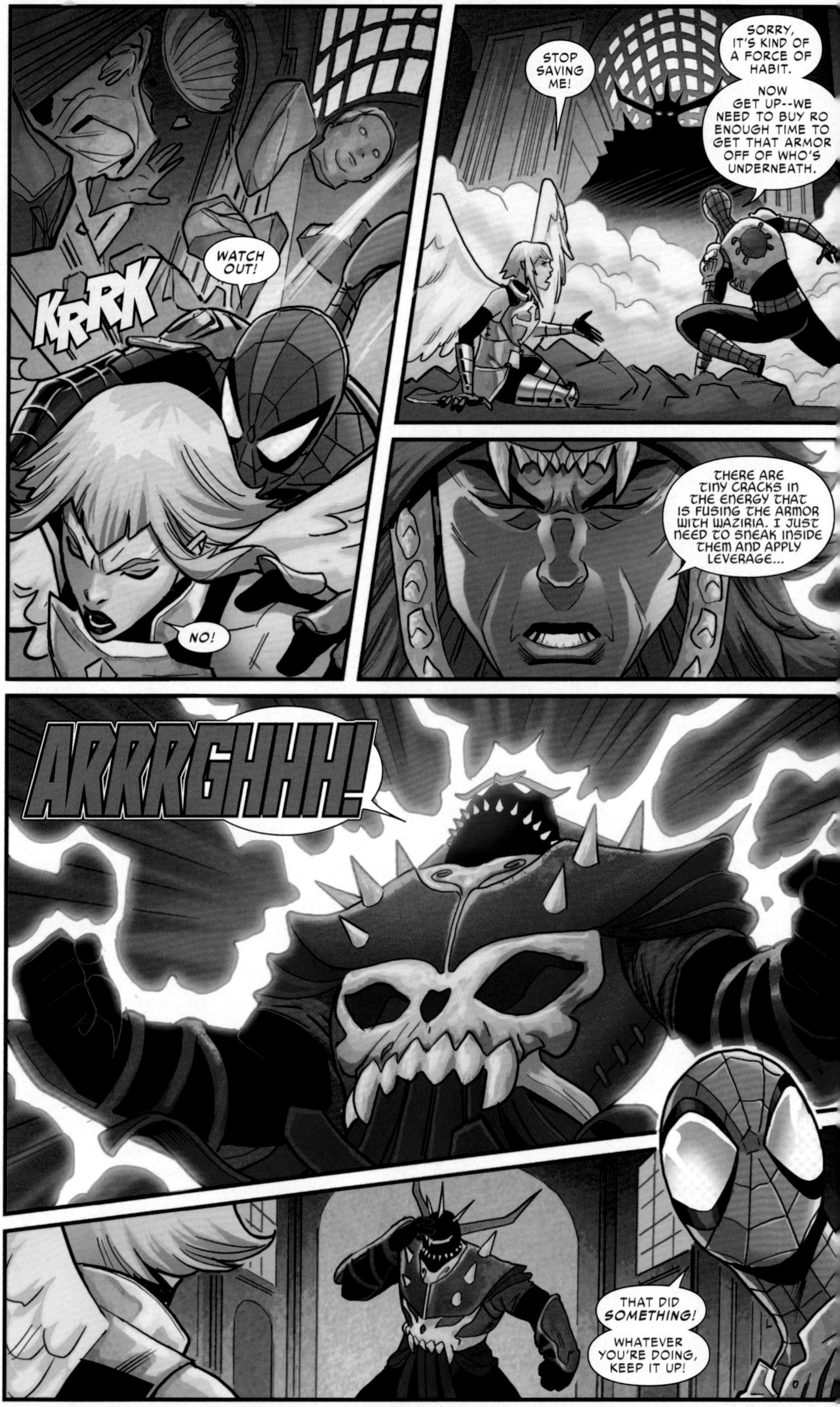

WATCH OUT!
KRRK
NO!
STOP SAVING ME!
SORRY, IT'S KIND OF A FORCE OF HABIT.
NOW GET UP--WE NEED TO BUY RO ENOUGH TIME TO GET THAT ARMOR OFF OF WHO'S UNDERNEATH.
THERE ARE TINY CRACKS IN THE ENERGY THAT IS FUSING THE ARMOR WITH WAZIRIA. I JUST NEED TO SNEAK INSIDE THEM AND APPLY LEVERAGE...
ARRRGHHH!
THAT DID SOMETHING!
WHATEVER YOU'RE DOING, KEEP IT UP!

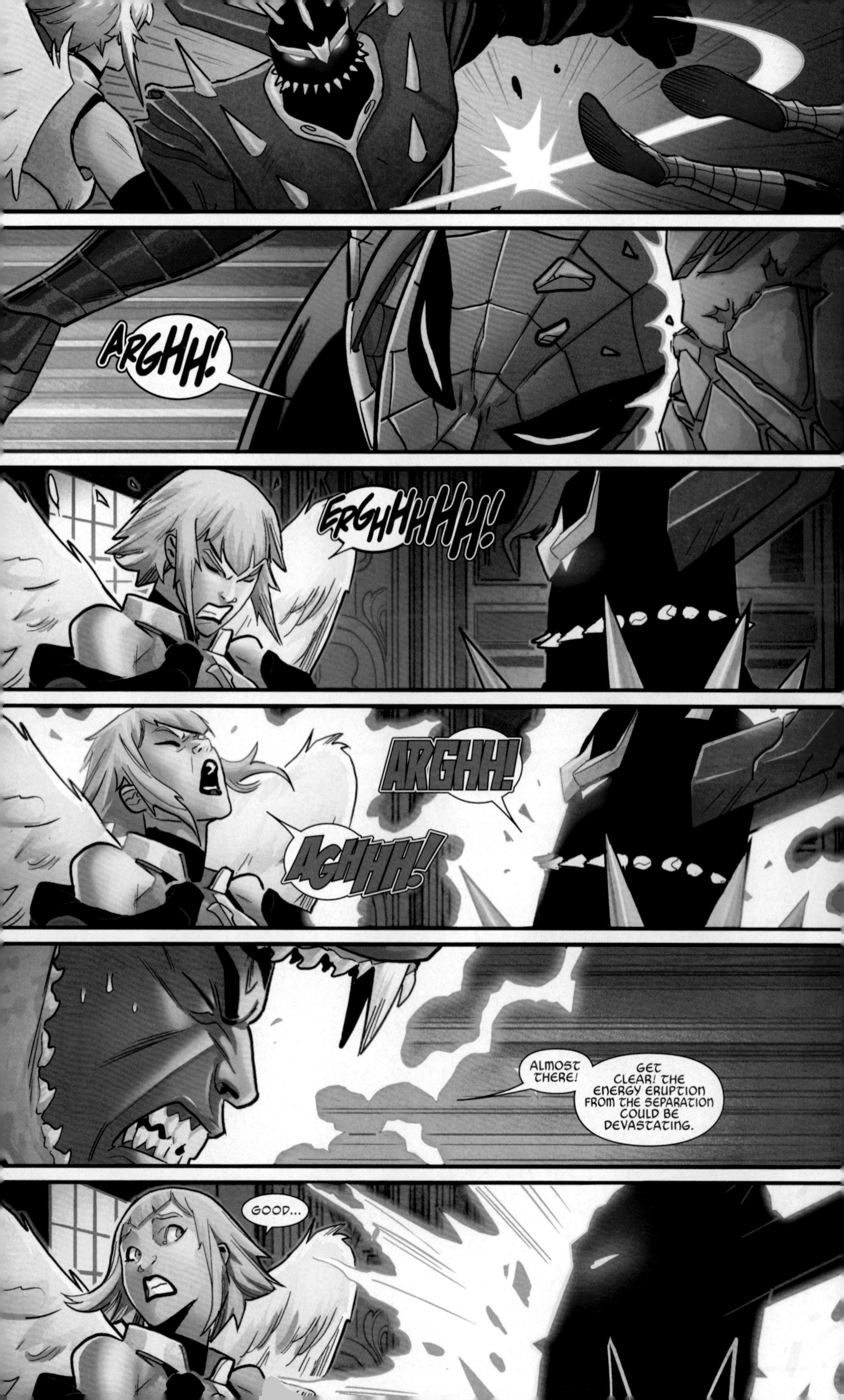
ARGHH!
ERGHHHHHH!
ARGHH!
AGHHH!
ALMOST THERE!
GET CLEAR! THE ENERGY ERUPTION FROM THE SEPARATION COULD BE DEVASTATING.
GOOD...

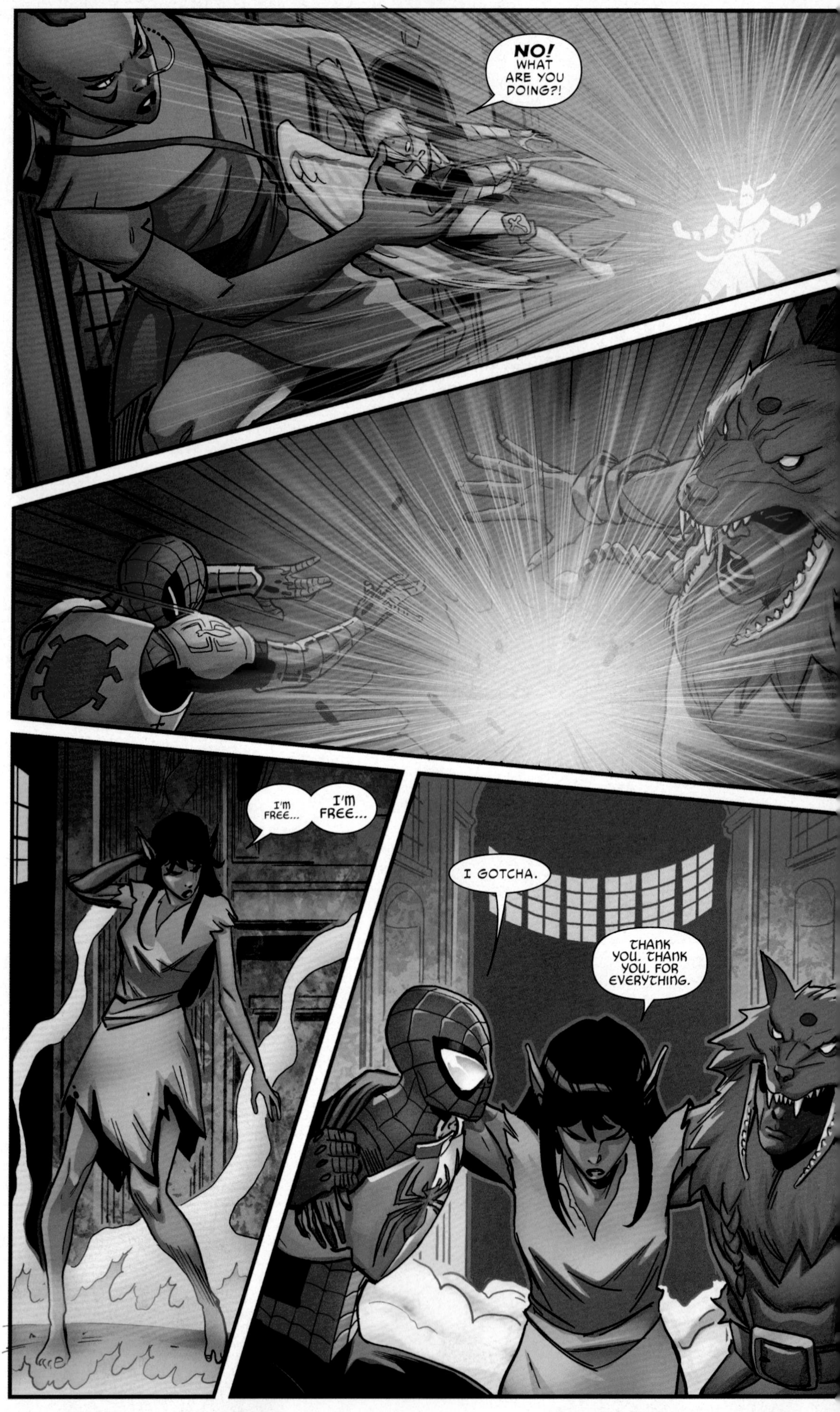
NO! WHAT ARE YOU DOING?!
I'M FREE...
I'M FREE...
I GOTCHA.
THANK YOU. THANK YOU. FOR EVERYTHING.

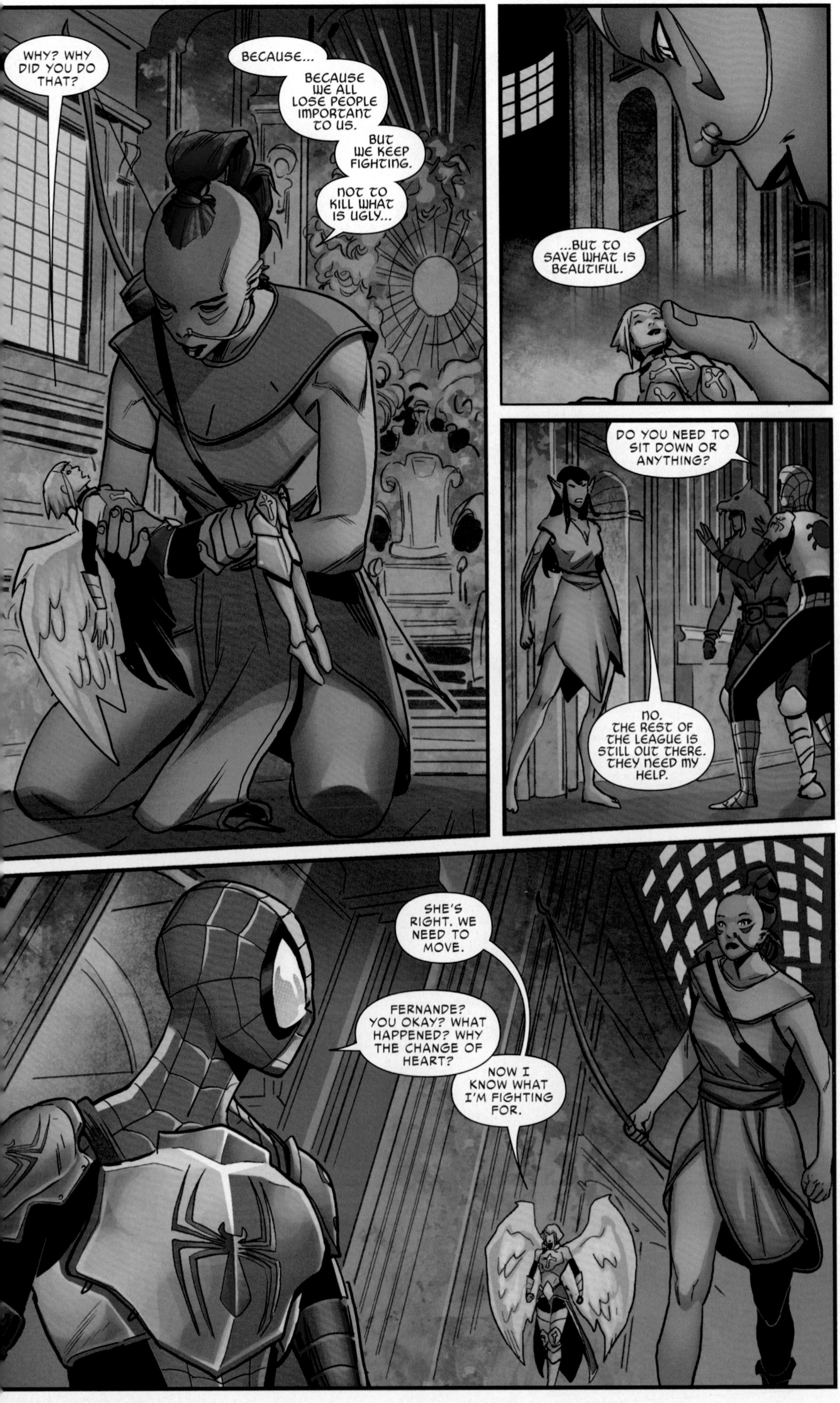
WHY? WHY DID YOU DO THAT?
BECAUSE...
BECAUSE WE ALL LOSE PEOPLE IMPORTANT TO US.
BUT WE KEEP FIGHTING.
NOT TO KILL WHAT IS UGLY...
...BUT TO SAVE WHAT IS BEAUTIFUL.
DO YOU NEED TO SIT DOWN OR ANYTHING?
NO. THE REST OF THE LEAGUE IS STILL OUT THERE. THEY NEED MY HELP.
SHE'S RIGHT. WE NEED TO MOVE.
FERNANDE? YOU OKAY? WHAT HAPPENED? WHY THE CHANGE OF HEART?
NOW I KNOW WHAT I'M FIGHTING FOR.

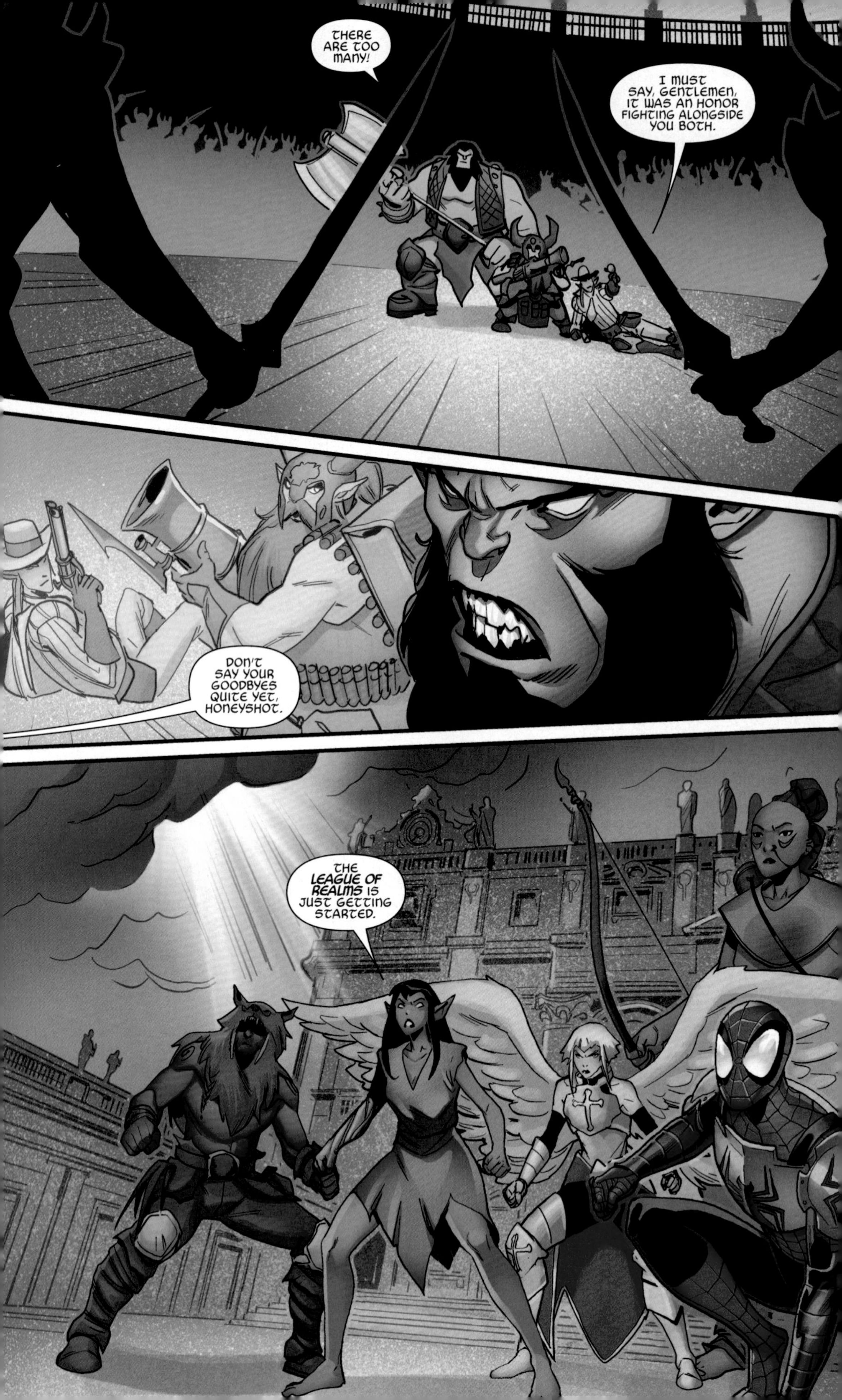
THERE ARE TOO MANY!
I MUST SAY, GENTLEMEN, IT WAS AN HONOR FIGHTING ALONGSIDE YOU BOTH.
DON'T SAY YOUR GOODBYES QUITE YET, HONEYSHOT.
THE LEAGUE OF REALMS IS JUST GETTING STARTED.

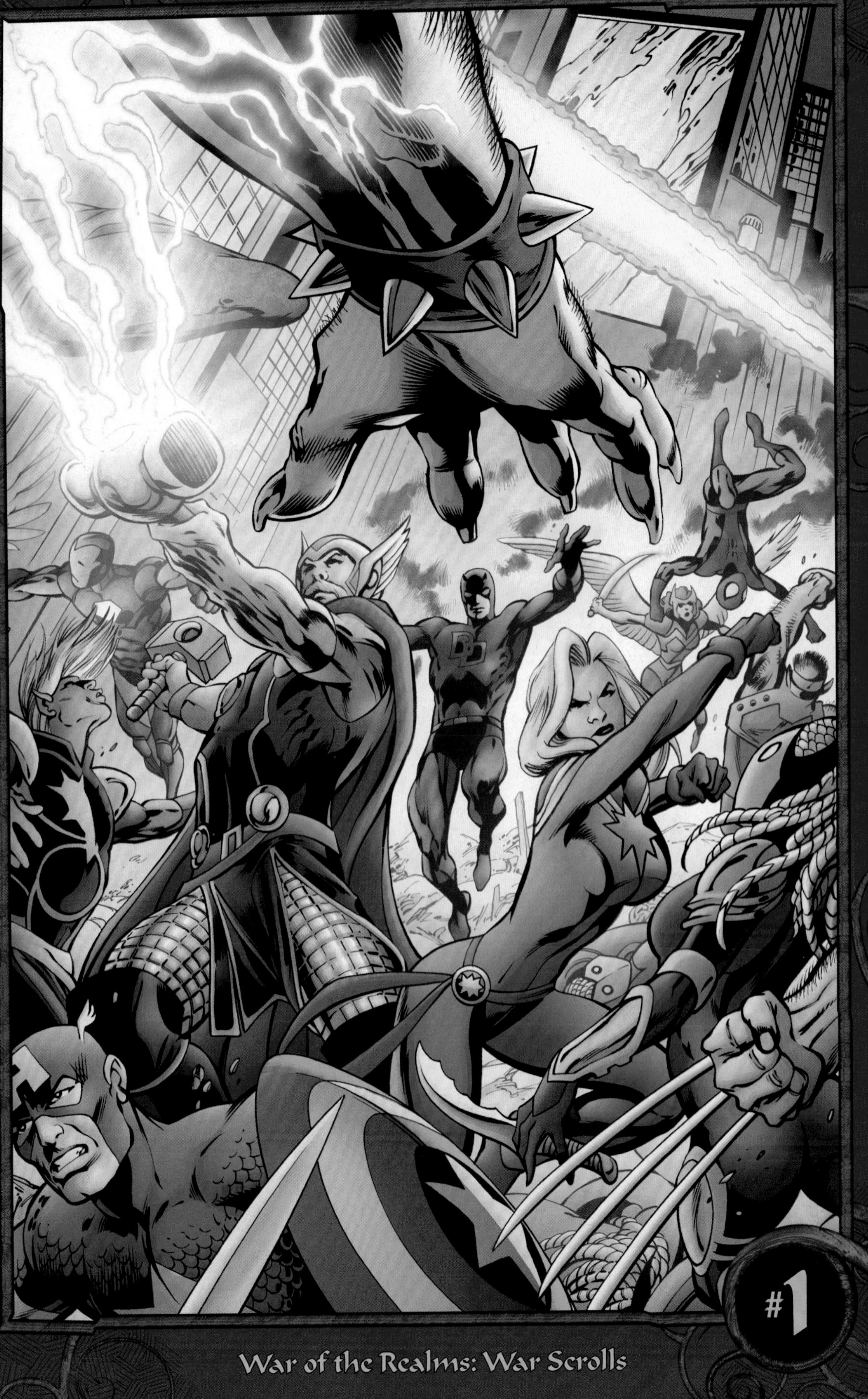
#1

War of the Realms: War Scrolls

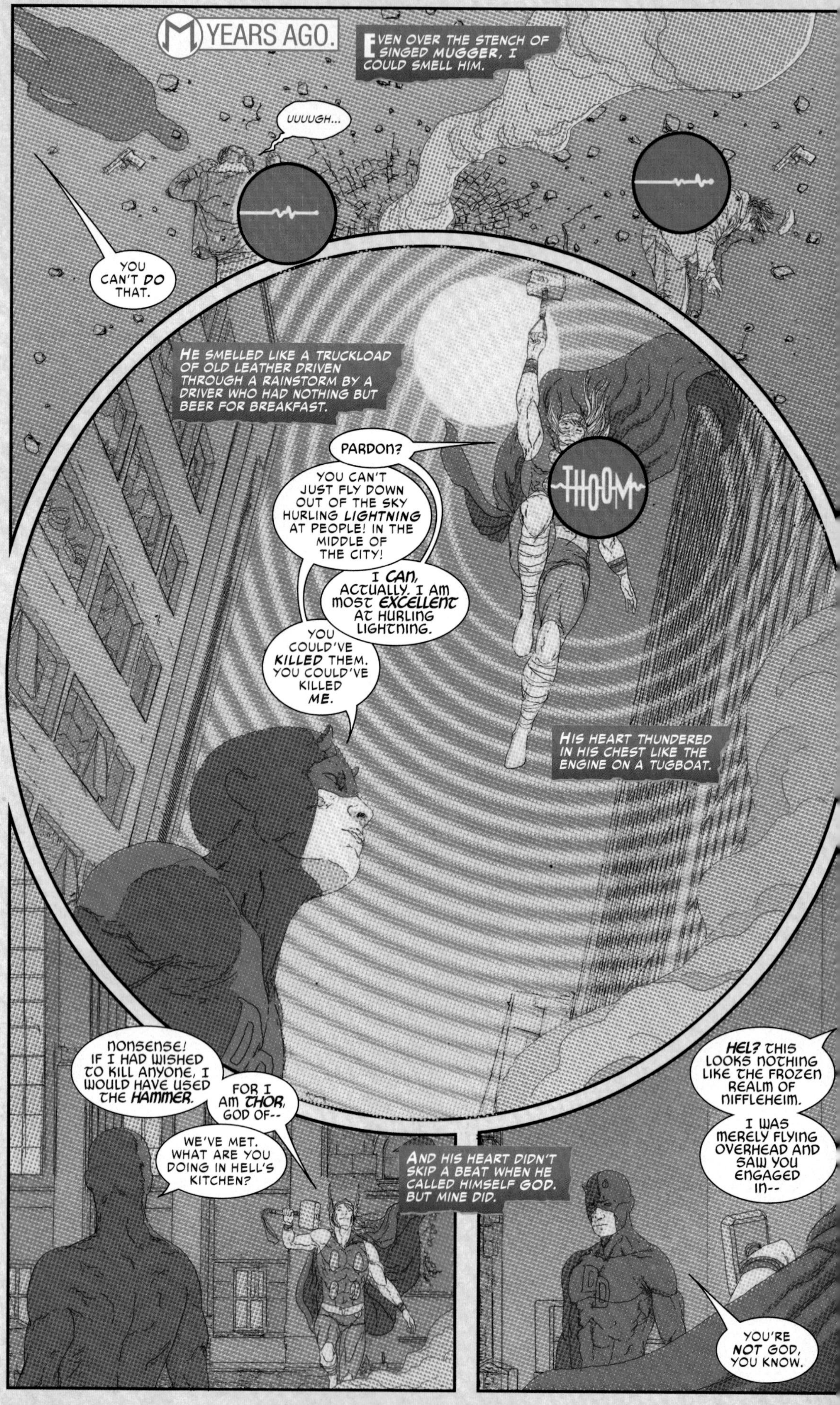
YEARS AGO.
EVEN OVER THE STENCH OF SINGED MUGGER, I COULD SMELL HIM.
UUUUGH...
YOU CAN'T DO THAT.
HE SMELLED LIKE A TRUCKLOAD OF OLD LEATHER DRIVEN THROUGH A RAINSTORM BY A DRIVER WHO HAD NOTHING BUT BEER FOR BREAKFAST.
PARDON?
THOOM
YOU CAN'T JUST FLY DOWN OUT OF THE SKY HURLING LIGHTNING AT PEOPLE! IN THE MIDDLE OF THE CITY!
I CAN, ACTUALLY. I AM MOST EXCELLENT AT HURLING LIGHTNING.
YOU COULD'VE KILLED THEM. YOU COULD'VE KILLED ME.
HIS HEART THUNDERED IN HIS CHEST LIKE THE ENGINE ON A TUGBOAT.
NONSENSE! IF I HAD WISHED TO KILL ANYONE, I WOULD HAVE USED THE HAMMER.
FOR I AM THOR, GOD OF--
WE'VE MET. WHAT ARE YOU DOING IN HELL'S KITCHEN?
AND HIS HEART DIDN'T SKIP A BEAT WHEN HE CALLED HIMSELF GOD. BUT MINE DID.
HEL? THIS LOOKS NOTHING LIKE THE FROZEN REALM OF NIFFLEHEIM.
I WAS MERELY FLYING OVERHEAD AND SAW YOU ENGAGED IN--
YOU'RE NOT GOD, YOU KNOW.

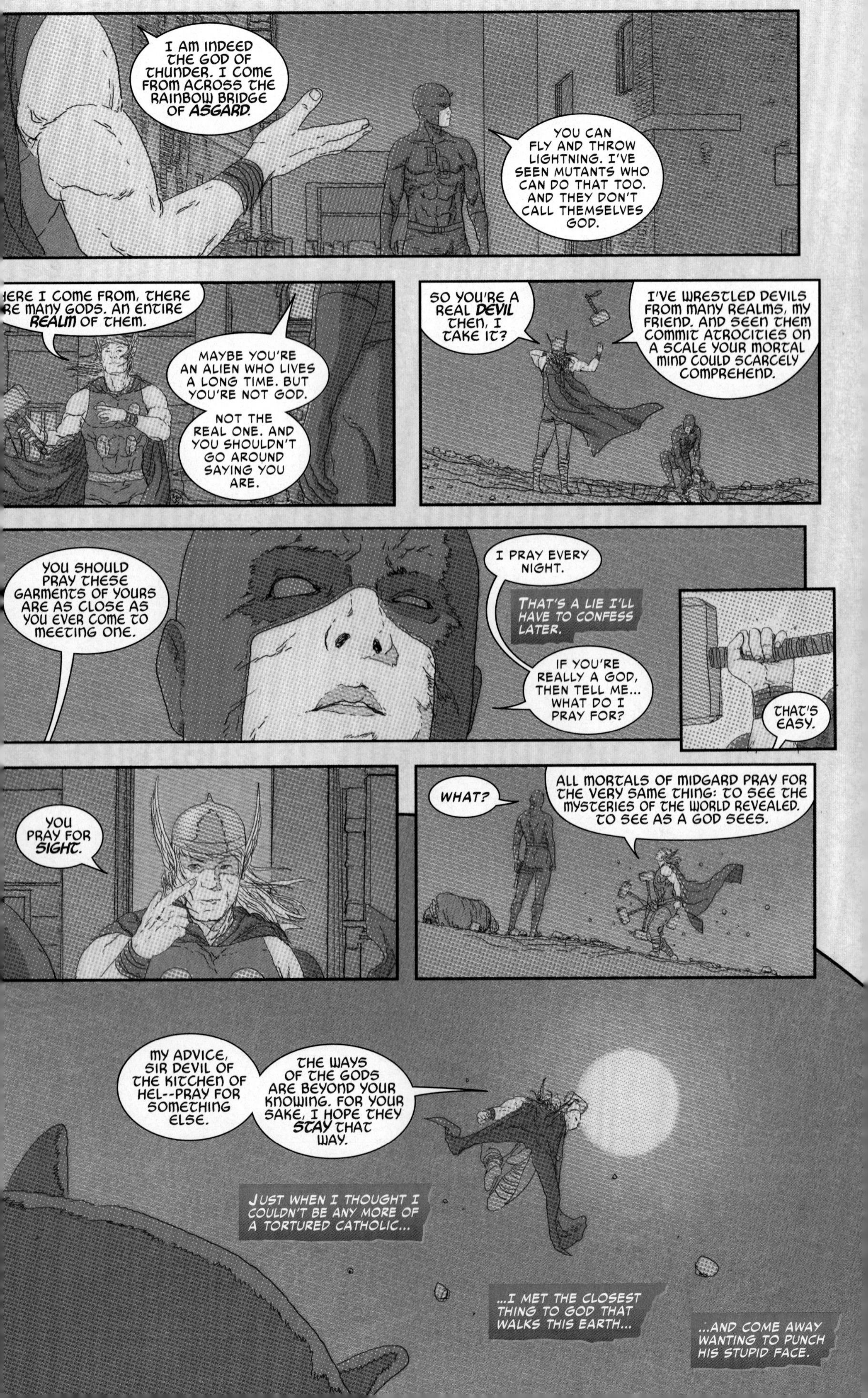
I AM INDEED THE GOD OF THUNDER. I COME FROM ACROSS THE RAINBOW BRIDGE OF ASGARD.
YOU CAN FLY AND THROW LIGHTNING. I'VE SEEN MUTANTS WHO CAN DO THAT TOO. AND THEY DON'T CALL THEMSELVES GOD.
ERE I COME FROM, THERE RE MANY GODS. AN ENTIRE REALM OF THEM.
MAYBE YOU'RE AN ALIEN WHO LIVES A LONG TIME. BUT YOU'RE NOT GOD.
NOT THE REAL ONE. AND YOU SHOULDN'T GO AROUND SAYING YOU ARE.
SO YOU'RE A REAL DEVIL THEN, I TAKE IT?
I'VE WRESTLED DEVILS FROM MANY REALMS, MY FRIEND. AND SEEN THEM COMMIT ATROCITIES ON A SCALE YOUR MORTAL MIND COULD SCARCELY COMPREHEND.
YOU SHOULD PRAY THESE GARMENTS OF YOURS ARE AS CLOSE AS YOU EVER COME TO MEETING ONE.
I PRAY EVERY NIGHT.
THAT'S A LIE I'LL HAVE TO CONFESS LATER.
IF YOU'RE REALLY A GOD, THEN TELL ME... WHAT DO I PRAY FOR?
THAT'S EASY.
YOU PRAY FOR SIGHT.
WHAT?
ALL MORTALS OF MIDGARD PRAY FOR THE VERY SAME THING: TO SEE THE MYSTERIES OF THE WORLD REVEALED. TO SEE AS A GOD SEES.
MY ADVICE, SIR DEVIL OF THE KITCHEN OF HEL--PRAY FOR SOMETHING ELSE.
THE WAYS OF THE GODS ARE BEYOND YOUR KNOWING. FOR YOUR SAKE, I HOPE THEY STAY THAT WAY.
JUST WHEN I THOUGHT I COULDN'T BE ANY MORE OF A TORTURED CATHOLIC...
...I MET THE CLOSEST THING TO GOD THAT WALKS THIS EARTH...
...AND COME AWAY WANTING TO PUNCH HIS STUPID FACE.

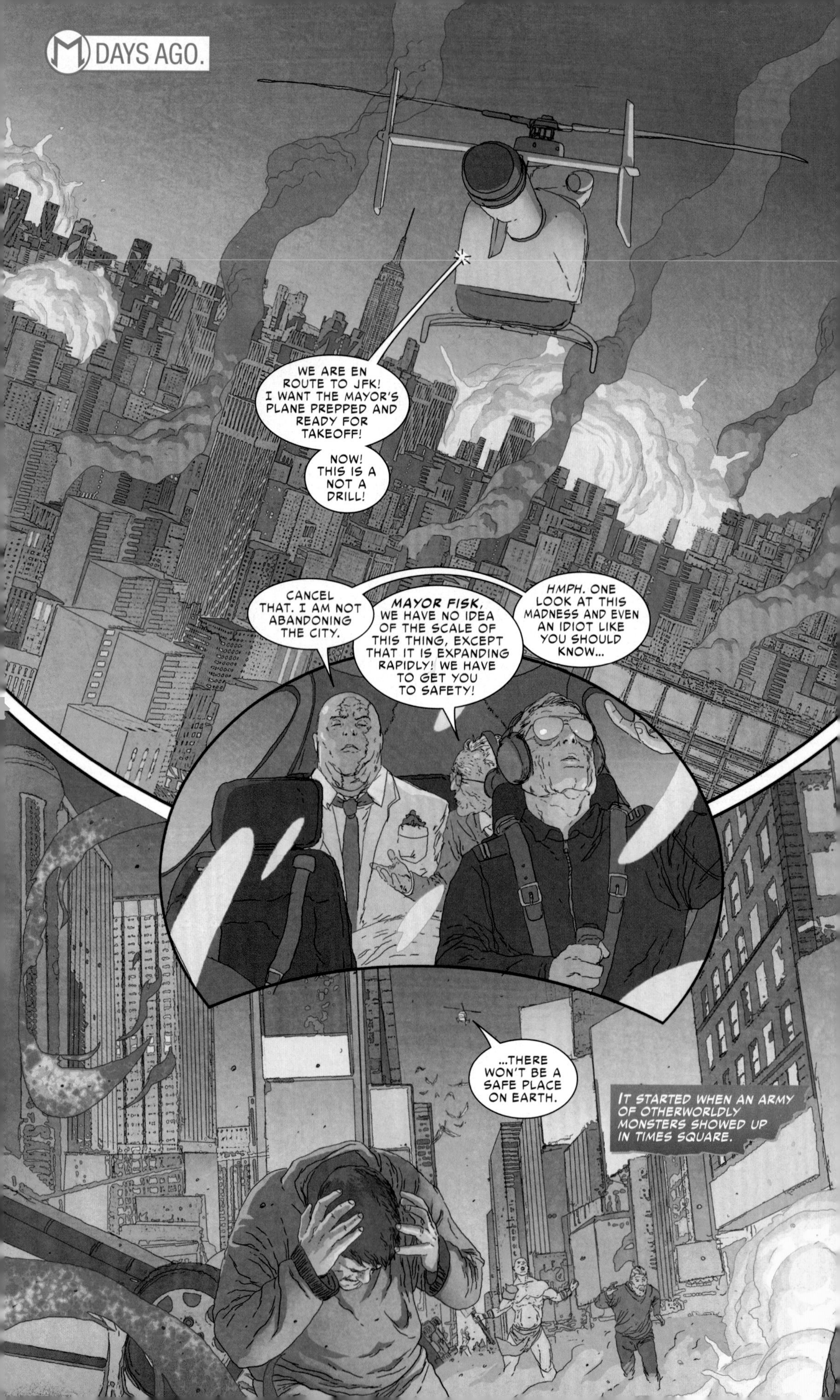
DAYS AGO.
WE ARE EN ROUTE TO JFK! I WANT THE MAYOR'S PLANE PREPPED AND READY FOR TAKEOFF!
NOW! THIS IS A NOT A DRILL!
CANCEL THAT. I AM NOT ABANDONING THE CITY.
MAYOR FISK, WE HAVE NO IDEA OF THE SCALE OF THIS THING, EXCEPT THAT IT IS EXPANDING RAPIDLY! WE HAVE TO GET YOU TO SAFETY!
HMPH. ONE LOOK AT THIS MADNESS AND EVEN AN IDIOT LIKE YOU SHOULD KNOW...
...THERE WON'T BE A SAFE PLACE ON EARTH.
IT STARTED WHEN AN ARMY OF OTHERWORLDLY MONSTERS SHOWED UP IN TIMES SQUARE.

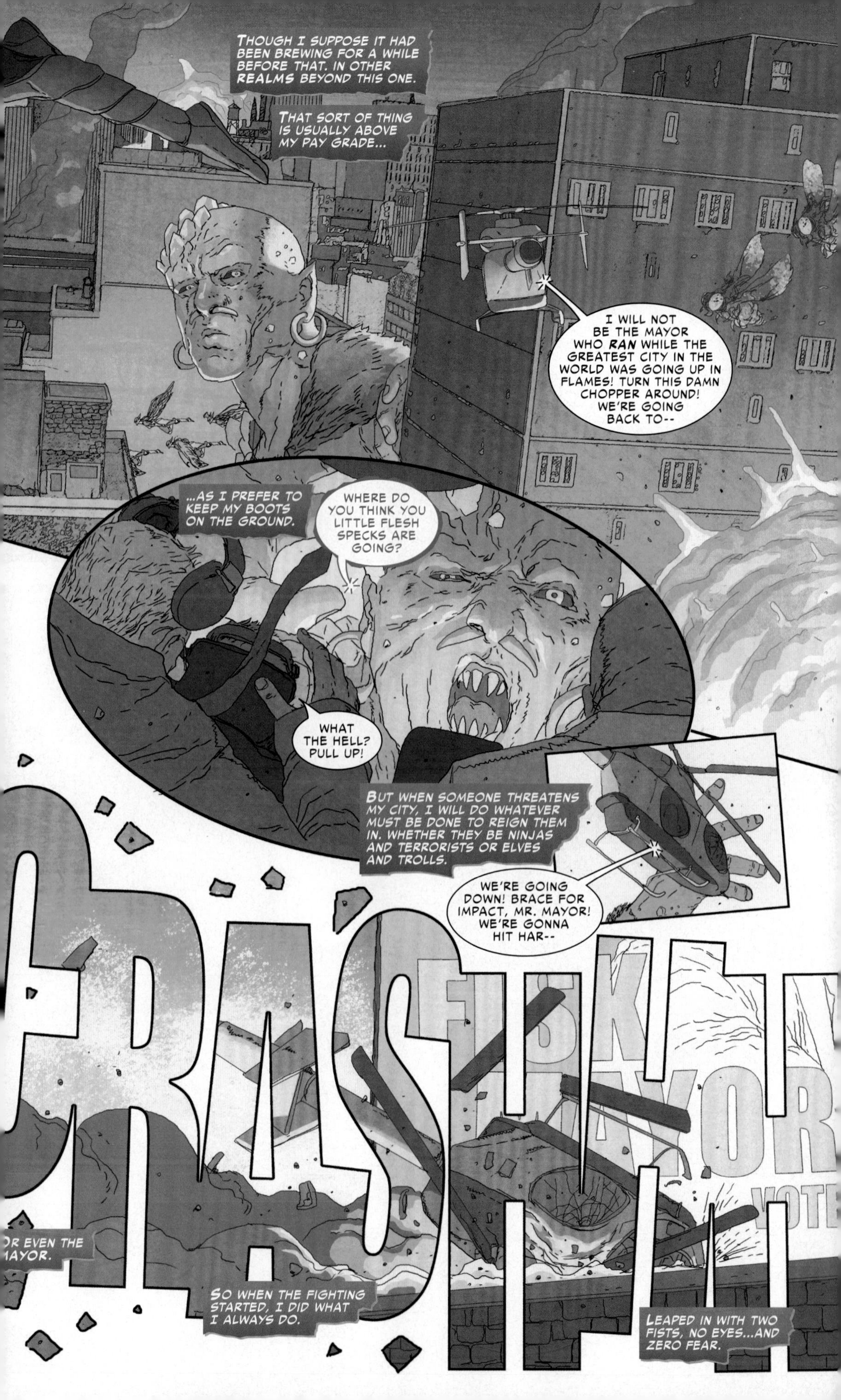
THOUGH I SUPPOSE IT HAD BEEN BREWING FOR A WHILE BEFORE THAT. IN OTHER REALMS BEYOND THIS ONE.
THAT SORT OF THING IS USUALLY ABOVE MY PAY GRADE...
I WILL NOT BE THE MAYOR WHO RAN WHILE THE GREATEST CITY IN THE WORLD WAS GOING UP IN FLAMES! TURN THIS DAMN CHOPPER AROUND! WE'RE GOING BACK TO--
...AS I PREFER TO KEEP MY BOOTS ON THE GROUND.
WHERE DO YOU THINK YOU LITTLE FLESH SPECKS ARE GOING?
WHAT THE HELL? PULL UP!
BUT WHEN SOMEONE THREATENS MY CITY, I WILL DO WHATEVER MUST BE DONE TO REIGN THEM IN. WHETHER THEY BE NINJAS AND TERRORISTS OR ELVES AND TROLLS.
WE'RE GOING DOWN! BRACE FOR IMPACT, MR. MAYOR! WE'RE GONNA HIT HAR--
OR EVEN THE MAYOR.
SO WHEN THE FIGHTING STARTED, I DID WHAT I ALWAYS DO.
LEAPED IN WITH TWO FISTS, NO EYES...AND ZERO FEAR.

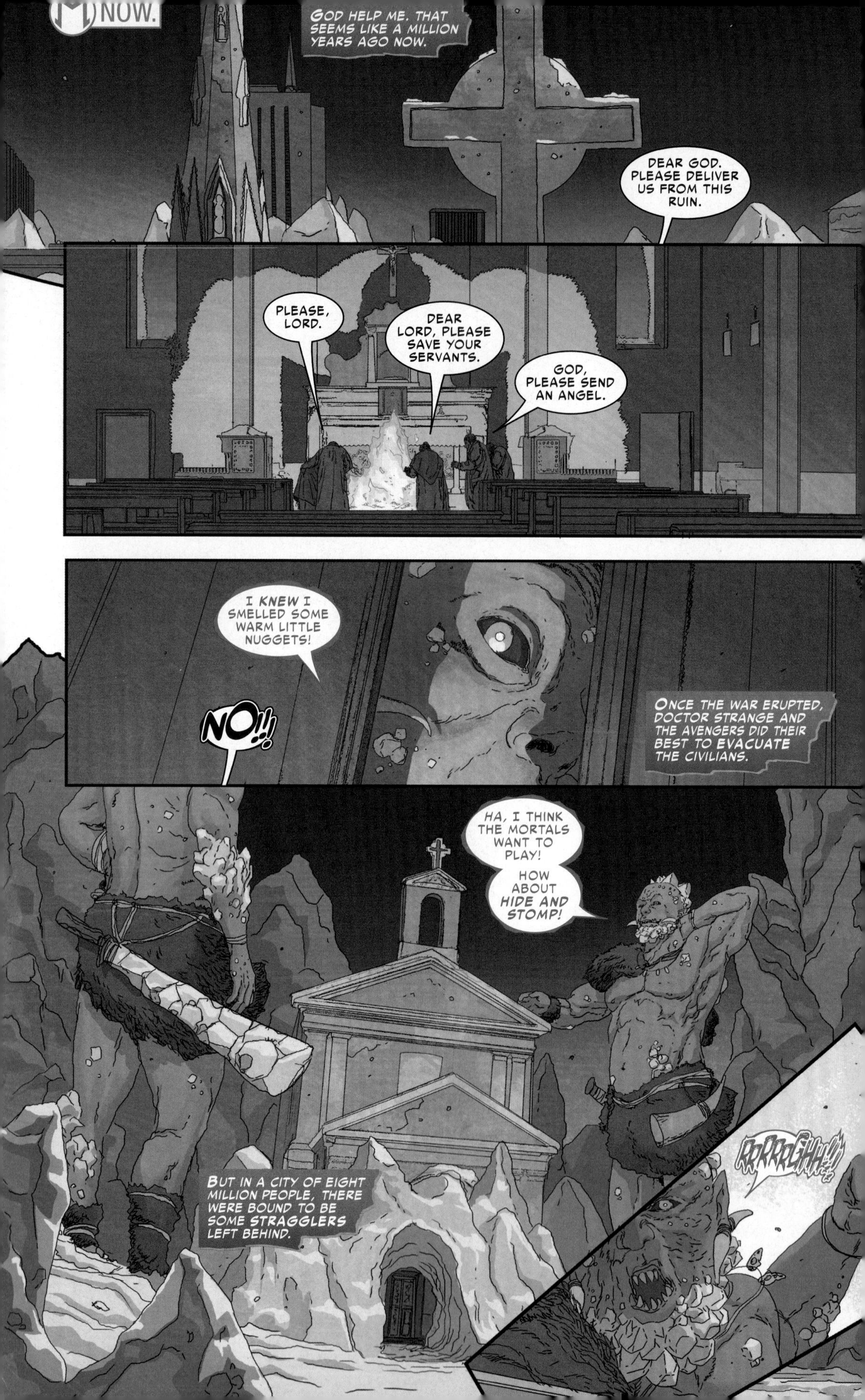
NOW.
GOD HELP ME. THAT SEEMS LIKE A MILLION YEARS AGO NOW.
DEAR GOD. PLEASE DELIVER US FROM THIS RUIN.
PLEASE, LORD.
DEAR LORD, PLEASE SAVE YOUR SERVANTS.
GOD, PLEASE SEND AN ANGEL.
I KNEW I SMELLED SOME WARM LITTLE NUGGETS!
NO!!!
ONCE THE WAR ERUPTED, DOCTOR STRANGE AND THE AVENGERS DID THEIR BEST TO EVACUATE THE CIVILIANS.
HA, I THINK THE MORTALS WANT TO PLAY!
HOW ABOUT HIDE AND STOMP!
BUT IN A CITY OF EIGHT MILLION PEOPLE, THERE WERE BOUND TO BE SOME STRAGGLERS LEFT BEHIND.
RRRRRGHHH!!

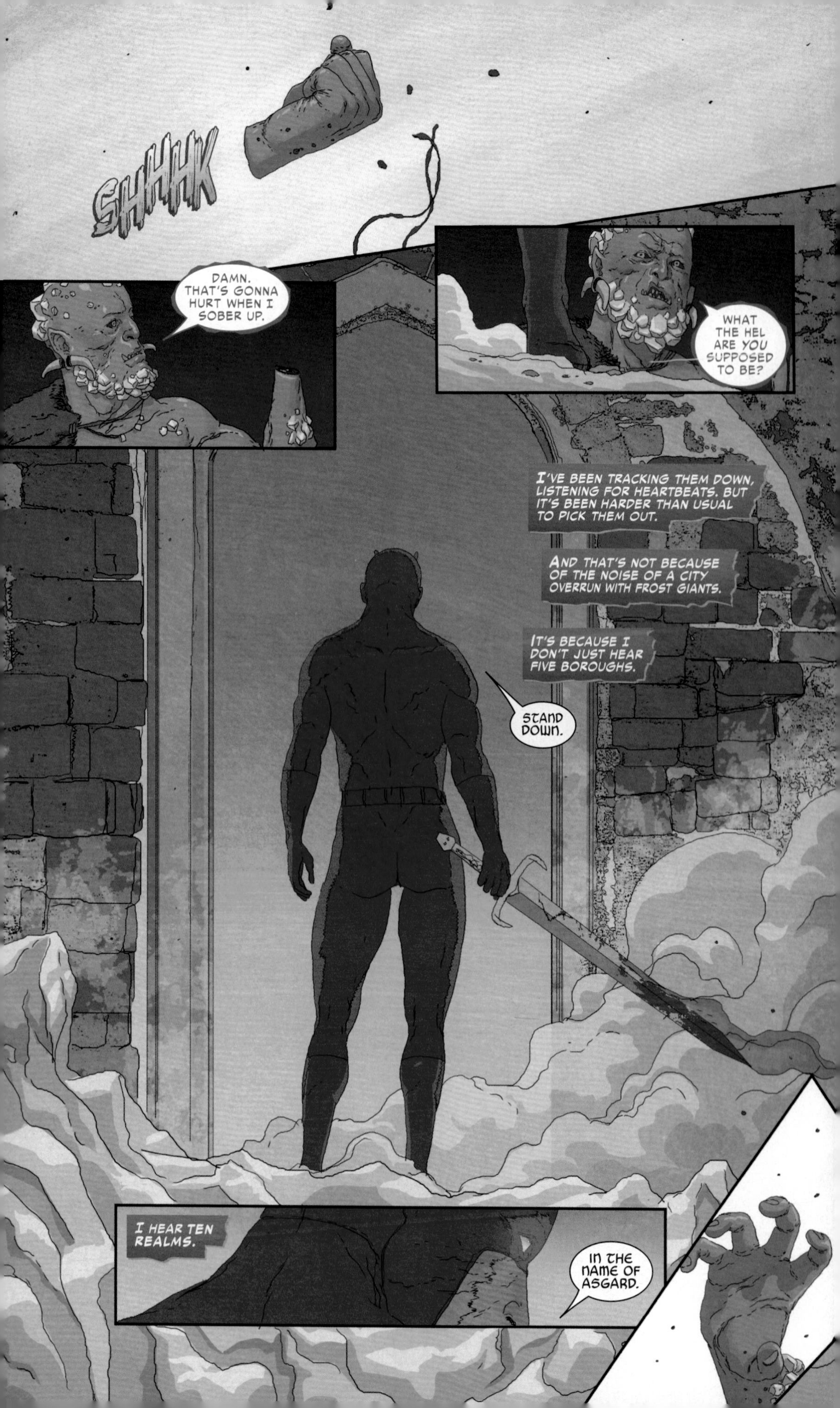

SHHHK
DAMN. THAT'S GONNA HURT WHEN I SOBER UP.
WHAT THE HEL ARE YOU SUPPOSED TO BE?
I'VE BEEN TRACKING THEM DOWN, LISTENING FOR HEARTBEATS. BUT IT'S BEEN HARDER THAN USUAL TO PICK THEM OUT.
AND THAT'S NOT BECAUSE OF THE NOISE OF A CITY OVERRUN WITH FROST GIANTS.
IT'S BECAUSE I DON'T JUST HEAR FIVE BOROUGHS.
STAND DOWN.
I HEAR TEN REALMS.
IN THE NAME OF ASGARD.

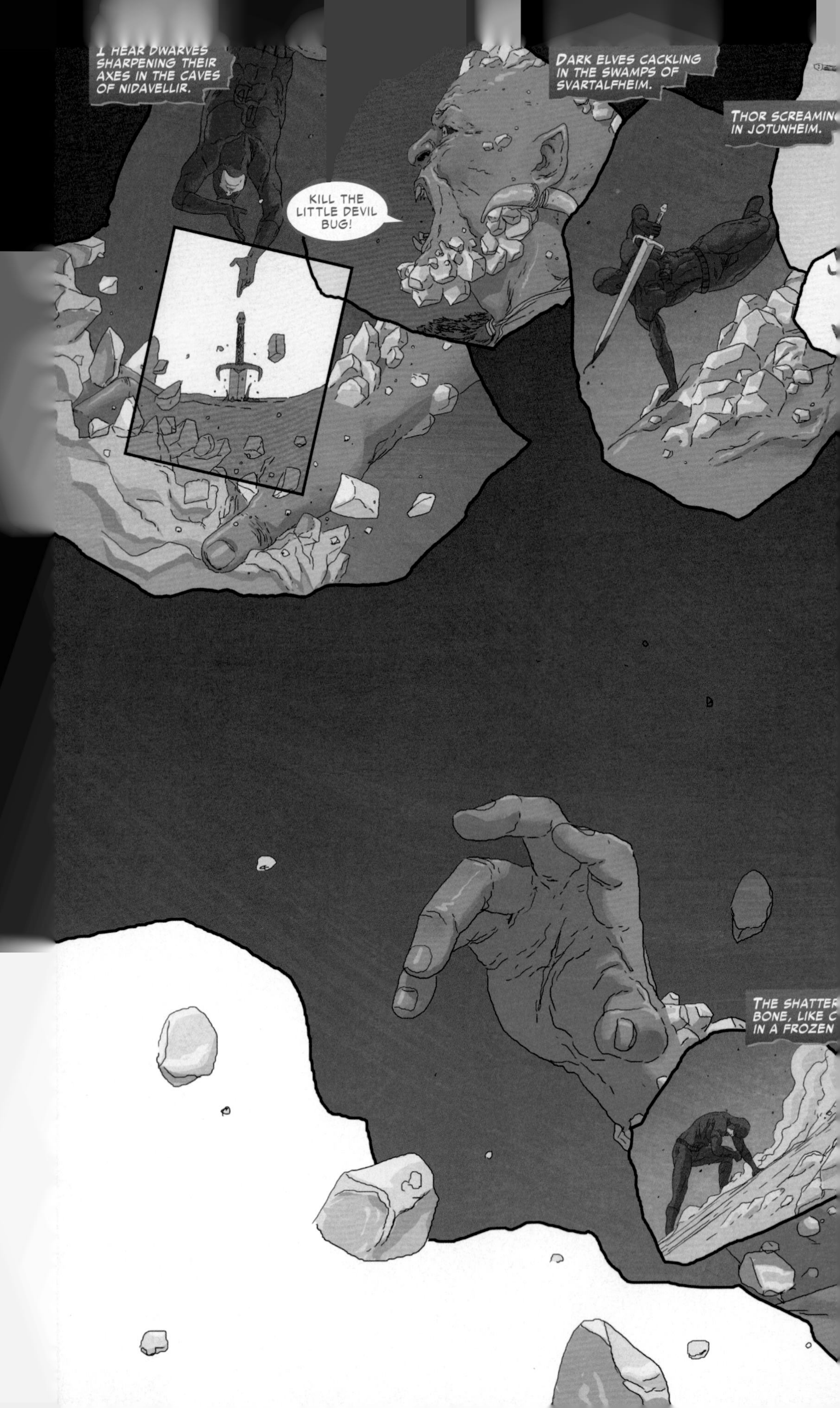
I HEAR DWARVES SHARPENING THEIR AXES IN THE CAVES OF NIDAVELLIR.
KILL THE LITTLE DEVIL BUG!
DARK ELVES CACKLING IN THE SWAMPS OF SVARTALFHEIM.
THOR SCREAMIN
IN JOTUNHEIM.
THE SHATTER
BONE, LIKE C
IN A FROZEN

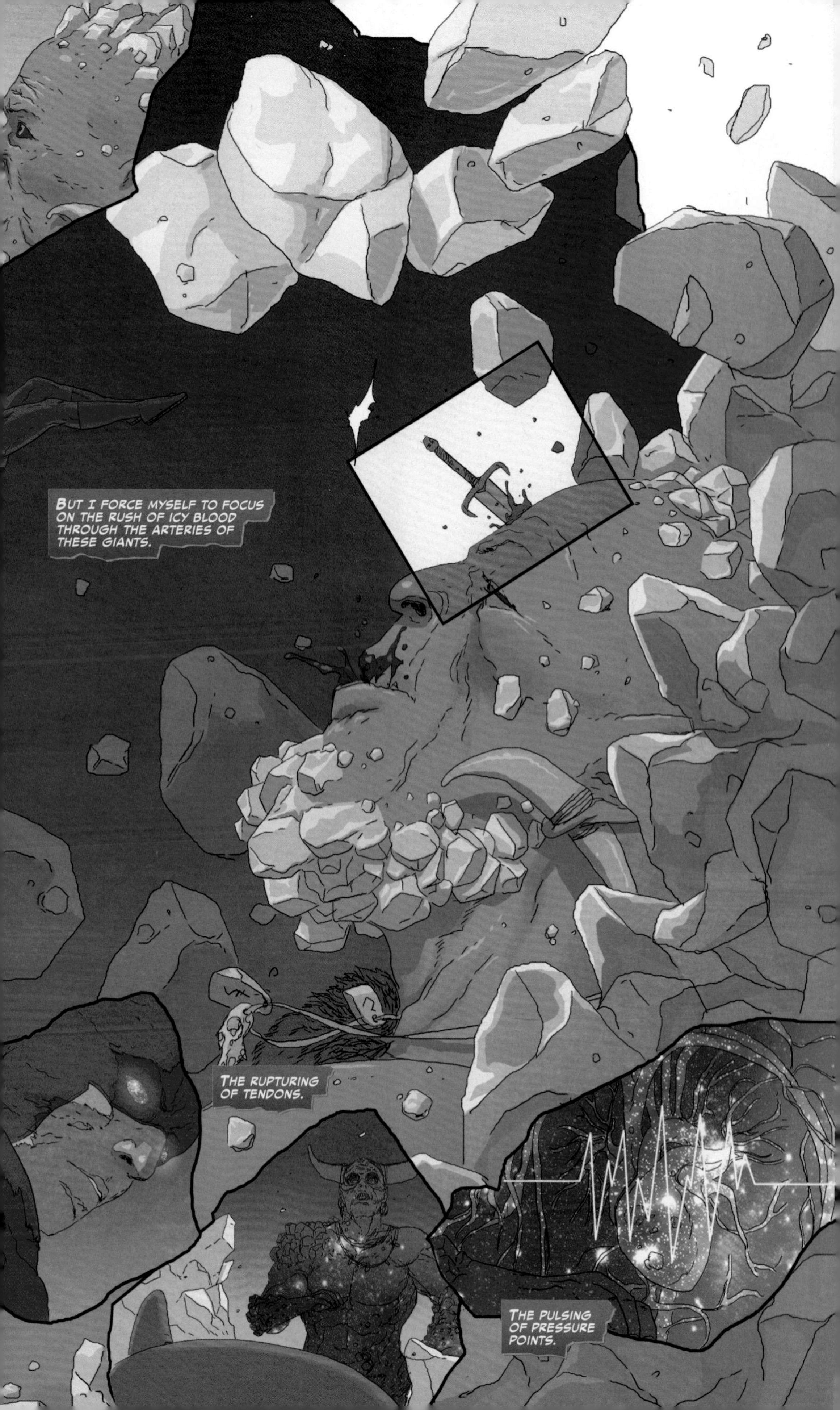
BUT I FORCE MYSELF TO FOCUS ON THE RUSH OF ICY BLOOD THROUGH THE ARTERIES OF THESE GIANTS.
THE RUPTURING OF TENDONS.
THE PULSING OF PRESSURE POINTS.

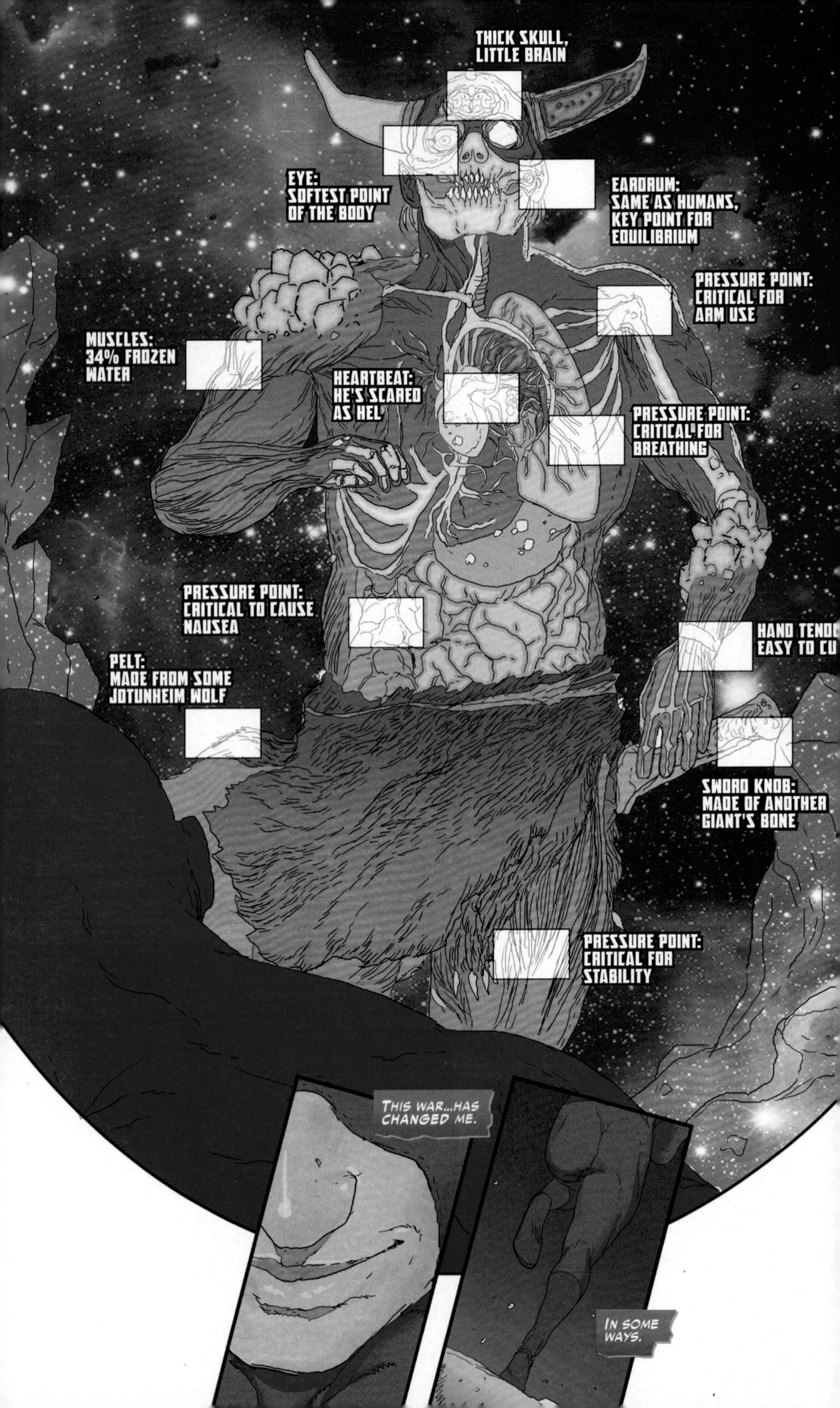
THICK SKULL, LITTLE BRAIN
EYE: SOFTEST POINT OF THE BODY
EARDRUM: SAME AS HUMANS, KEY POINT FOR EQUILIBRIUM
PRESSURE POINT: CRITICAL FOR ARM USE
MUSCLES: 34% FROZEN WATER
HEARTBEAT: HE'S SCARED AS HEL
PRESSURE POINT: CRITICAL FOR BREATHING
PRESSURE POINT: CRITICAL TO CAUSE NAUSEA
HAND TEND EASY TO CU
PELT: MADE FROM SOME JOTUNHEIM WOLF
SWORD KNOB: MADE OF ANOTHER GIANT'S BONE
PRESSURE POINT: CRITICAL FOR STABILITY
THIS WAR...HAS CHANGED ME.
IN SOME WAYS.

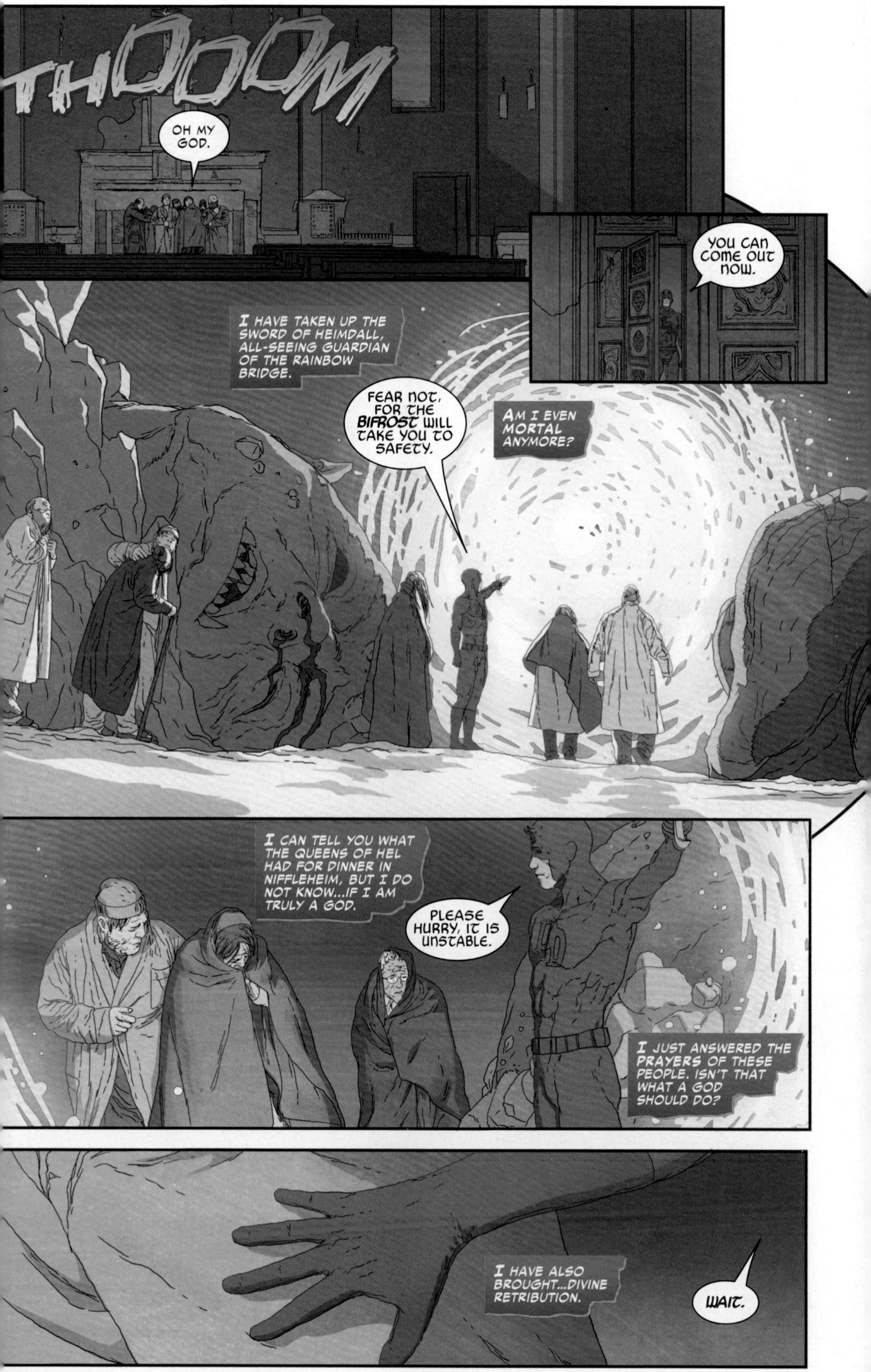
THOOOM
OH MY GOD.
YOU CAN COME OUT NOW.
I HAVE TAKEN UP THE SWORD OF HEIMDALL, ALL-SEEING GUARDIAN OF THE RAINBOW BRIDGE.
FEAR NOT, FOR THE BIFROST WILL TAKE YOU TO SAFETY.
AM I EVEN MORTAL ANYMORE?
I CAN TELL YOU WHAT THE QUEENS OF HEL HAD FOR DINNER IN NIFFLEHEIM, BUT I DO NOT KNOW...IF I AM TRULY A GOD.
PLEASE HURRY, IT IS UNSTABLE.
I JUST ANSWERED THE PRAYERS OF THESE PEOPLE. ISN'T THAT WHAT A GOD SHOULD DO?
I HAVE ALSO BROUGHT...DIVINE RETRIBUTION.
WAIT.

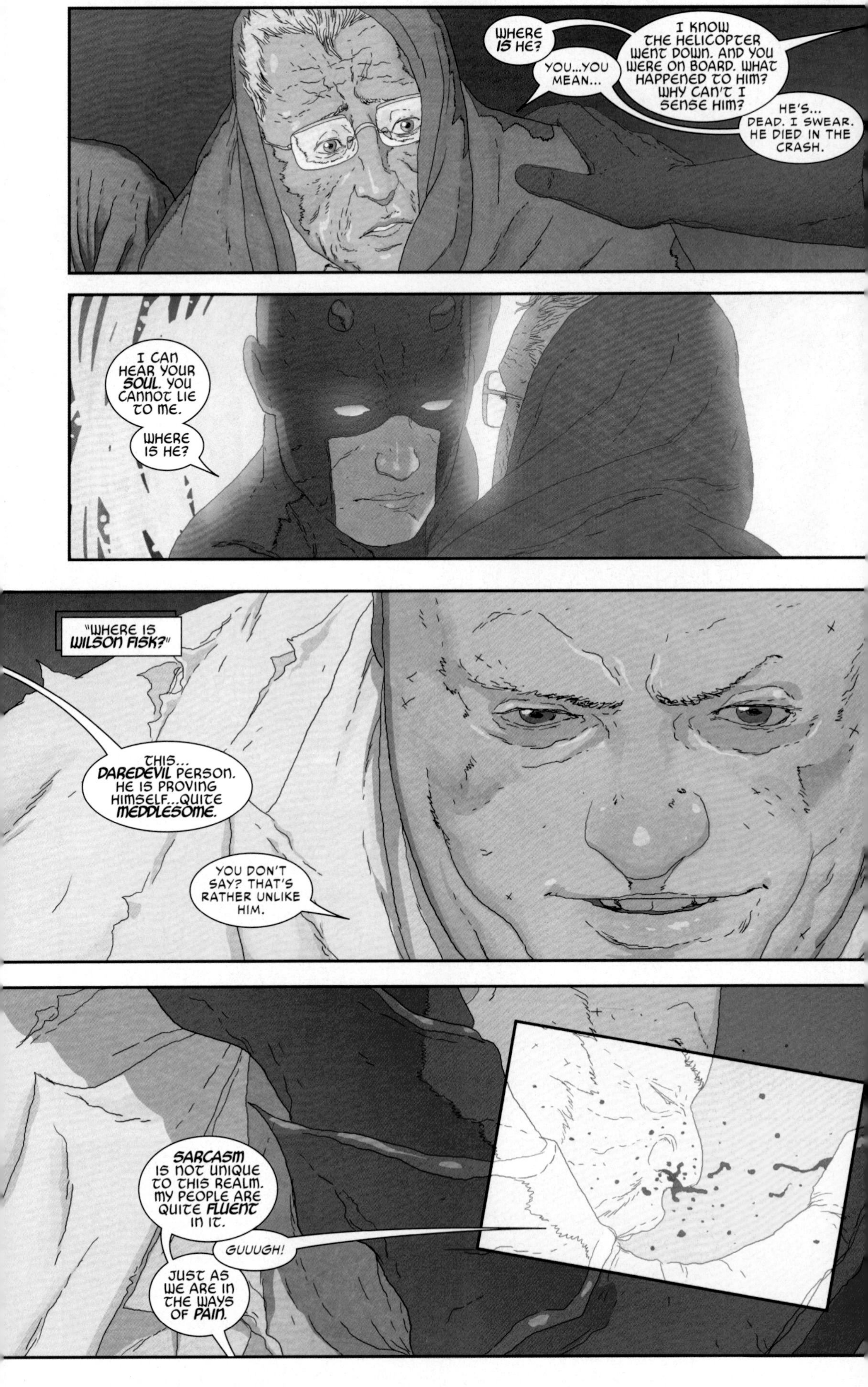
WHERE IS HE?
YOU...YOU MEAN...
I KNOW THE HELICOPTER WENT DOWN. AND YOU WERE ON BOARD. WHAT HAPPENED TO HIM? WHY CAN'T I SENSE HIM?
HE'S... DEAD. I SWEAR. HE DIED IN THE CRASH.
I CAN HEAR YOUR SOUL. YOU CANNOT LIE TO ME.
WHERE IS HE?
"WHERE IS WILSON FISK?"
THIS... DAREDEVIL PERSON. HE IS PROVING HIMSELF...QUITE MEDDLESOME.
YOU DON'T SAY? THAT'S RATHER UNLIKE HIM.
SARCASM IS NOT UNIQUE TO THIS REALM. MY PEOPLE ARE QUITE FLUENT IN IT.
GUUUGH!
JUST AS WE ARE IN THE WAYS OF PAIN.

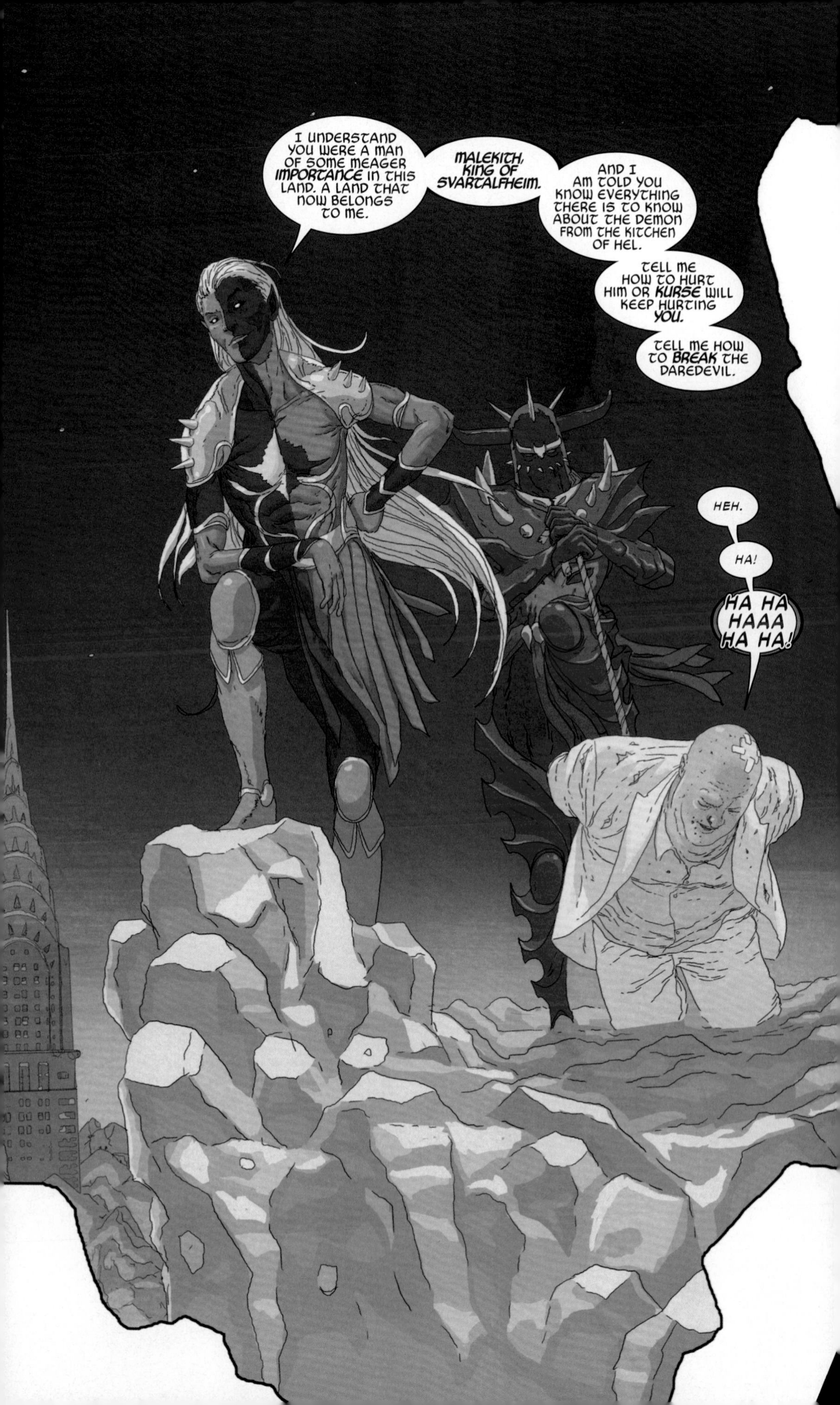
I UNDERSTAND YOU WERE A MAN OF SOME MEAGER IMPORTANCE IN THIS LAND. A LAND THAT NOW BELONGS TO ME.
MALEKITH, KING OF SVARTALFHEIM.
AND I AM TOLD YOU KNOW EVERYTHING THERE IS TO KNOW ABOUT THE DEMON FROM THE KITCHEN OF HEL.
TELL ME HOW TO HURT HIM OR KURSE WILL KEEP HURTING YOU.
TELL ME HOW TO BREAK THE DAREDEVIL.
HEH.
HA!
HA HA HAAA HA HA!

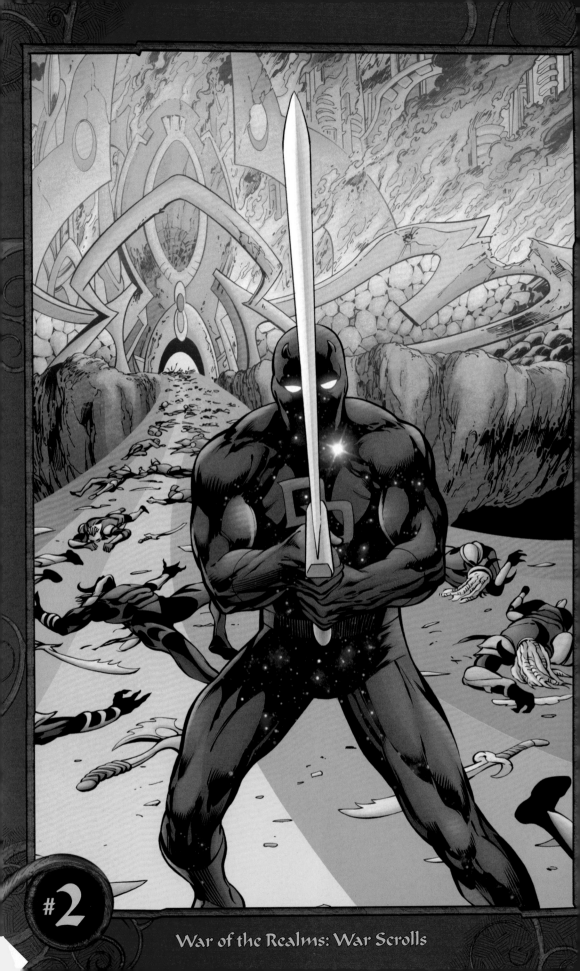

#2

War of the Realms: War Scrolls

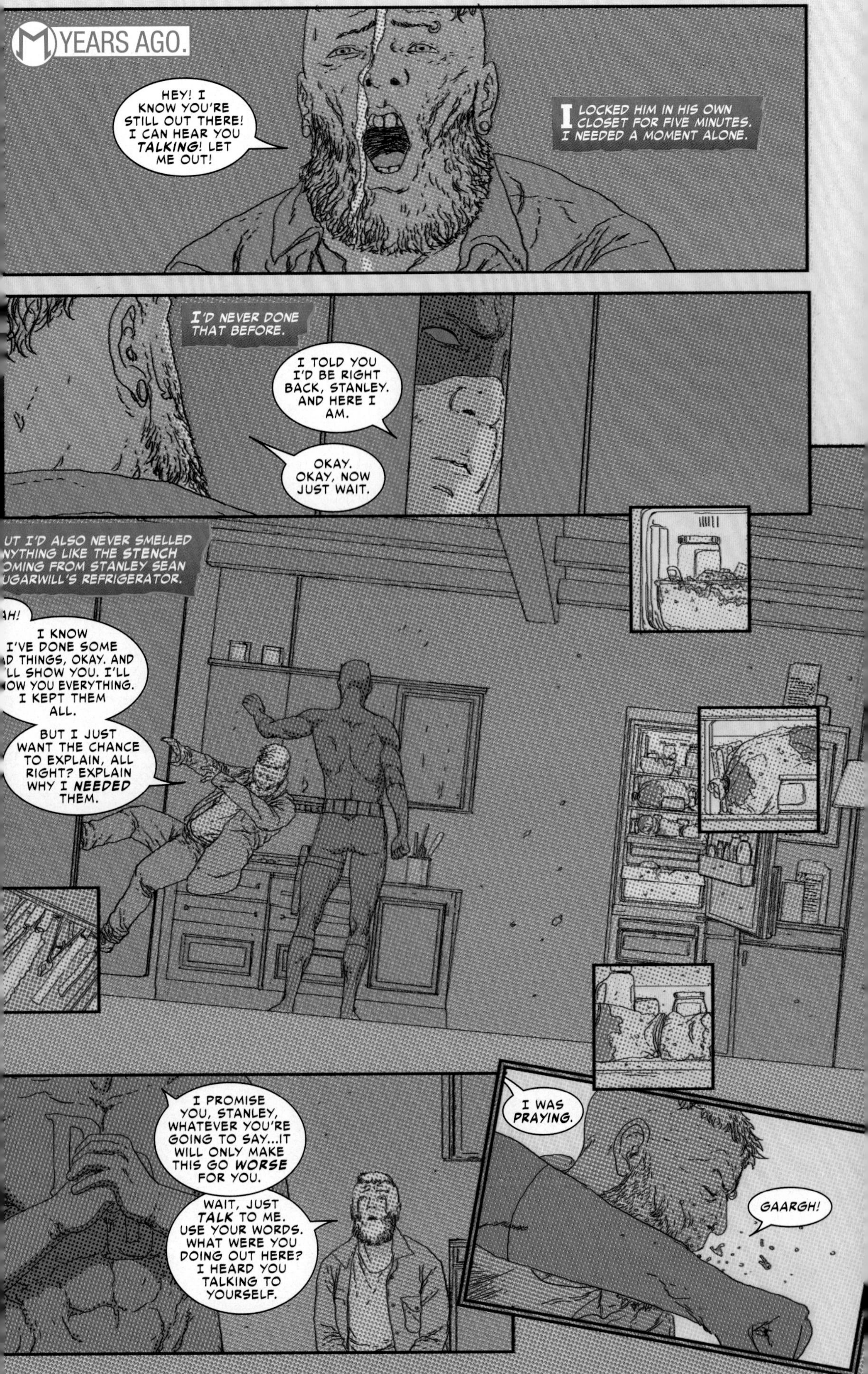

YEARS AGO.
HEY! I KNOW YOU'RE STILL OUT THERE! I CAN HEAR YOU TALKING! LET ME OUT!
I LOCKED HIM IN HIS OWN CLOSET FOR FIVE MINUTES. I NEEDED A MOMENT ALONE.
I'D NEVER DONE THAT BEFORE.
I TOLD YOU I'D BE RIGHT BACK, STANLEY. AND HERE I AM.
OKAY. OKAY, NOW JUST WAIT.
UT I'D ALSO NEVER SMELLED NYTHING LIKE THE STENCH OMING FROM STANLEY SEAN UGARWILL'S REFRIGERATOR.
AH!
I KNOW I'VE DONE SOME D THINGS, OKAY. AND LL SHOW YOU. I'LL OW YOU EVERYTHING. I KEPT THEM ALL.
BUT I JUST WANT THE CHANCE TO EXPLAIN, ALL RIGHT? EXPLAIN WHY I NEEDED THEM.
I PROMISE YOU, STANLEY, WHATEVER YOU'RE GOING TO SAY...IT WILL ONLY MAKE THIS GO WORSE FOR YOU.
WAIT, JUST TALK TO ME. USE YOUR WORDS. WHAT WERE YOU DOING OUT HERE? I HEARD YOU TALKING TO YOURSELF.
I WAS PRAYING.
GAARGH!

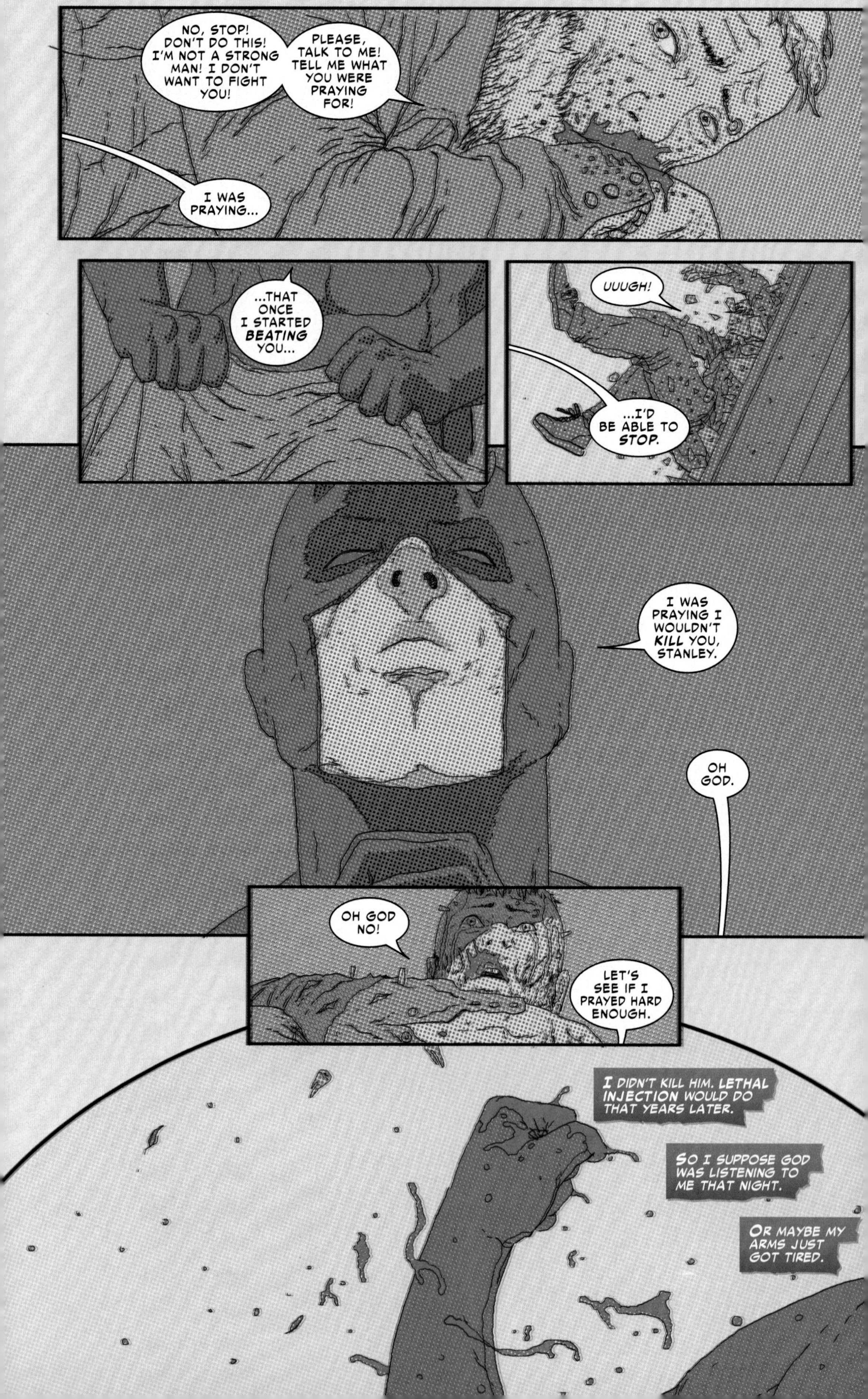
NO, STOP! DON'T DO THIS! I'M NOT A STRONG MAN! I DON'T WANT TO FIGHT YOU!
PLEASE, TALK TO ME! TELL ME WHAT YOU WERE PRAYING FOR!
I WAS PRAYING...
...THAT ONCE I STARTED BEATING YOU...
UUUGH!
...I'D BE ABLE TO STOP.
I WAS PRAYING I WOULDN'T KILL YOU, STANLEY.
OH GOD.
OH GOD NO!
LET'S SEE IF I PRAYED HARD ENOUGH.
I DIDN'T KILL HIM. LETHAL INJECTION WOULD DO THAT YEARS LATER.
SO I SUPPOSE GOD WAS LISTENING TO ME THAT NIGHT.
OR MAYBE MY ARMS JUST GOT TIRED.

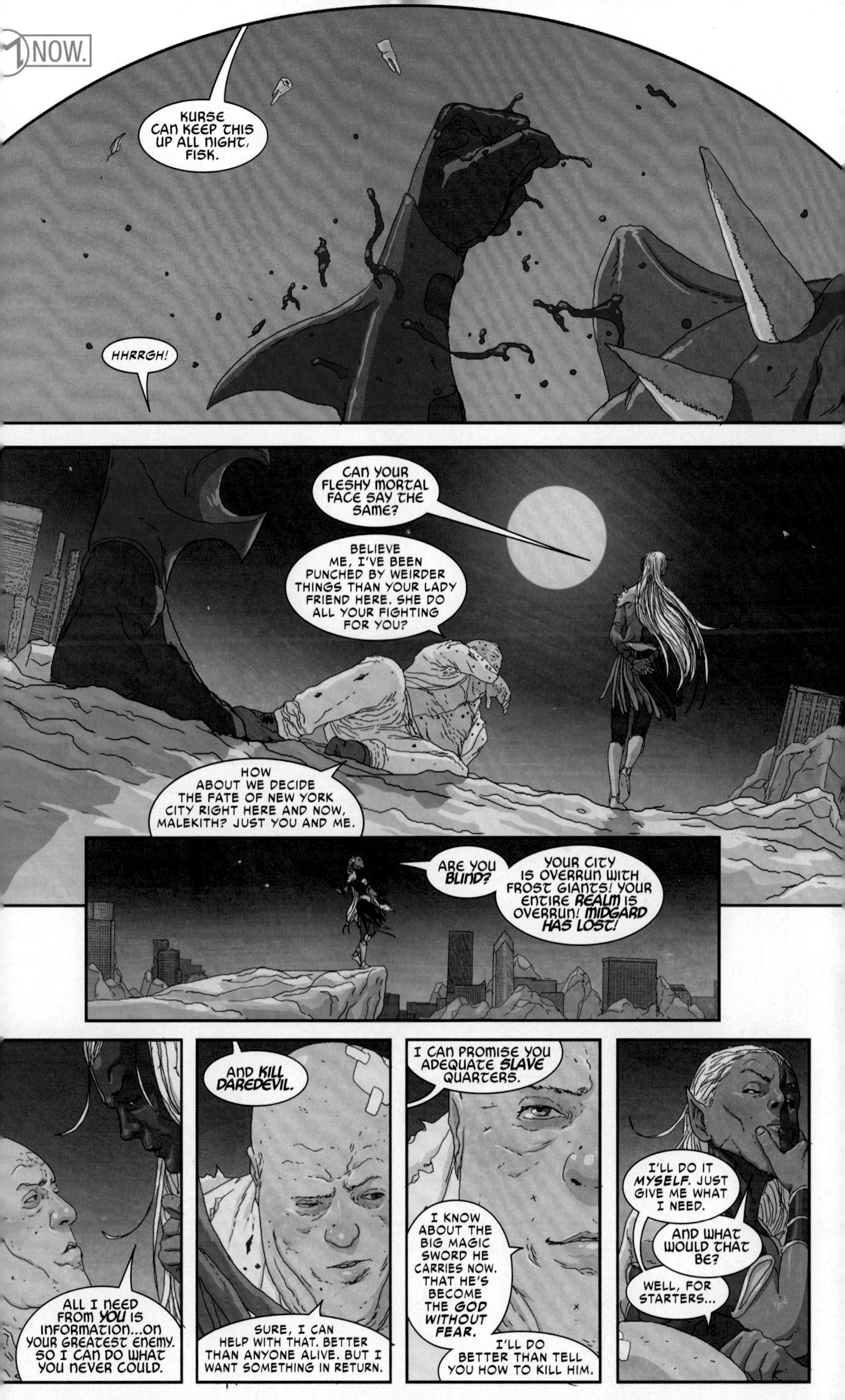
NOW.
KURSE CAN KEEP THIS UP ALL NIGHT, FISK.
HHRRGH!
CAN YOUR FLESHY MORTAL FACE SAY THE SAME?
BELIEVE ME, I'VE BEEN PUNCHED BY WEIRDER THINGS THAN YOUR LADY FRIEND HERE. SHE DO ALL YOUR FIGHTING FOR YOU?
HOW ABOUT WE DECIDE THE FATE OF NEW YORK CITY RIGHT HERE AND NOW, MALEKITH? JUST YOU AND ME.
ARE YOU BLIND?
YOUR CITY IS OVERRUN WITH FROST GIANTS! YOUR ENTIRE REALM IS OVERRUN! MIDGARD HAS LOST!
ALL I NEED FROM YOU IS INFORMATION...ON YOUR GREATEST ENEMY. SO I CAN DO WHAT YOU NEVER COULD.
AND KILL DAREDEVIL.
SURE, I CAN HELP WITH THAT. BETTER THAN ANYONE ALIVE. BUT I WANT SOMETHING IN RETURN.
I CAN PROMISE YOU ADEQUATE SLAVE QUARTERS.
I KNOW ABOUT THE BIG MAGIC SWORD HE CARRIES NOW. THAT HE'S BECOME THE GOD WITHOUT FEAR.
I'LL DO BETTER THAN TELL YOU HOW TO KILL HIM.
I'LL DO IT MYSELF. JUST GIVE ME WHAT I NEED.
AND WHAT WOULD THAT BE?
WELL, FOR STARTERS...

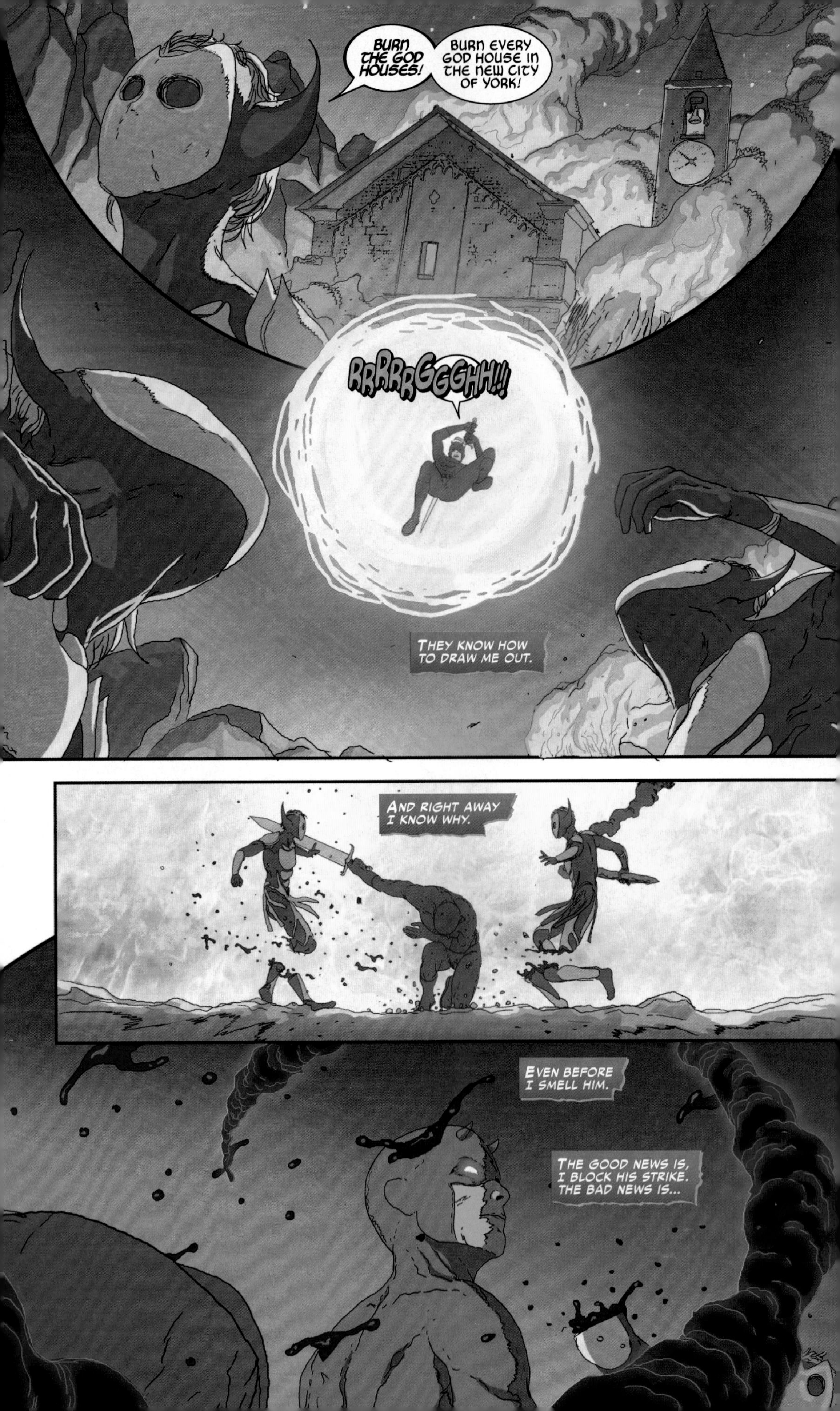
BURN THE GOD HOUSES!
BURN EVERY GOD HOUSE IN THE NEW CITY OF YORK!
RRRRRGGGHH!!!
THEY KNOW HOW TO DRAW ME OUT.
AND RIGHT AWAY I KNOW WHY.
EVEN BEFORE I SMELL HIM.
THE GOOD NEWS IS, I BLOCK HIS STRIKE. THE BAD NEWS IS...

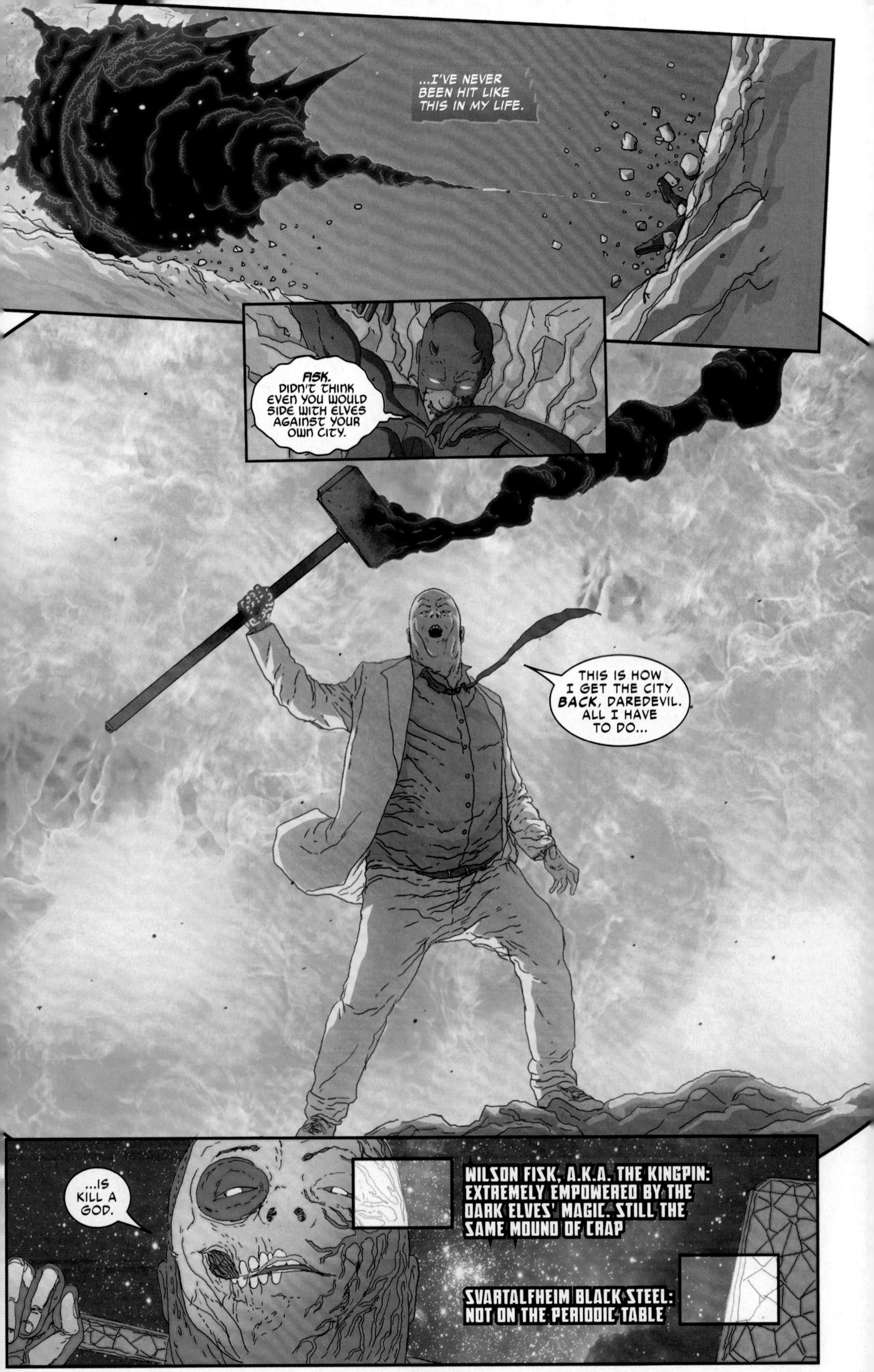
...I'VE NEVER BEEN HIT LIKE THIS IN MY LIFE.
FISK. DIDN'T THINK EVEN YOU WOULD SIDE WITH ELVES AGAINST YOUR OWN CITY.
THIS IS HOW I GET THE CITY BACK, DAREDEVIL. ALL I HAVE TO DO...
...IS KILL A GOD.
WILSON FISK, A.K.A. THE KINGPIN: EXTREMELY EMPOWERED BY THE DARK ELVES' MAGIC. STILL THE SAME MOUND OF CRAP
SVARTALFHEIM BLACK STEEL: NOT ON THE PERIODIC TABLE

NICE, RIGHT? IT'S SOME KINDA MAGIC ELF HAMMER!
I DON'T KNOW, I WASN'T REALLY LISTENING DURING THAT PART. BUT I TELL YA...
THOOM
...I CAN SEE WHY THOR LIKES THIS SO MUCH!

NO NO NO, THIS IS NO GOOD. WE CAN'T DO THIS IN THE SUBWAY...
...I NEED YOU UP IN THE-- UNH!
THOOM
I'VE PUNCHED PEOPLE EVERY KINDA WAY YOU CAN IMAGINE.
BUT I'VE NEVER PUNCHED ANYONE THROUGH A BUILDING BEFORE.
IT'S TERRIFYING, THAT POWER.
IT'S TERRIFYING HOW QUICKLY YOU GET USED TO IT.
IT DOESN'T MATTER HOW POWERFUL THAT HAMMER MAKES YOU!

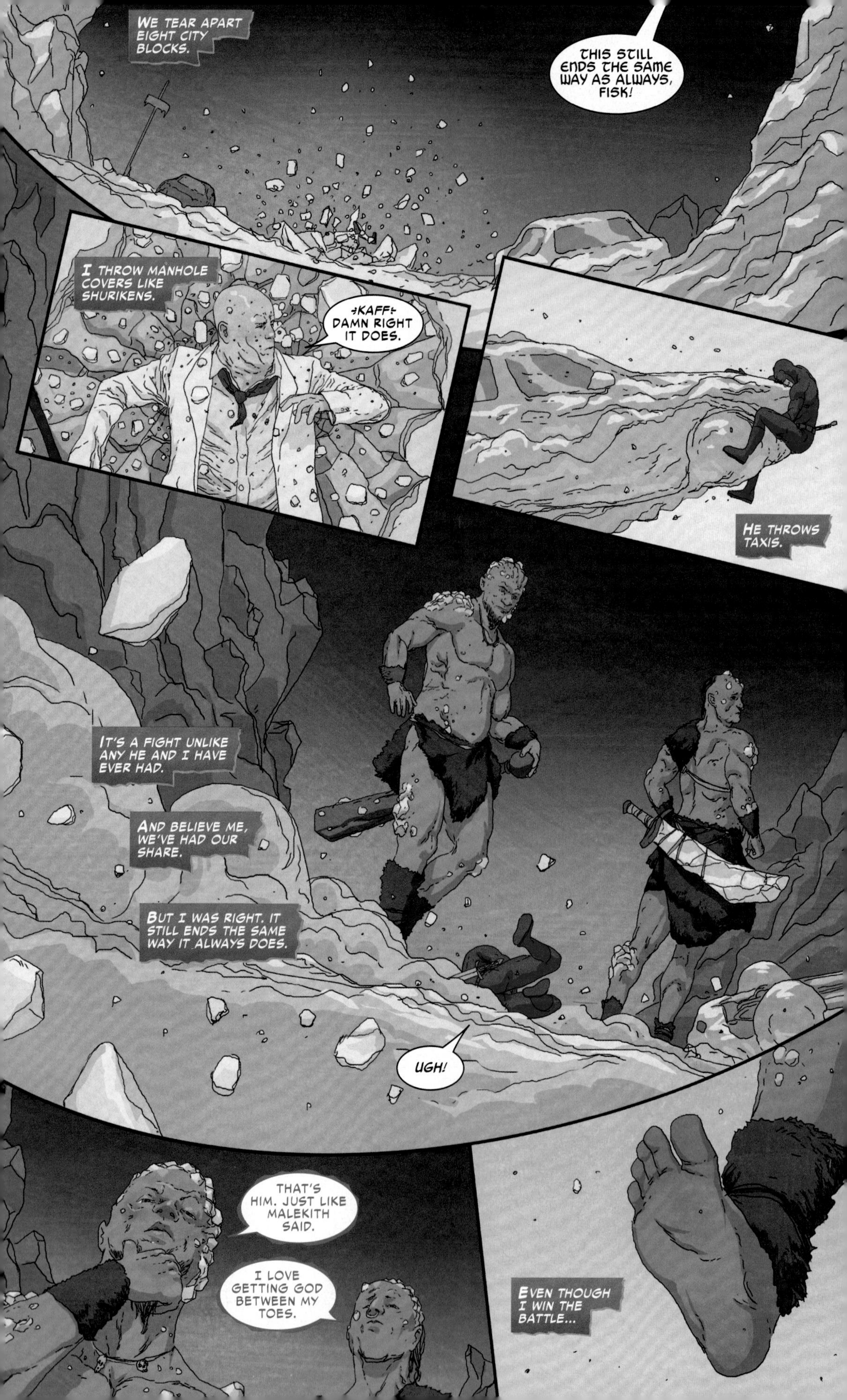

WE TEAR APART EIGHT CITY BLOCKS.
THIS STILL ENDS THE SAME WAY AS ALWAYS, FISK!
I THROW MANHOLE COVERS LIKE SHURIKENS.
KAFF DAMN RIGHT IT DOES.
HE THROWS TAXIS.
IT'S A FIGHT UNLIKE ANY HE AND I HAVE EVER HAD.
AND BELIEVE ME, WE'VE HAD OUR SHARE.
BUT I WAS RIGHT. IT STILL ENDS THE SAME WAY IT ALWAYS DOES.
UGH!
THAT'S HIM. JUST LIKE MALEKITH SAID.
I LOVE GETTING GOD BETWEEN MY TOES.
EVEN THOUGH I WIN THE BATTLE...

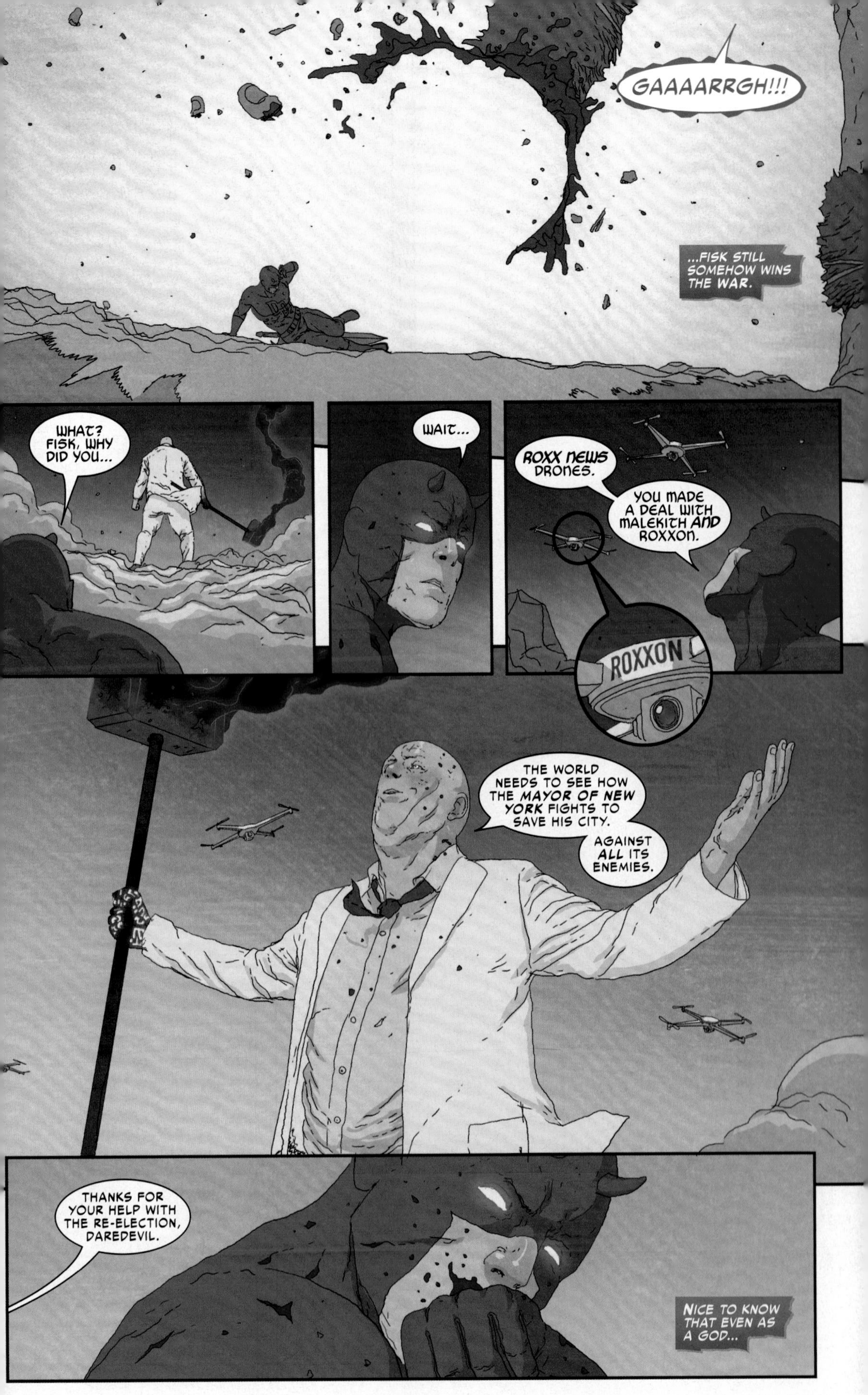
GAAAARRGH!!!
...FISK STILL SOMEHOW WINS THE WAR.
WHAT? FISK, WHY DID YOU...
WAIT...
ROXX NEWS DRONES.
YOU MADE A DEAL WITH MALEKITH AND ROXXON.
ROXXON
THE WORLD NEEDS TO SEE HOW THE MAYOR OF NEW YORK FIGHTS TO SAVE HIS CITY.
AGAINST ALL ITS ENEMIES.
THANKS FOR YOUR HELP WITH THE RE-ELECTION, DAREDEVIL.
NICE TO KNOW THAT EVEN AS A GOD...

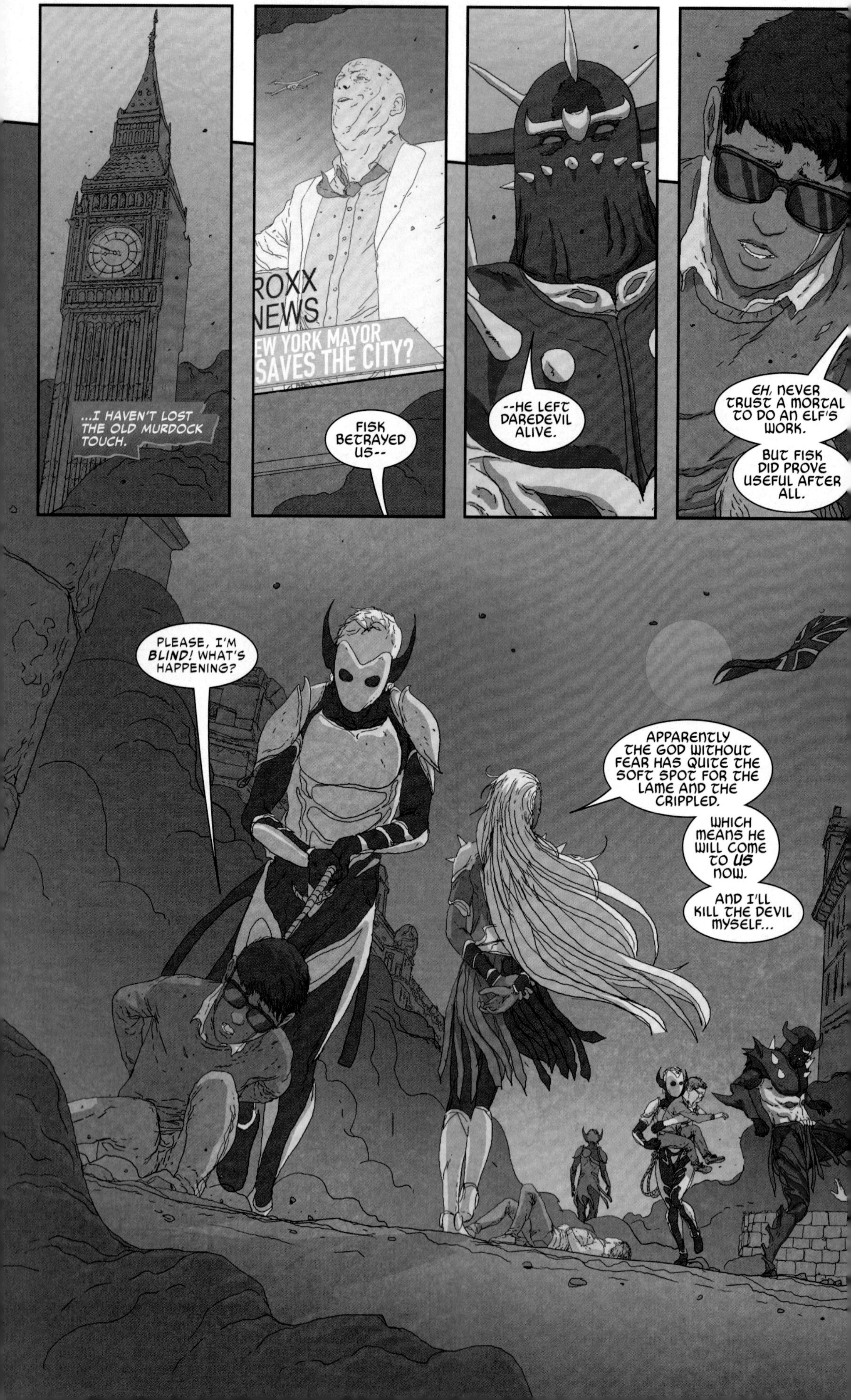

...I HAVEN'T LOST THE OLD MURDOCK TOUCH.
ROXX NEWS
EW YORK MAYOR SAVES THE CITY?
FISK BETRAYED US--
--HE LEFT DAREDEVIL ALIVE.
EH, NEVER TRUST A MORTAL TO DO AN ELF'S WORK.
BUT FISK DID PROVE USEFUL AFTER ALL.
PLEASE, I'M BLIND! WHAT'S HAPPENING?
APPARENTLY THE GOD WITHOUT FEAR HAS QUITE THE SOFT SPOT FOR THE LAME AND THE CRIPPLED.
WHICH MEANS HE WILL COME TO US NOW.
AND I'LL KILL THE DEVIL MYSELF...

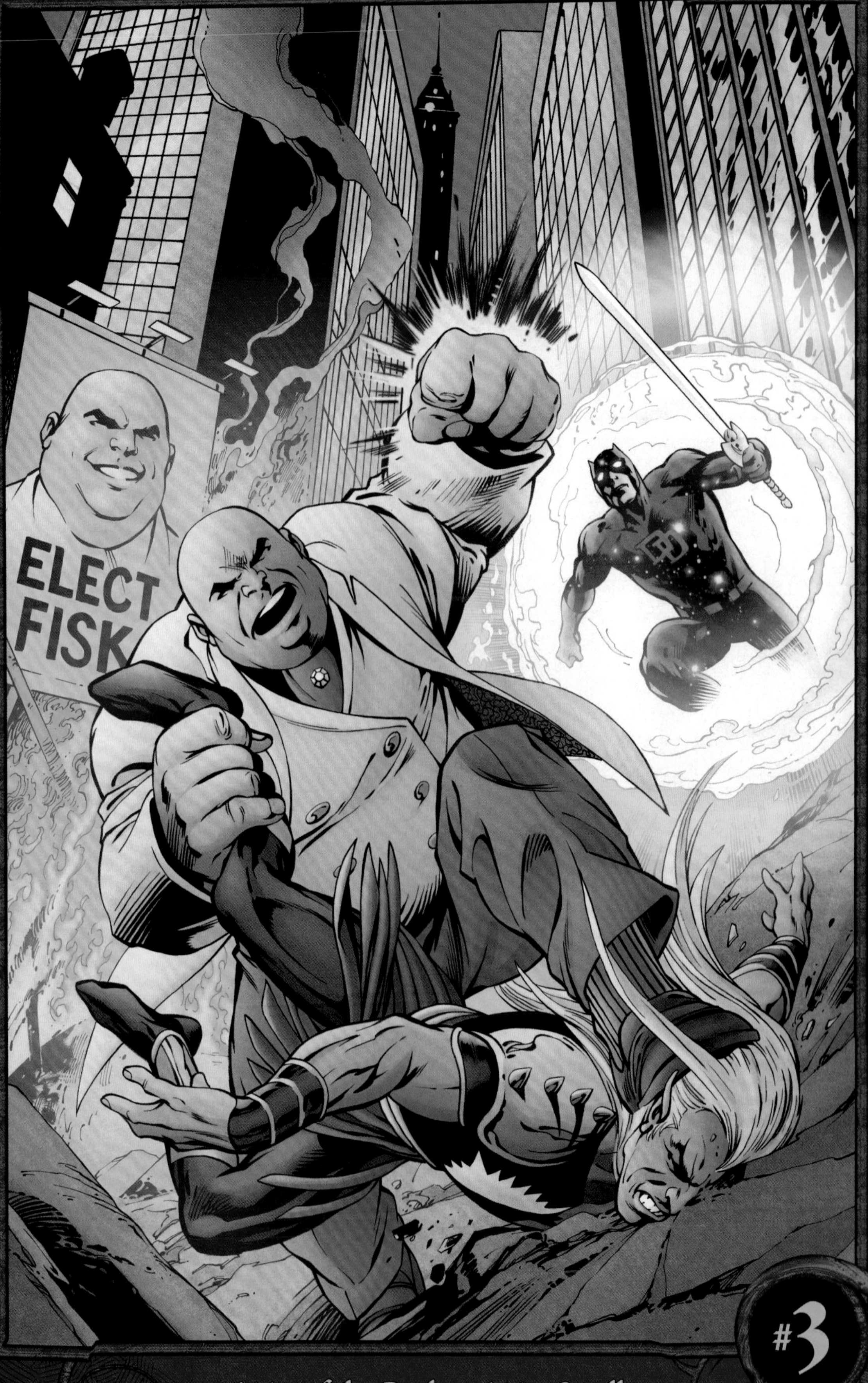
ELECT
FISK
#3

War of the Realms: War Scrolls

THIS IS A WASTE OF TIME. THERE'S A WAR TO BE FOUGHT.

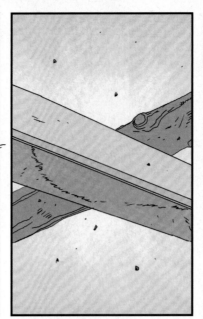

ASGARD

AND I'VE BEEN TRAINING FOR YEARS TO--

GAAAGH!

YOU'VE BEEN TRAINING TO FIGHT AS A *BLIND MORTAL* WITH SUPER-SENSES, SIR MURDOCK. BUT NOW YOU'RE A BLIND *GOD* WHO'S *ALL-SEEING*.

AND ONE CAN BECOME BLINDED BY SEEING TOO MUCH.

THAT'S... A PIECE OF *THE WORLD TREE* YOU JUST HIT ME WITH. IT'S GROWING OUT OF THE SUN NOW, YOU KNOW.

THAT IS EXACTLY WHAT I MEAN. YOU ARE NOT FOCUSED.

YOU'RE RIGHT, HEIMDALL, BUT I'M NOT WORRIED ABOUT SEEING TOO MUCH. RIGHT NOW MY PROBLEM IS THAT I CAN'T SEE *MALEKITH*.

HE'S SOMEHOW USING HIS MAG[IC] TO HIDE FROM--

WAIT...THAT SONUVA...

I JUST FOUND HIM.

WHATEVER YOU'RE SEEING, YOU REALIZE OF COURSE IT'S A *TRAP*.

YES. AND *YOU* REALIZE I STILL HAVE TO GO.

BUT YOU HITTING ME WITH THE WORLD TREE GAVE ME AN IDEA. SO WITH YOUR PERMISSION...

...I WON'T BE GOING EMPTY-HANDED.

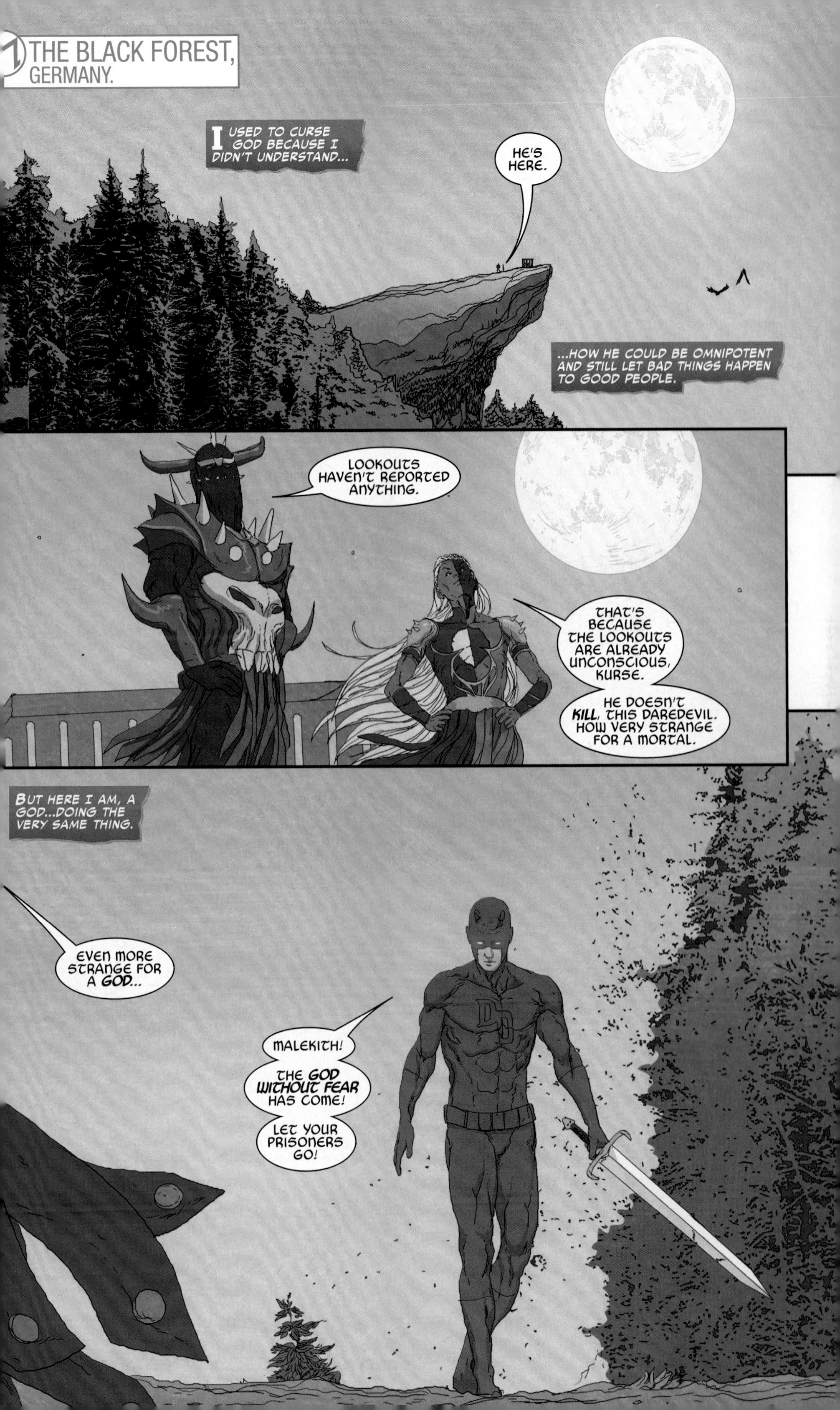

THE BLACK FOREST, GERMANY.
I USED TO CURSE GOD BECAUSE I DIDN'T UNDERSTAND...
HE'S HERE.
...HOW HE COULD BE OMNIPOTENT AND STILL LET BAD THINGS HAPPEN TO GOOD PEOPLE.
LOOKOUTS HAVEN'T REPORTED ANYTHING.
THAT'S BECAUSE THE LOOKOUTS ARE ALREADY UNCONSCIOUS, KURSE.
HE DOESN'T KILL, THIS DAREDEVIL. HOW VERY STRANGE FOR A MORTAL.
BUT HERE I AM, A GOD...DOING THE VERY SAME THING.
EVEN MORE STRANGE FOR A GOD...
MALEKITH!
THE GOD WITHOUT FEAR HAS COME!
LET YOUR PRISONERS GO!

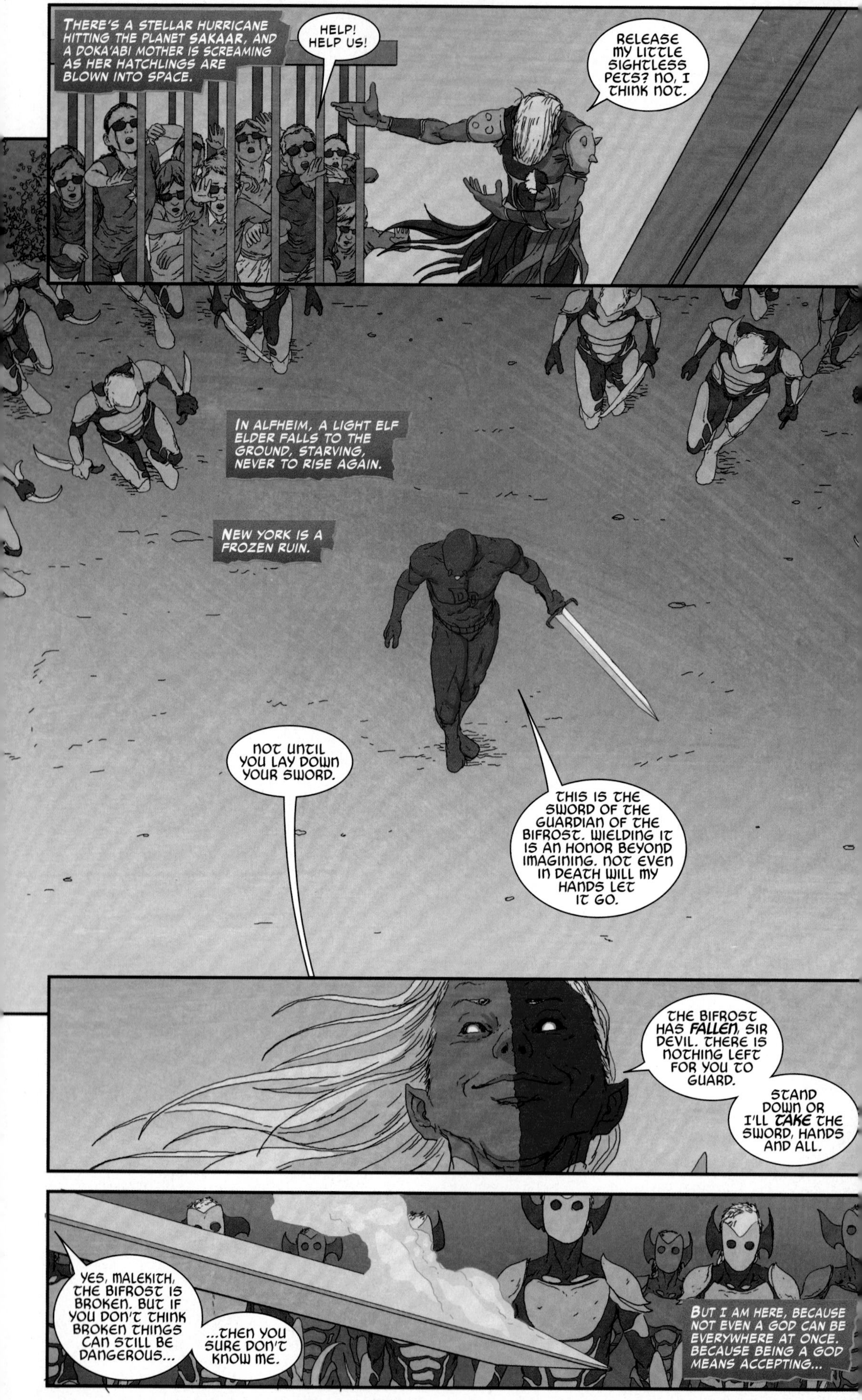
THERE'S A STELLAR HURRICANE HITTING THE PLANET SAKAAR, AND A DOKA'ABI MOTHER IS SCREAMING AS HER HATCHLINGS ARE BLOWN INTO SPACE.
HELP! HELP US!
RELEASE MY LITTLE SIGHTLESS PETS? NO, I THINK NOT.
IN ALFHEIM, A LIGHT ELF ELDER FALLS TO THE GROUND, STARVING, NEVER TO RISE AGAIN.
NEW YORK IS A FROZEN RUIN.
NOT UNTIL YOU LAY DOWN YOUR SWORD.
THIS IS THE SWORD OF THE GUARDIAN OF THE BIFROST. WIELDING IT IS AN HONOR BEYOND IMAGINING. NOT EVEN IN DEATH WILL MY HANDS LET IT GO.
THE BIFROST HAS FALLEN, SIR DEVIL. THERE IS NOTHING LEFT FOR YOU TO GUARD.
STAND DOWN OR I'LL TAKE THE SWORD, HANDS AND ALL.
YES, MALEKITH, THE BIFROST IS BROKEN. BUT IF YOU DON'T THINK BROKEN THINGS CAN STILL BE DANGEROUS...
...THEN YOU SURE DON'T KNOW ME.
BUT I AM HERE, BECAUSE NOT EVEN A GOD CAN BE EVERYWHERE AT ONCE. BECAUSE BEING A GOD MEANS ACCEPTING...

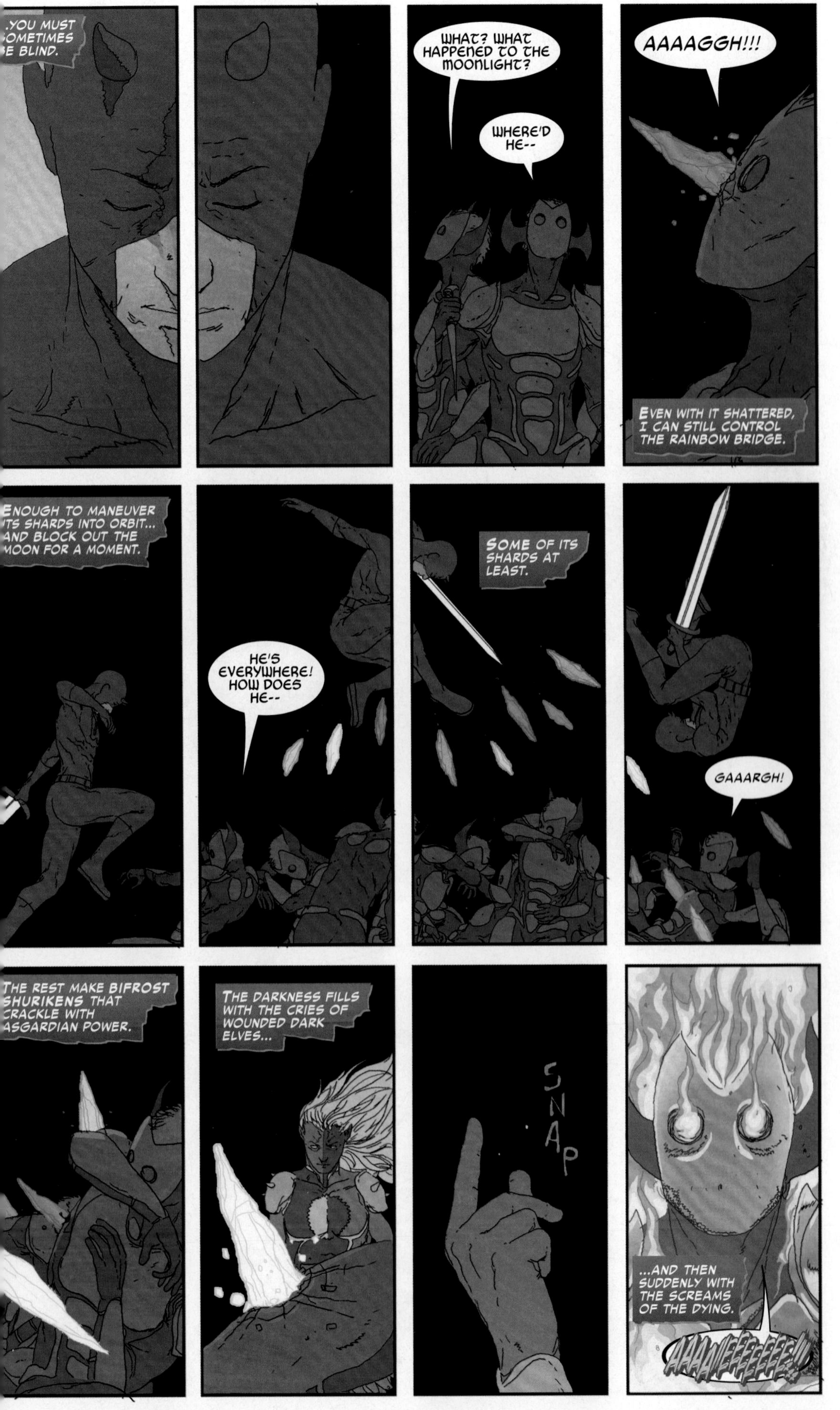

...YOU MUST SOMETIMES BE BLIND.
WHAT? WHAT HAPPENED TO THE MOONLIGHT?
WHERE'D HE--
AAAAGGH!!!
EVEN WITH IT SHATTERED, I CAN STILL CONTROL THE RAINBOW BRIDGE.
ENOUGH TO MANEUVER ITS SHARDS INTO ORBIT... AND BLOCK OUT THE MOON FOR A MOMENT.
HE'S EVERYWHERE! HOW DOES HE--
SOME OF ITS SHARDS AT LEAST.
GAAARGH!
THE REST MAKE BIFROST SHURIKENS THAT CRACKLE WITH ASGARDIAN POWER.
THE DARKNESS FILLS WITH THE CRIES OF WOUNDED DARK ELVES...
SNAP
...AND THEN SUDDENLY WITH THE SCREAMS OF THE DYING.
AAAAIEEEEEEE!!!

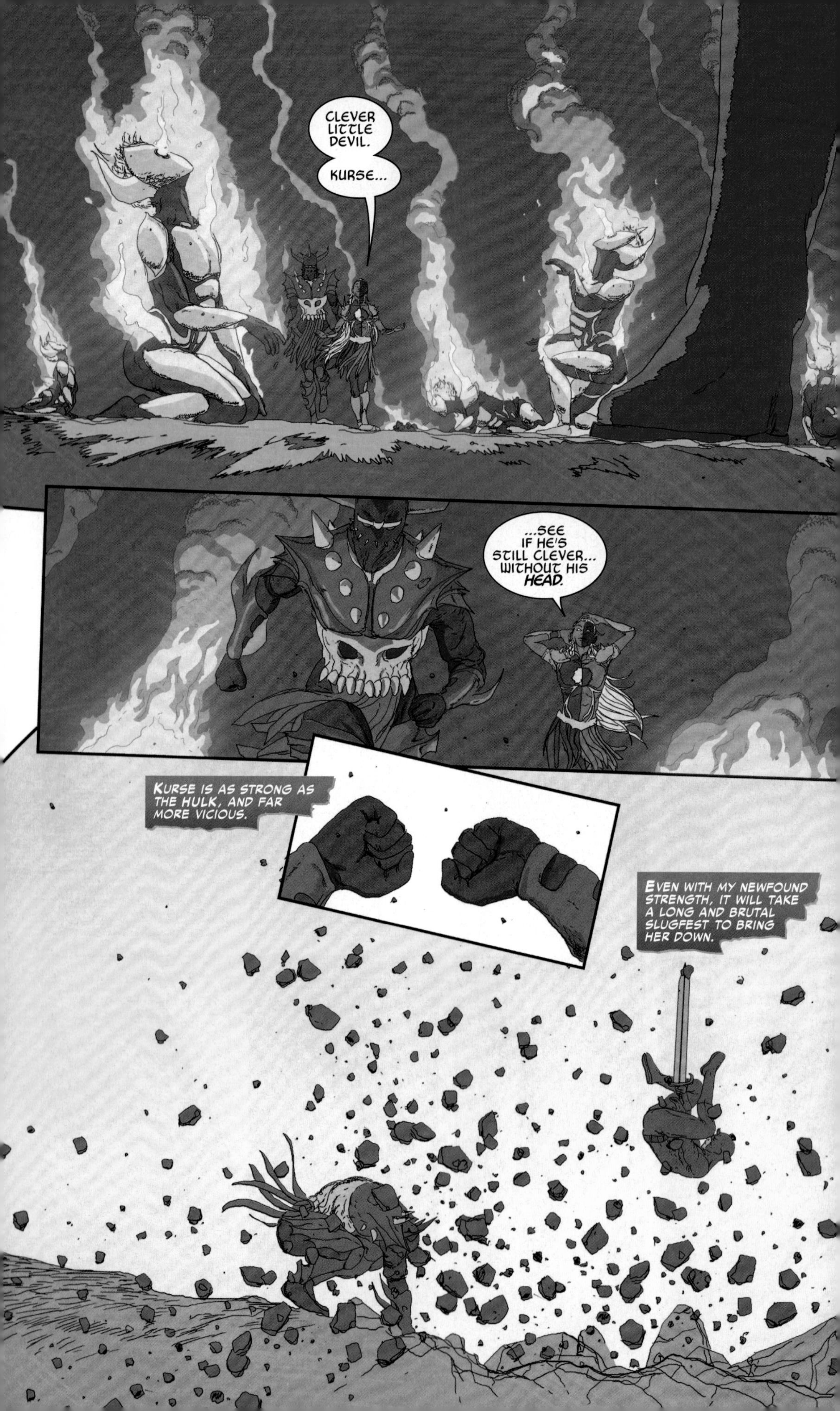

CLEVER LITTLE DEVIL.
KURSE...
...SEE IF HE'S STILL CLEVER... WITHOUT HIS HEAD.
KURSE IS AS STRONG AS THE HULK, AND FAR MORE VICIOUS.
EVEN WITH MY NEWFOUND STRENGTH, IT WILL TAKE A LONG AND BRUTAL SLUGFEST TO BRING HER DOWN.

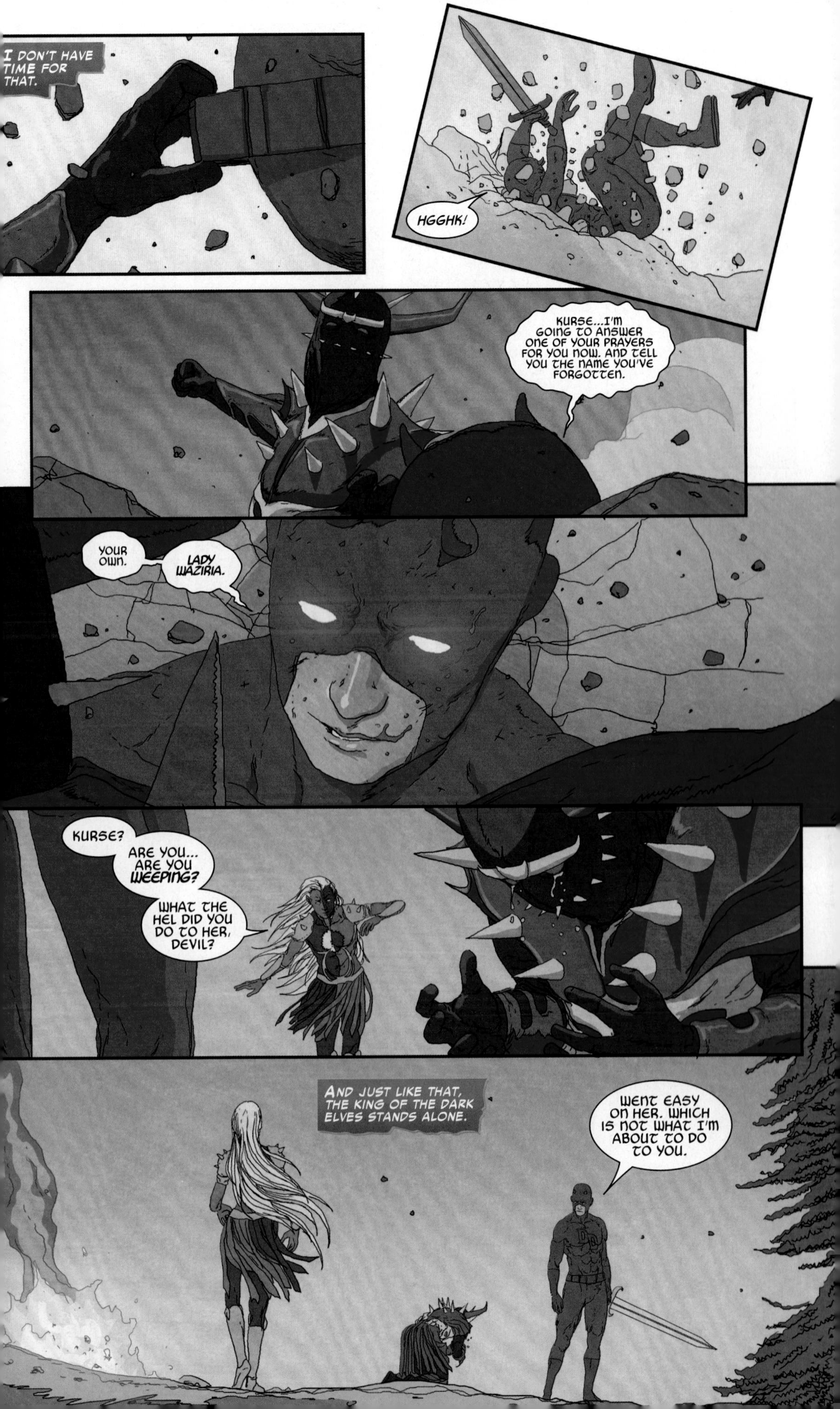
I DON'T HAVE TIME FOR THAT.
HGGHK!
KURSE...I'M GOING TO ANSWER ONE OF YOUR PRAYERS FOR YOU NOW. AND TELL YOU THE NAME YOU'VE FORGOTTEN.
YOUR OWN.
LADY WAZIRIA.
KURSE?
ARE YOU... ARE YOU WEEPING?
WHAT THE HEL DID YOU DO TO HER, DEVIL?
AND JUST LIKE THAT, THE KING OF THE DARK ELVES STANDS ALONE.
WENT EASY ON HER. WHICH IS NOT WHAT I'M ABOUT TO DO TO YOU.

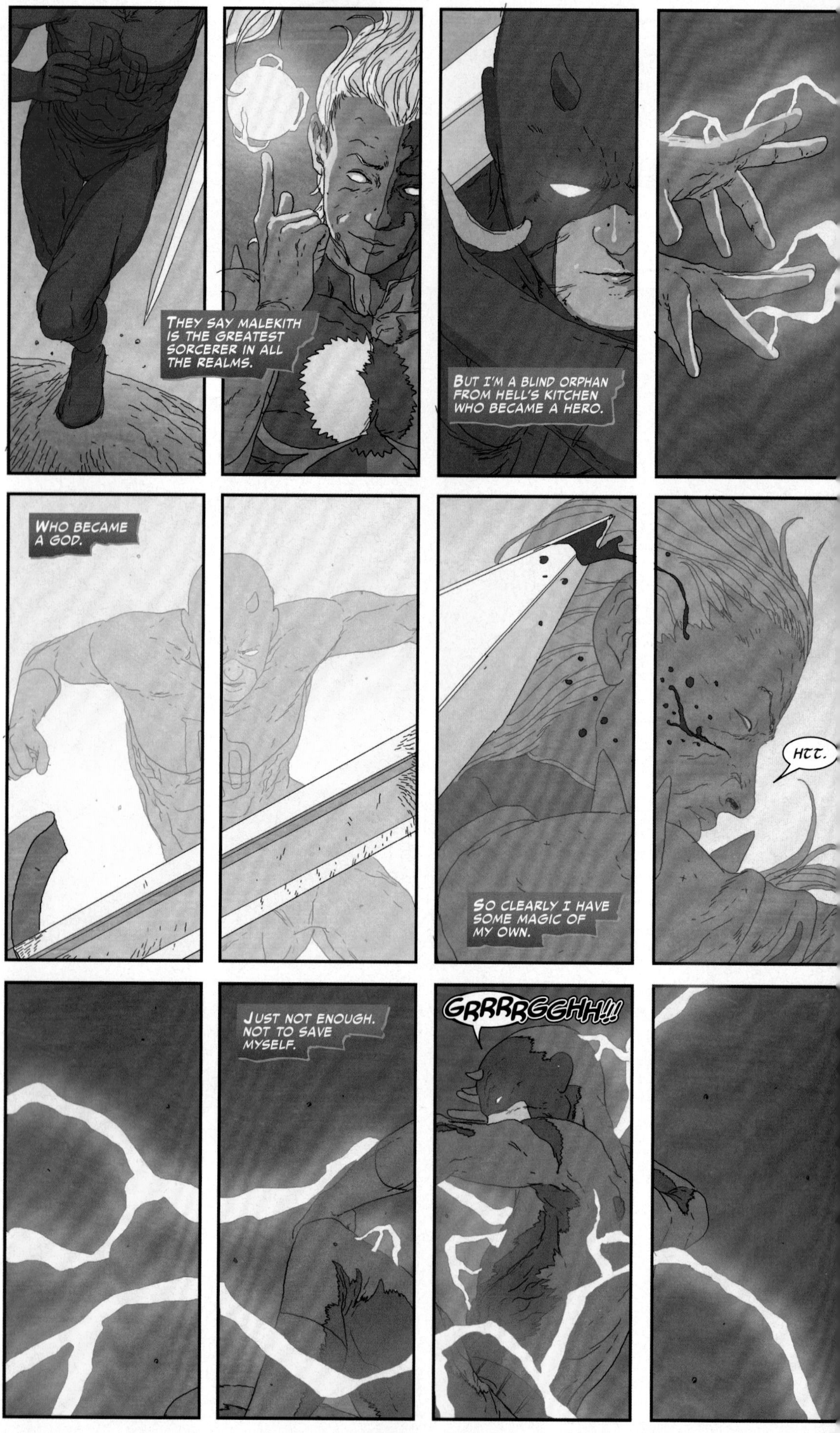
THEY SAY MALEKITH IS THE GREATEST SORCERER IN ALL THE REALMS.
BUT I'M A BLIND ORPHAN FROM HELL'S KITCHEN WHO BECAME A HERO.
WHO BECAME A GOD.
SO CLEARLY I HAVE SOME MAGIC OF MY OWN.
HTT.
JUST NOT ENOUGH. NOT TO SAVE MYSELF.
GRRRRGGHH!!!

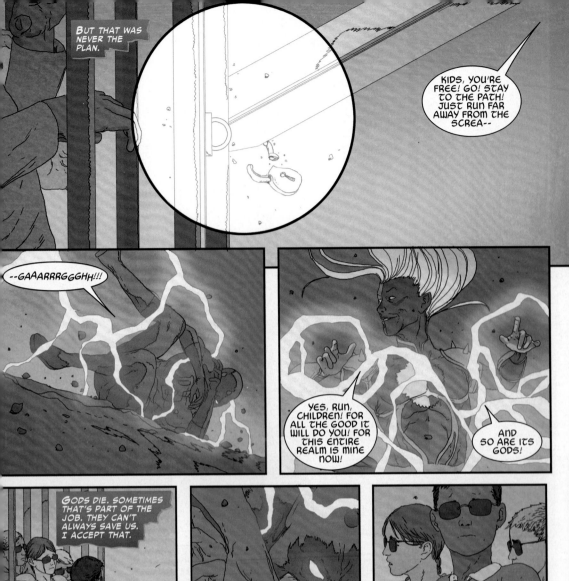

BUT THAT WAS NEVER THE PLAN.

KIDS, YOU'RE FREE! GO! STAY TO THE PATH! JUST RUN FAR AWAY FROM THE SCREA--

--GAAARRRGGGHH!!!

YES, RUN, CHILDREN! FOR ALL THE GOOD IT WILL DO YOU! FOR THIS ENTIRE REALM IS MINE NOW!

AND SO ARE ITS GODS!

GODS DIE. SOMETIMES THAT'S PART OF THE JOB. THEY CAN'T ALWAYS SAVE US. I ACCEPT THAT.

I SUPPOSE WHAT I DIDN'T EXPECT...WAS THAT SOMETIMES MORE IMPORTANT THAN SALVATION...

...IS DIVINE INSPIRATION.

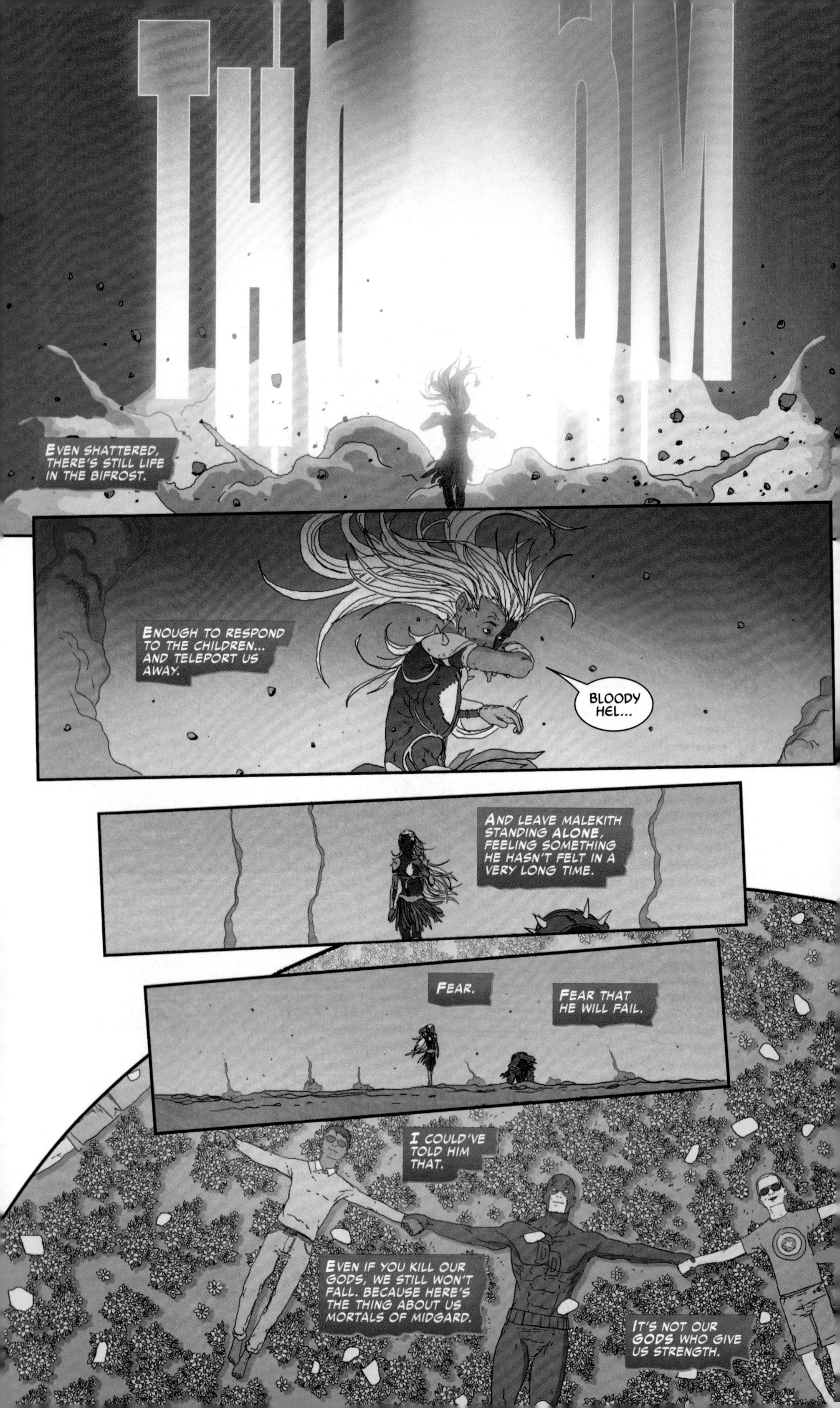
EVEN SHATTERED, THERE'S STILL LIFE IN THE BIFROST.
ENOUGH TO RESPOND TO THE CHILDREN... AND TELEPORT US AWAY.
BLOODY HEL...
AND LEAVE MALEKITH STANDING ALONE, FEELING SOMETHING HE HASN'T FELT IN A VERY LONG TIME.
FEAR.
FEAR THAT HE WILL FAIL.
I COULD'VE TOLD HIM THAT.
EVEN IF YOU KILL OUR GODS, WE STILL WON'T FALL. BECAUSE HERE'S THE THING ABOUT US MORTALS OF MIDGARD.
IT'S NOT OUR GODS WHO GIVE US STRENGTH.

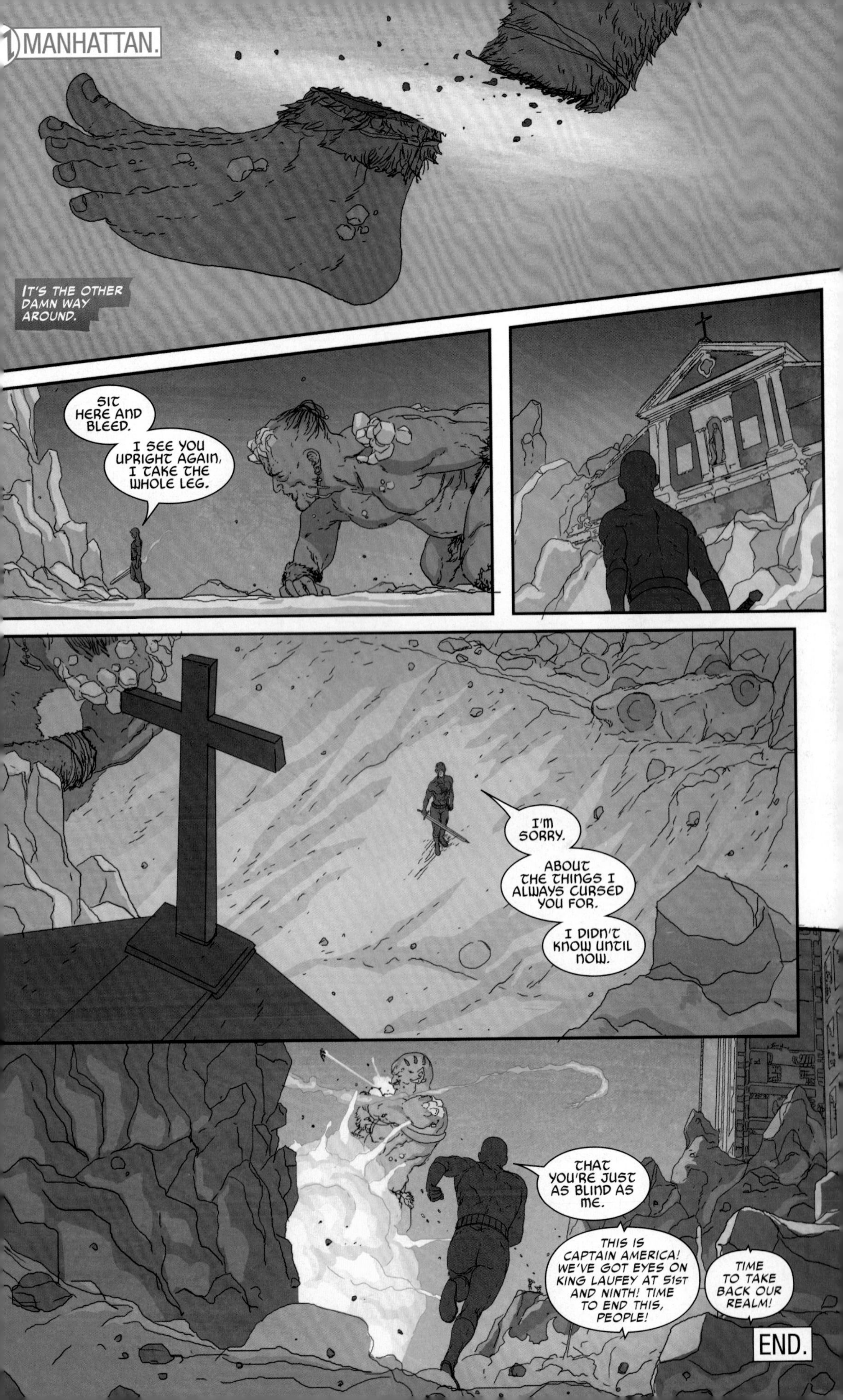

MANHATTAN.
IT'S THE OTHER DAMN WAY AROUND.
SIT HERE AND BLEED.
I SEE YOU UPRIGHT AGAIN, I TAKE THE WHOLE LEG.
I'M SORRY.
ABOUT THE THINGS I ALWAYS CURSED YOU FOR.
I DIDN'T KNOW UNTIL NOW.
THAT YOU'RE JUST AS BLIND AS ME.
THIS IS CAPTAIN AMERICA! WE'VE GOT EYES ON KING LAUFEY AT 51ST AND NINTH! TIME TO END THIS, PEOPLE!
TIME TO TAKE BACK OUR REALM!
END.

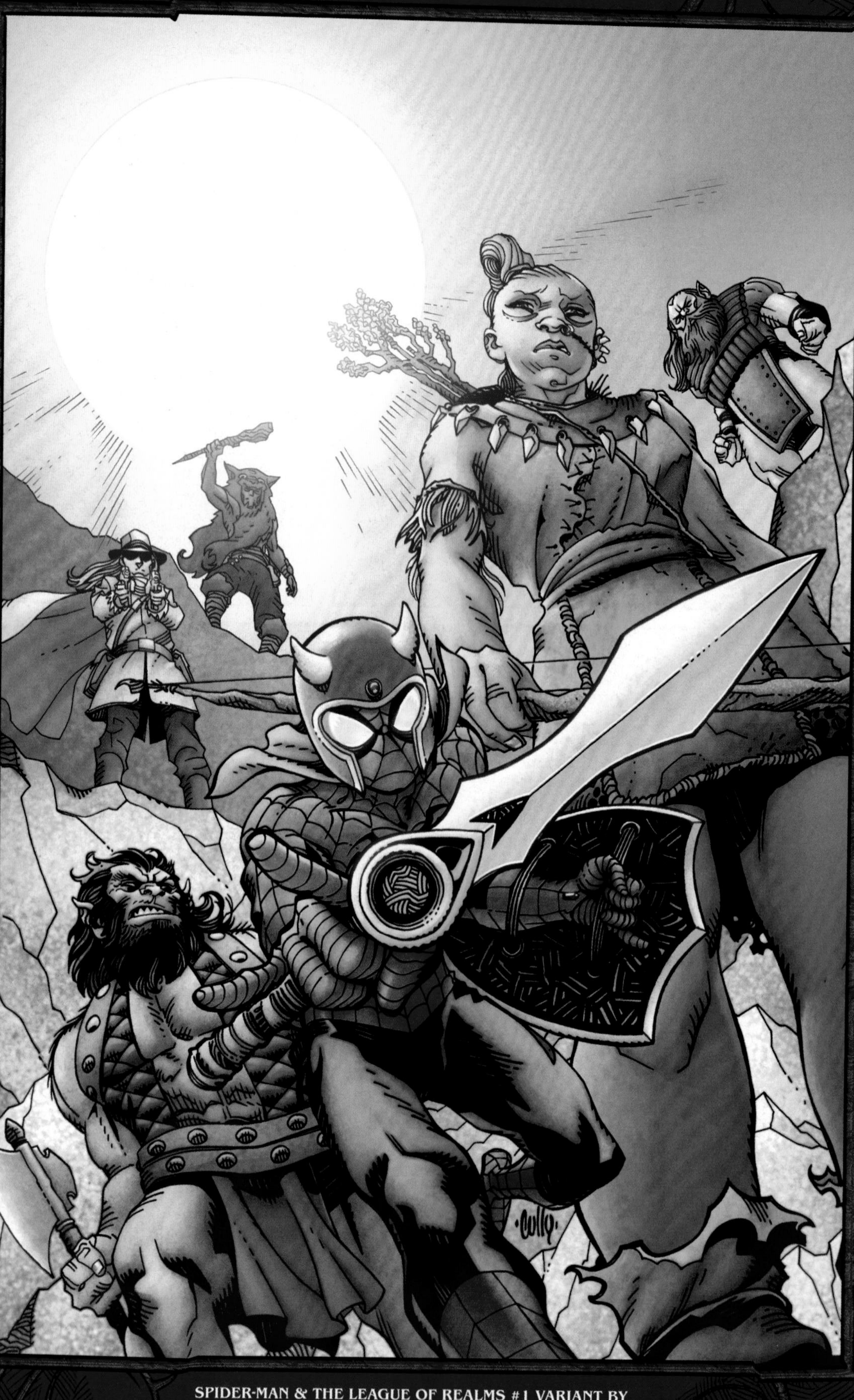

SPIDER-MAN & THE LEAGUE OF REALMS #1 VARIANT BY
Cully Hamner & Morry Hollowell

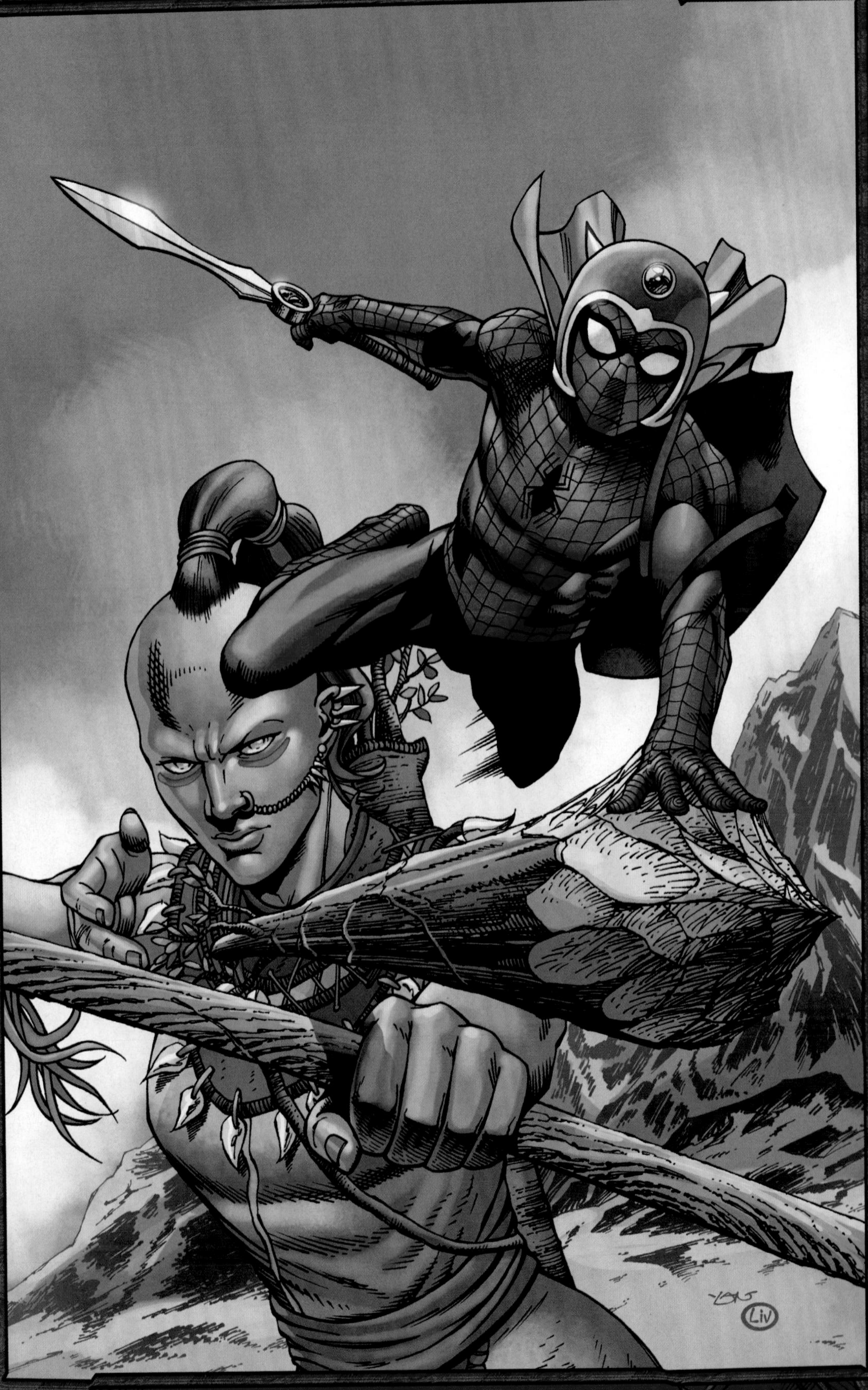

SPIDER-MAN & THE LEAGUE OF REALMS #2 VARIANT BY
Lan Medina, Livesay & Brian Reber

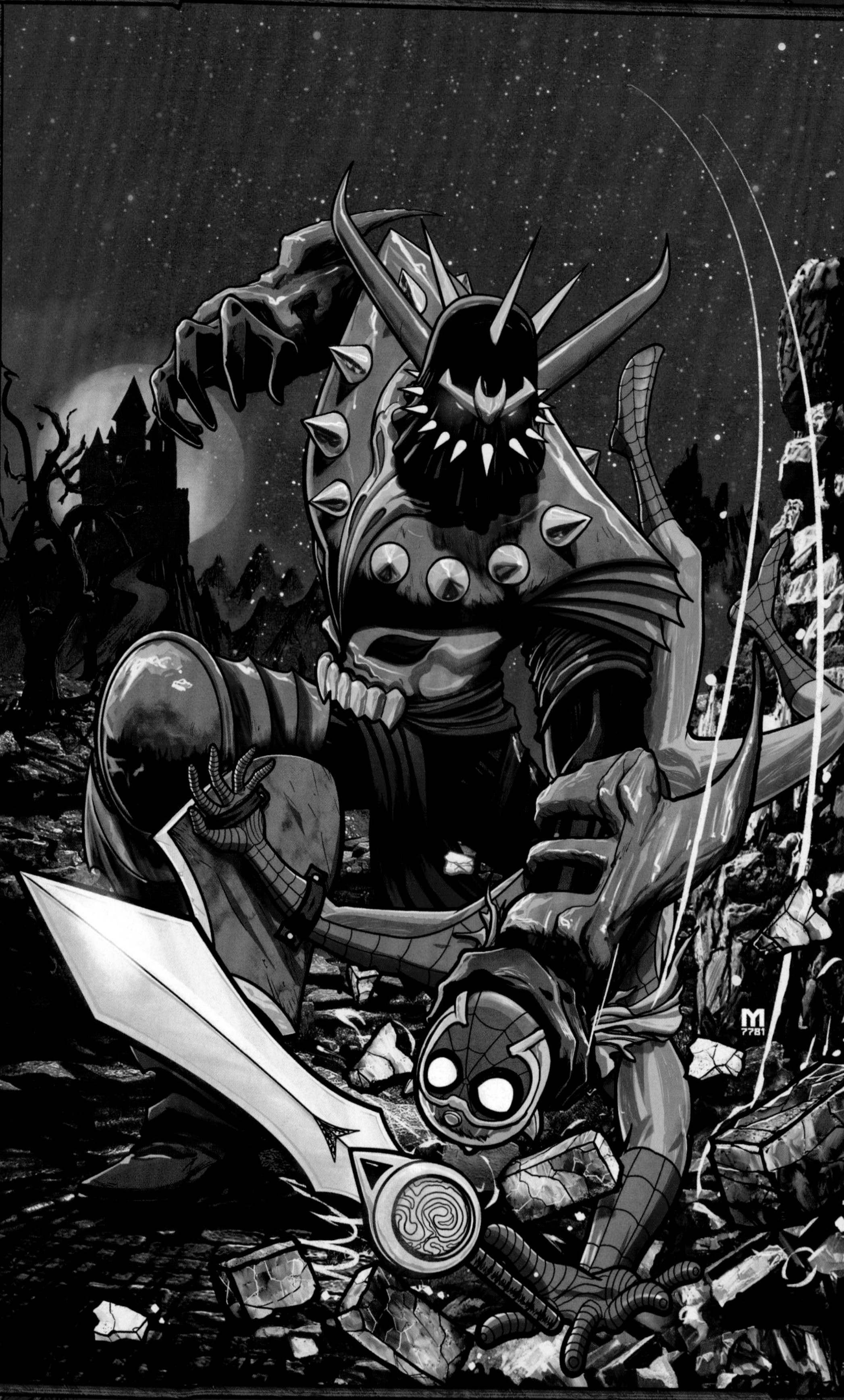

SPIDER-MAN & THE LEAGUE OF REALMS #3 VARIANT BY
Cully Hamner & Morry Hollowell

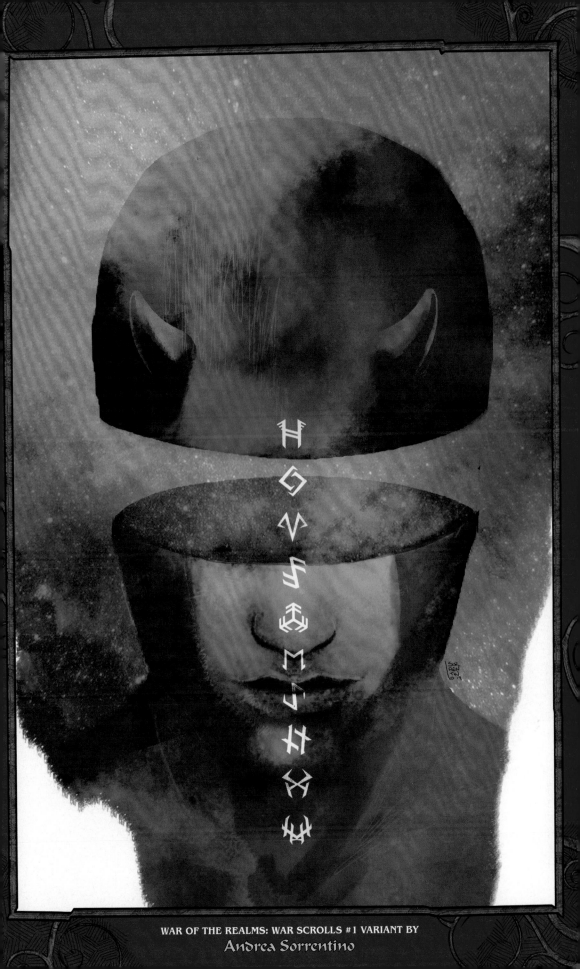

WAR OF THE REALMS: WAR SCROLLS #1 VARIANT BY
Andrea Sorrentino

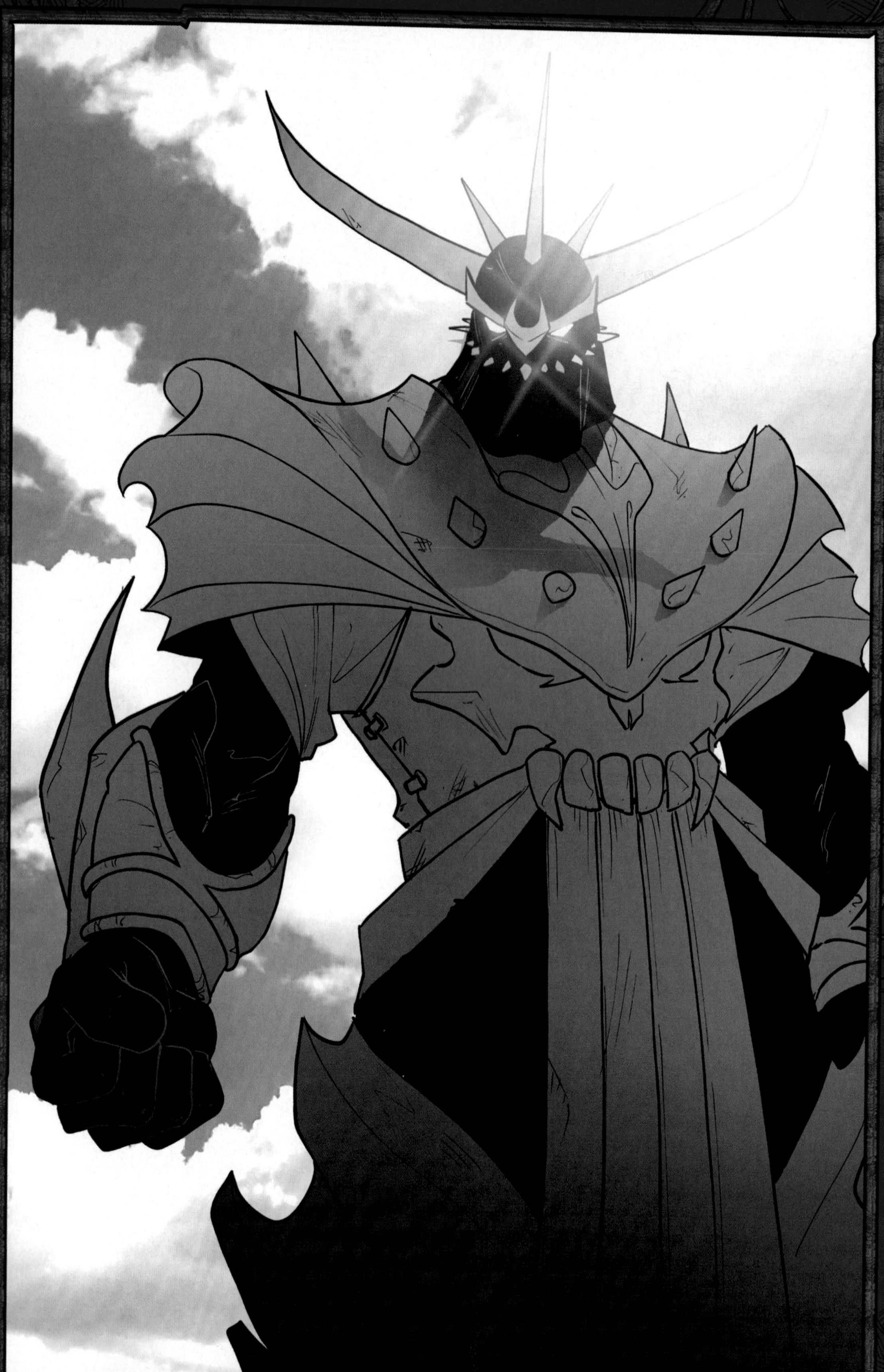

SPIDER-MAN & THE LEAGUE OF REALMS #1, PAGE 20 ART BY
Nico Leon

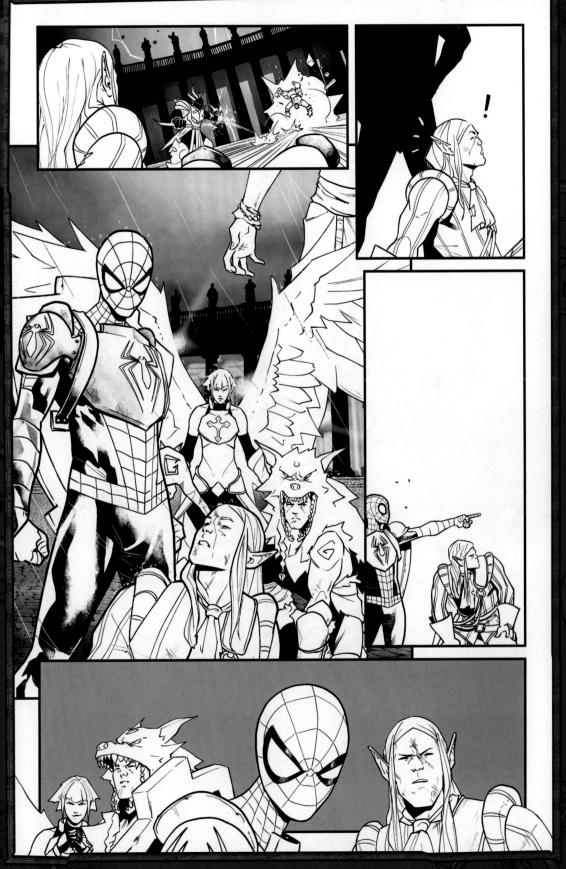

SPIDER-MAN & THE LEAGUE OF REALMS #3, PAGE 8 ART BY
Nico Leon

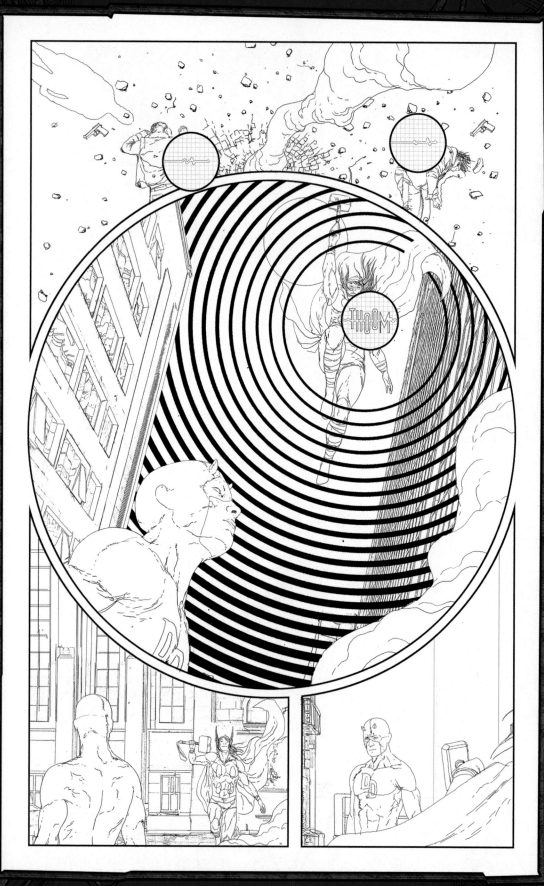

WAR OF THE REALMS: WAR SCROLLS #1, PAGE 1 ART BY
Andrea Sorrentino

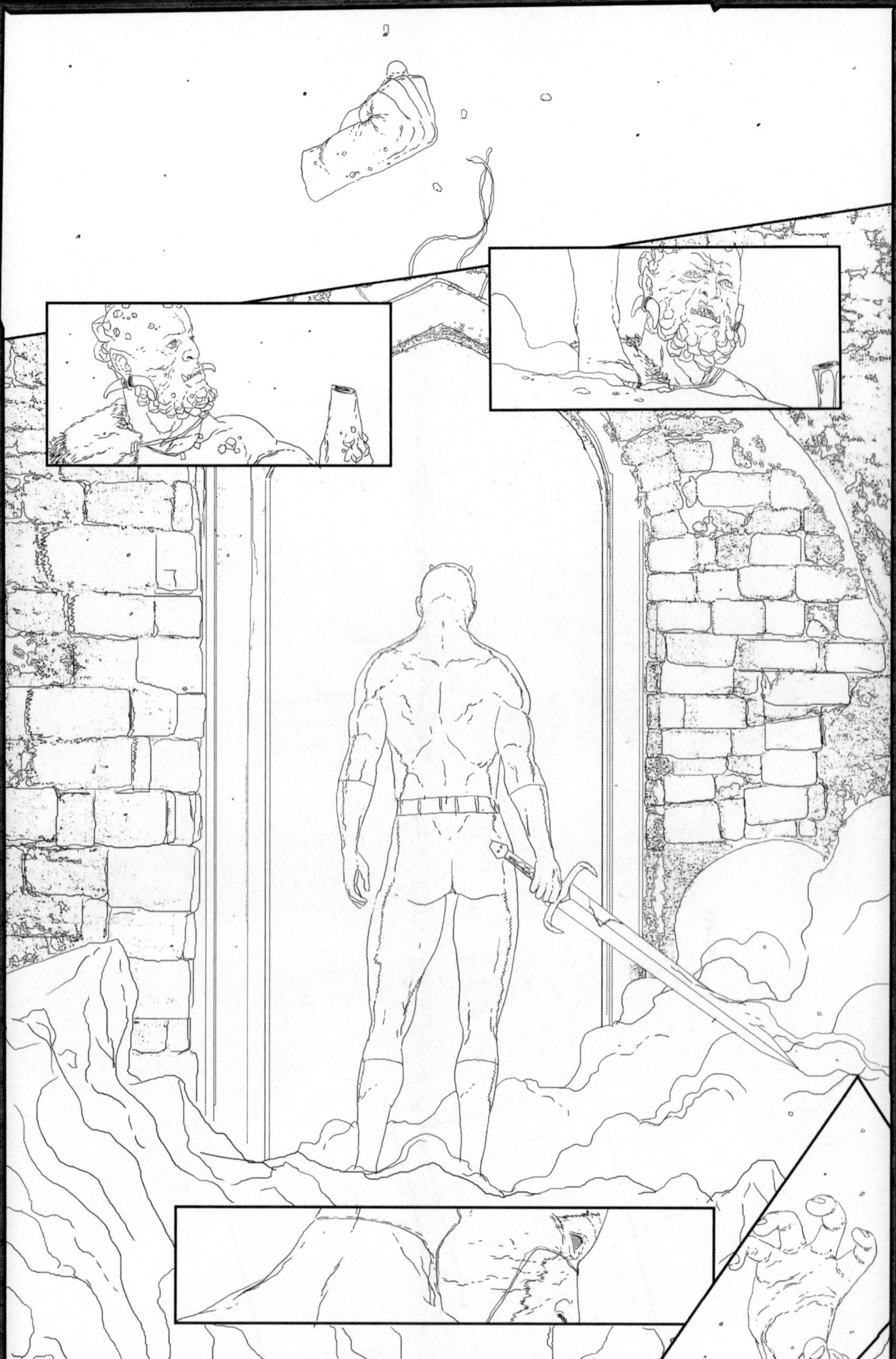

WAR OF THE REALMS: WAR SCROLLS #1, PAGE 6 ART BY
Andrea Sorrentino

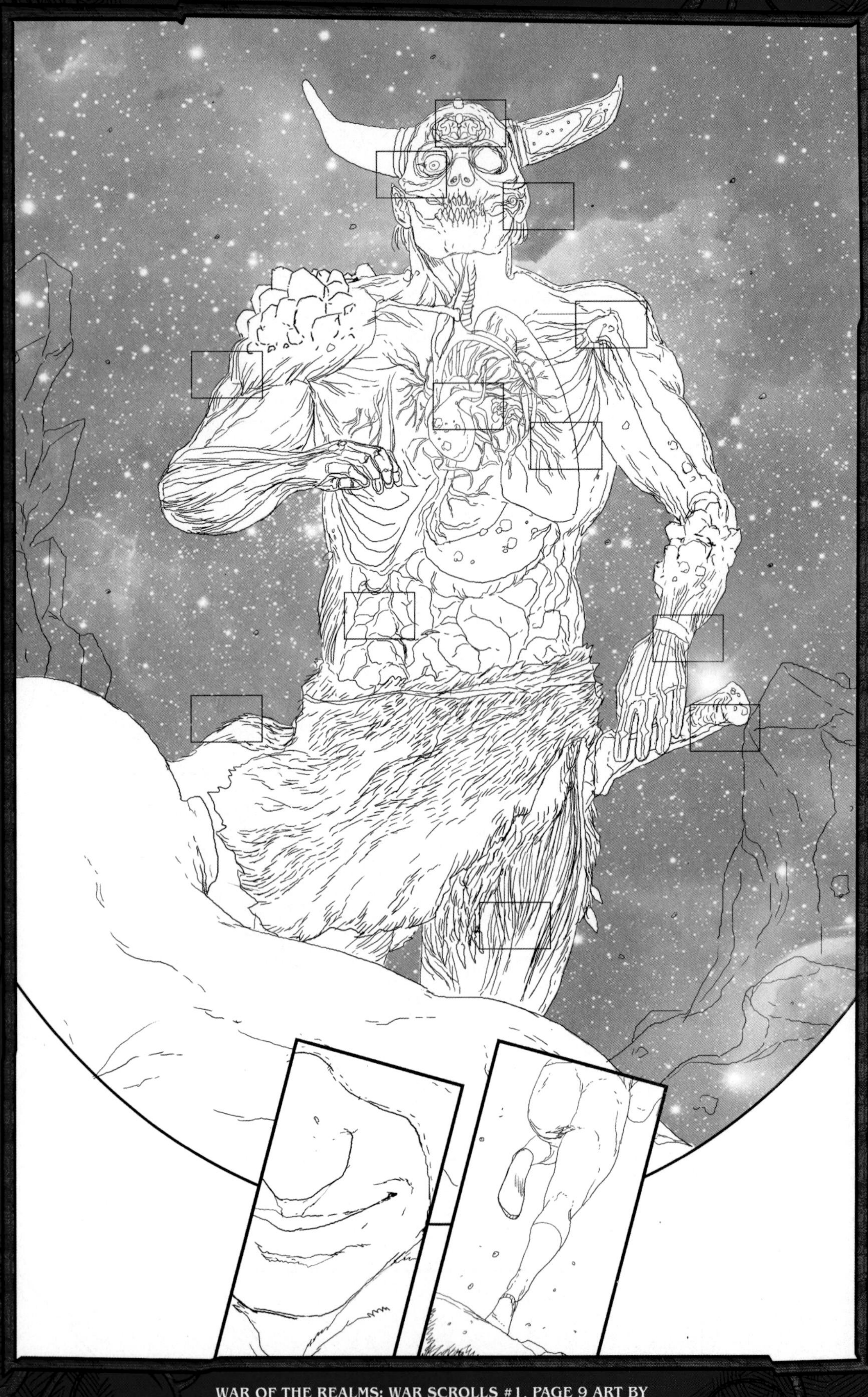

WAR OF THE REALMS: WAR SCROLLS #1, PAGE 9 ART BY
Andrea Sorrentino

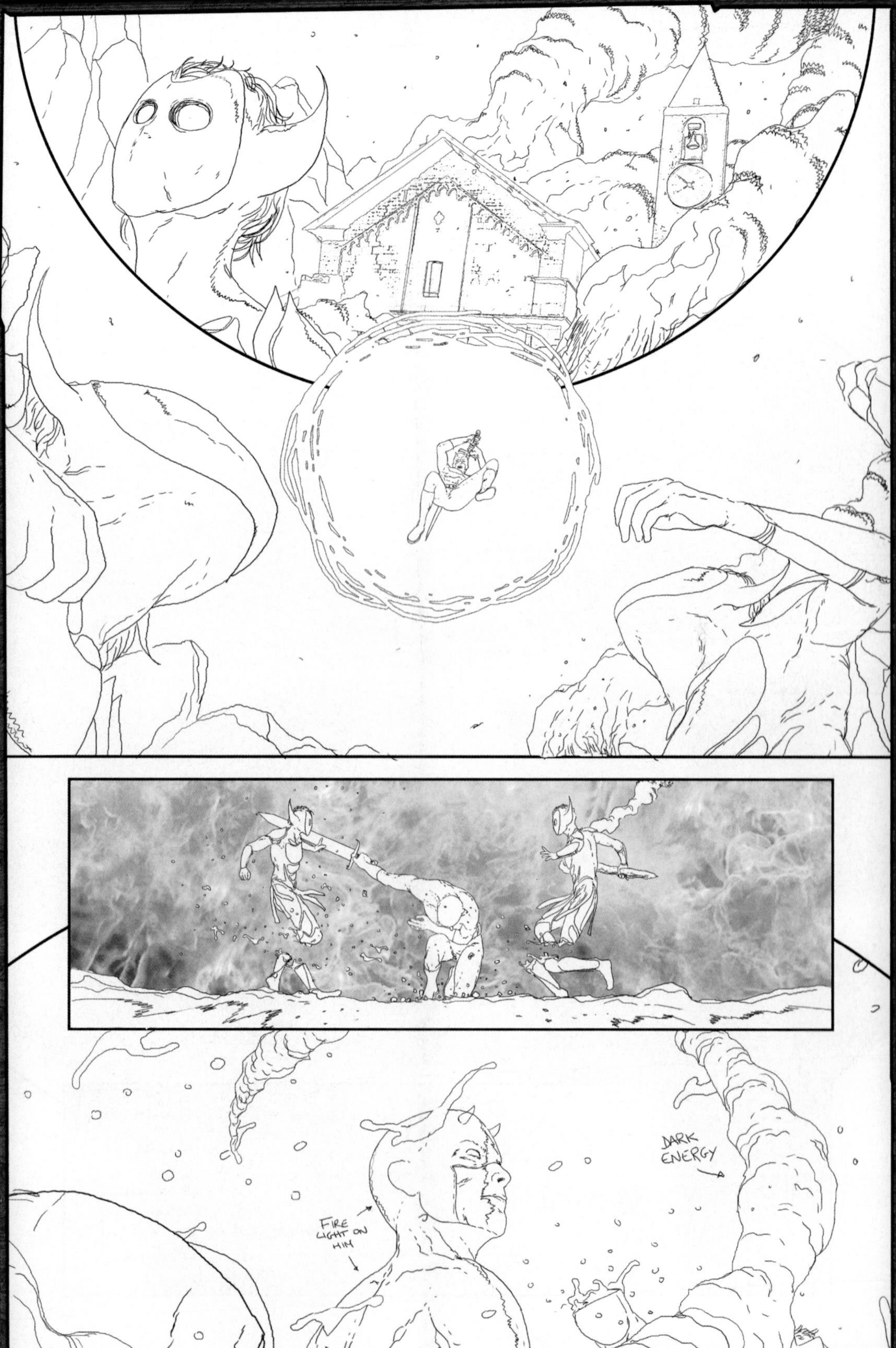
FIRE
LIGHT ON
HIM
DARK
ENERGY

WAR OF THE REALMS: WAR SCROLLS #2, PAGE 4 ART BY
Andrea Sorrentino

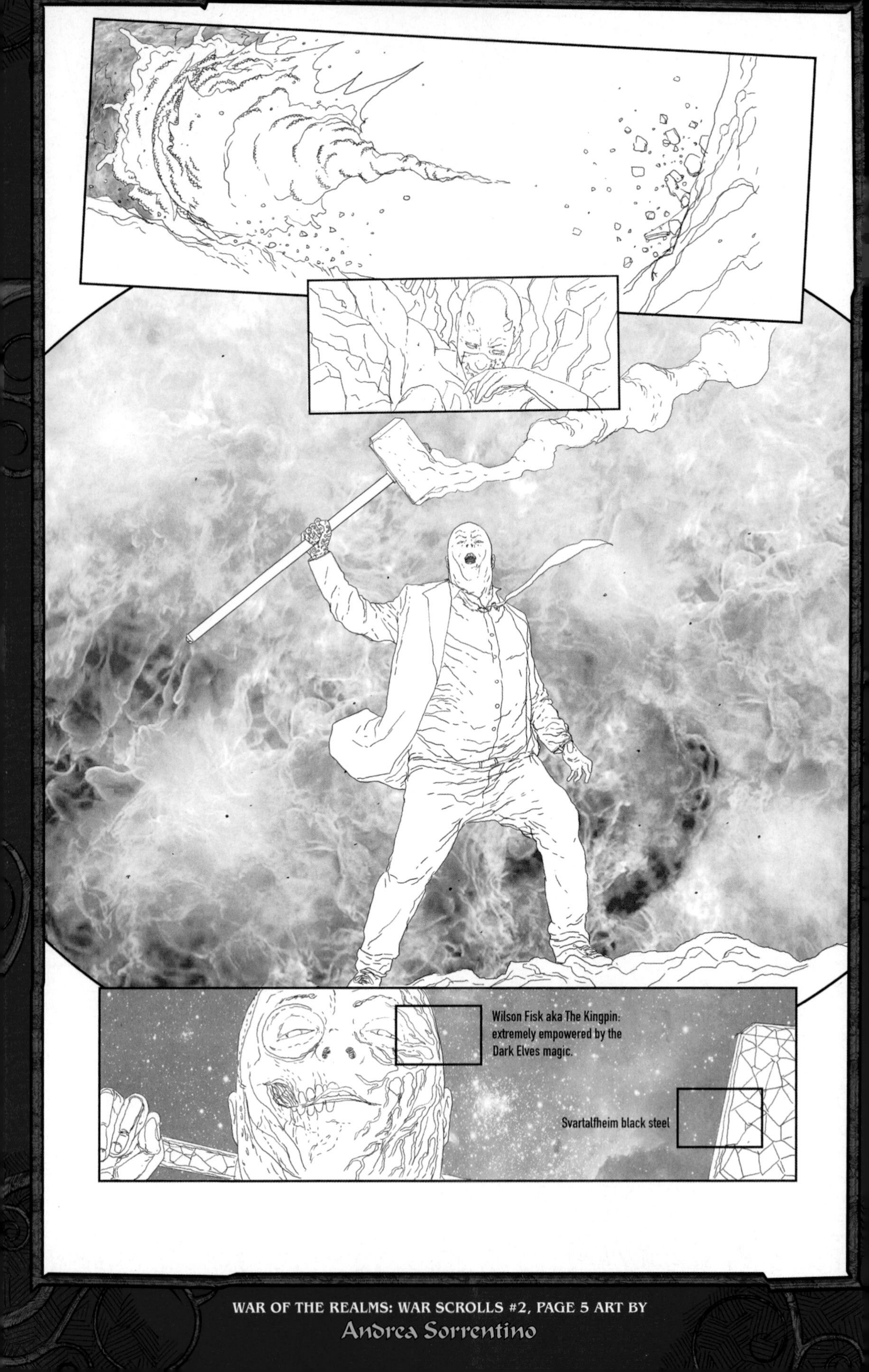
Wilson Fisk aka The Kingpin: extremely empowered by the Dark Elves magic.
Svartalfheim black steel

WAR OF THE REALMS: WAR SCROLLS #2, PAGE 5 ART BY
Andrea Sorrentino